PARENTS
UNDER
PRESSURE

Parents Under Pressure

Struggling to Raise Children
in an Unequal America

Karen Zilberstein

Levellers Press

AMHERST, MASSACHUSETTS

Levellers Press · Amherst, Massachusetts

ISBN 978-1-945473-79-1

If I could prevent one person from going through what I went through, I'd tell my story a million times.

—*Diana*, Chapter Three

As long as I change one person's life, I'll be alright.

—*Sophia*, Chapter Six

In recognition of the families who gave their
time and stories to this project, all author
proceeds will be donated to charities
that aid parents and youth.

Contents

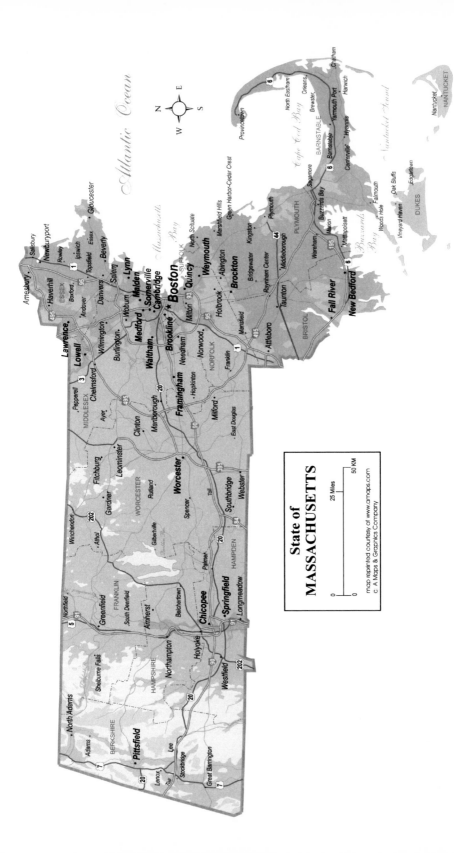

State of
MASSACHUSETTS

0   25 Miles
0   50 KM

map reprinted courtesy of www.amaps.com
c A Maps & Graphics Company

1. Introduction

Evolving Expectations and Difficulties Fulfilling Them

WHEN MY DAUGHTER fell ill with an autoimmune disease at age fourteen, it took my husband and me well over a year to sort through competing diagnoses and treatments, and restore her life to working order. We spent hours in waiting rooms, sitting in chairs invariably upholstered red or blue, with magazines piled beside them. We settled into the hard seats of examination rooms, the walls sparsely clad with pictures and explanations of bodily ills, and watched and listened as doctors checked our daughter's symptoms, ordered tests, and offered advice. We held her hand through numerous needle pricks and blood tests, applied hot compresses to her aching body, mourned when early treatment attempts failed, and railed at the injustice of her disease and diminished energy. When she required hospitalization the week before high school began, we took turns shuttling between the hospital, work, and our two boys at home, juggling the load as best we could.

Coming home one day and observing strain on our sons' faces, we realized the regimen was unsustainable. We told the hospital to discharge our daughter. She was sufficiently recovered to be cared for at home, and we needed to function again as a family. She stabilized soon after, and family life resumed a more normal routine. Even then, ongoing needs for treatment, monitoring, correcting insurance bungles, school coordination, and medical setbacks sporadically assailed us. It was a time-consuming process, unfolding under an exhausting cloud of anxiety.

But we knew we were lucky. We enjoyed good medical insurance, flexible, secure jobs, an income that could absorb the medical deductibles and copays, and a car that could withstand multiple drives to a specialist over an hour away. Our older son provided competent childcare to our youngest, and our knowledge and professional contacts located the best medical care for her condition. We realized, then, how easily a family without those benefits could collapse, driven over a cascading edge of demands.

The insight was not novel, just forcefully impressed in a new way. As a psychotherapist working with children and parents, my profession brings me into contact with many struggling families. They face numerous pressures: financial hardship, limited supports, traumas, illness, mental illness, and disability. Some of their children require extensive commitments for acute emotional, physical, or cognitive challenges. Over and over again, I encounter families confronting situations of such high demand and low resources that they simply cannot keep up. Aware that they and their children are falling short, parents feel inadequate, drained, and judged by family, friends, and professionals who question their choices and abilities.

Many of the families' needs bring them, and me, into contact with numerous state systems, from schools struggling to meet the educational requirements of diverse students, to the Department of Developmental Services (DDS), which provides for children with disabilities, to the mental health system, which offers various types of psychotherapies, as well as the Department of Children and Families (DCF) and court systems that intervene in families' lives when abuse or neglect is suspected or custody disputed.

Sometimes parents find knowledgeable, hard-working professionals who provide crucial services and supports. Too often, they feel entwined in bulky bureaucracies that cannot bend sufficiently to their needs. Promised services never materialize, are hard to access, or do not provide comprehensive or expert enough coverage. Inexperienced staff turn over, creating instability. Programs hold unrealistic expectations, pushing parents into untenable positions. Well-off parents and those with college educations generally fare better than poorer ones, readily challenging decisions with which they disagree, sometimes by hiring advocates or lawyers to bolster their causes. What has become clear is that systems of care have not kept pace with the challenges confronting families, nor do public policies appear poised to alleviate parents' toils. In twenty-first century America, access to means, resources, and knowledge are not evenly distributed, benefiting some families while leaving others behind.

This is a book about struggling parents, disadvantaged by hard circumstances, and how they rear children while striving to survive. It is not a book about families who have persevered and beat the odds. Although inspiring, those stories tend to obscure the impediments many families confront. It is also not a book about parents who have given up, neglecting their children and abdicating responsibilities. Instead, based on extensive, recorded interviews with a few dozen parents facing difficult conditions, as well as with professionals and researchers, it highlights the experiences of six representative families hindered by low income, racial discrimination, disabilities, trauma, and/or children with extraordinary needs who are slogging through the cracks in America's support systems.* It is a book about the dreams they hold, the efforts they make, the systemic barriers they face, and the personal price they pay for their commitment.

The parents in this book contend with circumstances that might appear extraordinary but are commonly seen by workers in human services. One in six American children live in poverty,[1] one in six struggle with a developmental disability,[2] and one in five will suffer a debilitating mental disorder at some point.[3] An estimated 70 percent of American adults have experienced a traumatic event and just under 20 percent develop posttraumatic stress disorder.[4] 38 percent of Americans identify as racial minorities, many of whom suffer negative health effects from experiencing racism.[5] Census data indicates that a full 29 percent of families report at least one of their members, whether a parent or child, struggles with a physical, mental, or emotional impairment.[6] Dislocation, violent communities, incarceration, as well as numerous other hardships impact families.

While all the parents profiled in this book reside in Massachusetts, similar, if not more dire, stories play out across the country. The 2017 Annie E. Casey Foundation's Kids Count Data Book ranks Massachu-

---

*None of the families portrayed in this book are, or have been, my psychotherapy clients. Names of the parents and children and identifying details have been left out or changed to protect their privacy. Names of professionals and researchers have not been changed.

setts as second-best in the country for overall child well-being, first in education, second in child health, seventh in terms of living in supportive communities and nurturing families, and thirteenth in economic well-being.[7] If Massachusetts ranks near the top, then parents in other parts of America grapple with even more extreme circumstances. Of course, families vary greatly in their difficulties and resources. However, far too many resemble the parents in this book who labor, with insufficient help, to reconcile their circumstances, to rear children in the face of obstacles, and to cope with the particular joys and hardships of their situations.

How did we, as a society, arrive at a place in which parents, contending with illness, disability, poverty, or other constraints, are expected to do so much with so little, where demands and expectations exceed the realms of possibility? In some sense, we have always been in this position. America never completely opened her arms or purse to help the vulnerable, despite Lady Liberty's invitation to "Give me your tired, your poor, your huddled masses ... the wretched refuse of your teeming shore." In fact, those huddled masses have received nominal welcome and little aid. Throughout American history, poverty and discrimination, including over two hundred years of slavery, hindered subclasses of mothers and fathers from fully discharging parental roles.[8] Although the twentieth century ushered in a period of increased governmental assistance and concern for the underprivileged, the movement has been halting, with forward steps followed by backward retreats.

At the same time, changing historical and cultural circumstances have reshaped expectations of parents, whittling and sharpening the demands placed upon them. Shifts, from large households to smaller, insular families, from emphasizing children's economic contributions to concern with their individual development, from confidence in boundless vocational opportunities to worries about the next generation's occupational chances, from faith in parental knowledge and authority to reliance on scientific and expert advice, have placed new pressures on parents, especially those raising children who require extraordinary care. Evolving expectations, and the difficulties fulfilling them, form the backdrop to the stories in this book.

Parenting has always changed according to time and circumstance. In our large and diverse country, populated first by Native Americans and then by immigrants who arrived from numerous homelands, no single pattern of parenting extends to all. However, the country's public policies and judgments do not represent that heterogeneity. Parenting norms trace to the country's founding by European settlers, and families' shifting fortunes and structure as industrialization progressed. To illustrate how those influences continue, and the relativity of parenting doctrines, a brief history of the American family is offered below.[9] Like any narrative, what it leaves out—the experiences of Native Americans, slaves, and other sidelined groups—speaks volumes about the voices and experiences considered normative.

Family composition and parenting goals in the seventeenth century New England colonies reflected the circumstances and beliefs of the settlers. Households were larger, consisting of parents, siblings, and resident non-family members, and centered around the homestead and patriarchal authority. Accountability for children's physical, educational, and spiritual needs, as well as their proper behavior, fell to fathers. Though responsible for child outcomes, fathers did not perform the lion's share of childrearing. Everyone who was able contributed to the family's caretaking and economic needs. Children worked and assumed responsibilities at young ages, either in their own or other households, sometimes living away from home. Although parents played an important role in children's upbringing, assistance was also provided by siblings, household members, or even other households in which the children lived.

Relationships between parents and children varied according to a family's social and geographic location, and religious affiliation. The Puritans believed children were born sinful, requiring strict moral education and the breaking of a child's will. Although they loved children, they shunned displays of doting and favored strict, and sometimes harsh, discipline. The less religious gentry showed more leniency. They showered children with affection and encouraged self-assertion, relegating discipline to tutors or servants. Outside of New England, the Quakers and Virginians held alternative beliefs. Quakers viewed children as harmless, not sinful, and thus needing less structure and strictness than the Puritans imposed. Virginians valued children's independence and strong-will, leading them both to indulge children and insist they submit to authority. Different strains of parenting thus flourished within the overall patriarchal and hierarchical structure of colonial families.

Over the course of the seventeenth and eighteenth centuries, conceptions of parenting changed as Enlightenment philosophers such as John Locke and Jean-Jacques Rousseau directed their ideas about rationality, tolerance, progress, and advancement of human potential towards the rearing of youngsters. They argued that children were born with innate goodness and distinct temperaments, whose natures parents should cultivate. Children were increasingly viewed as innocent, dependent on the skillful and deliberate molding of their characters. Locke believed in allowing children freedom to run and explore, but also that building integrity necessitated hardship and denial, lest a spoiled child become a willful, selfish adult. Toys, children's literature, and clothing that allowed children more flexibility of movement proliferated as means to achieve those ends. Good parenting consisted of mingling discipline with freedom and exploration.

Enlightenment philosophies bred nineteenth century, child-centered parenting that focused on the nurturance of children. A decidedly middle class phenomena, child-centered parenting was honed in a society sharply changed by the scientific and industrial revolutions. Moving from rural homesteads to urban centers, fathers now worked outside of the home, in factories and offices. As incomes rose, the need for youth to work declined, and advances in medicine assured higher childhood survival rates, families became smaller, and parents invested more in their offspring. The family also became more isolated and nuclear, with the burden of parenting falling squarely on the mother.

While poor women and children also worked, women of means stayed home and took care of their children, claiming control over the home as their own domain. Maternal love and devotion became especially valued as a necessary condition for childrearing. Characterizing women as "semi-divine," and their gentle, nurturing natures as the most essential ingredient in fostering morality, motherhood became exalted.[10] Although plenty of mothers disciplined with a harsh hand, the new branding was widely trumpeted. As writer and editor S.G. Goodrich wrote in 1856, "a majority of mothers do in fact temper their conduct to their children, so as, on the whole, to exercise…a saving, redeeming, regenerating influence on them."[11] Idealism conquered reality.

Social activism during the Progressive Era (late nineteenth and early twentieth century), aimed to extend middle class parenting to working class and farming families. As rapid urbanization and industrialization created urban poverty and plight, reformers turned their sights on rescuing children and improving society. Labor unions demanded a "family wage" so that males could support their families, and women could stay home and nurture their young. Concerned with children's welfare, the government built playgrounds and daycares, passed laws establishing compulsory education and limiting child labor, and prolonged schooling through high school. Public health measures reduced infant mortality.

Viewing poverty as a disease, reformers strove to foist middle class values on families deemed inadequate due to race, class, religion, immigrant status, and ethnicity, by dictating proper norms of home and childcare. Delinquent children were placed in foster care and other programs, in the hope they could be rehabilitated. From 1854 to 1929, "orphan trains" took homeless and destitute children off the streets of New York and relocated them with families in the Midwest. While some children thrived in their new homes, others were used on farms for slave labor, faced stigma and suspicion, and struggled with the separation from their families. Reformers' well-intentioned, but not always well-constructed, efforts both helped and hurt.

Continued urbanization and the expanding entrepreneurial economy of the twentieth century heightened Americans' respect for individuality. Success in business required sociability, self-direction, and sound judgment. Parenting methods changed in tandem. Starting in the 1930s, parenting aims included cultivating affable and autonomous children through affectionate and indulgent practices that focused on the individual child's emotional life and the internalization of skills. Good parents were expected to joyfully make sacrifices in order to inculcate these traits, and in doing so, ensure the morality and prosperity of the next generation.

Demands on the American family changed once again during and after World War II when men joined the armed services and women increasingly entered the workforce to support the war effort. At the war's end, as returning veterans took back jobs, displacing some female workers, women were encouraged to retreat home and start families. To incentivize the trend, raising children once again became glorified as a task requiring women's full mental and physical energies.

Parenting ideals got a boost and another makeover once the subject came under scientific scrutiny. Beginning in the nineteenth century, the burgeoning field of psychology turned to mapping stages of childhood development, in physical, social, emotional, cognitive, and behavioral spheres, thus suggesting a normal course to maturity and providing established signposts for parents. Much of that research was directed towards middle-class families and had the effect of creating further expectations for both parenting and children's achievements. Early recommendations focused on developing regularity and self-control through strict feeding, toileting, and sleeping schedules. Later instructions individualized through feeding on demand and following a child's lead. The field also sought to determine the causes of childhood maladjustment and to offer solutions.

While advances have undoubtedly been made that helped many children and families, psychology's early methods and findings underwent a bumpy rollout, full of cultural and value-driven assumptions. The field discovered a prime suspect for psychological disorders: mothers. If they were primarily responsible for the next generation, and esteemed for their successes, then poor outcomes could only be ascribed to their shortcomings. Scattering blame near and far, the psychiatric establishment alternately portrayed mothers, and sometimes fathers, as harsh, rejecting, or overly enmeshed—each prospect interfering with children's growth and development.

In 1949, the psychiatrist Leo Kanner erroneously identified the causes of autism as "parental coldness, obsessiveness, and a mechanical type of attention to material needs only.... Their withdrawal seems to be an act of turning away from such a situation to seek comfort in solitude."[12] Within a few years, the accusation pointed more specifically at "refrigerator mothers" who lacked maternal warmth.

Poor mothering was suspected to be the cause of numerous childhood problems, diverse as disability, schizophrenia, delinquent behavior, sexual difficulties, and health disparities. In this climate. parents were no longer considered capable of raising children without professional input. As Ray Lyman Wilbur, a doctor and President of Stamford University stated in 1930, "It is beyond the capacity of the individual parent to train her child to fit into the intricate, interwoven and interdependent social and economic system we have developed."[13]

Ironically, science and culture elevated the work of parenting at the same time as they cast doubt upon parents' abilities. With the added burdens of devoting their full energies to raising children, educating themselves about child development, seeking out experts, titrating parenting methods to be neither too intrusive nor too detached, and implementing the latest parenting fads, parenting became increasingly scrutinized and intensive.

Despite ongoing cultural and economic changes at the end of the twentieth century and beginning of the twenty-first, including the doubling of women in the workplace, many of those ideas about parenthood remain dominant.[14] Etched into collective American expectations is the view that parenthood, and in particular, motherhood, can provide fulfillment and mold children into better adults; that sacrifice and dedication ultimately makes or breaks children's outcomes. In addition, most Americans aspire to parenting in an insular family in which the parents take primary responsibility. This vision both inspires and constrains. It inspires because it promises purpose, direction, and a sense of connection and security that too often has been absent in many lives. It constrains because its achievement is predicated on circumstances not entirely within everyone's control.

Rosy images of happy homemakers hardly describe the day-to-day experiences of many parents. Poorer parents, and those handicapped by health, disability, or discrimination, often cannot afford the luxury of intensive and indulgent child-rearing practices. Even those with more means sometimes find the required sacrifices too great. Starting in the 1960s, some middle-class women, feeling stifled by high expectations of domesticity, sought a broader definition of motherhood and opportunities to pursue diverse identities and roles. Nonetheless, as a dominant ideology, lofty standards for parental effort and sacrifice have trickled into policies and services.[15] Despite parents' different circumstances, they are often blamed for their offspring's troubles, as if parental efforts alone can fully protect and shape children. Left out of that conception is the clear influence of genetics, neighborhoods, schools, peers, economics, nutrition, and the physical environment on child development.[16]

Part of what fuels judgments against struggling parents is America's belief that individuals should pull themselves up by their own bootstraps, that hard work inevitably produces the proper bounty, and that those who founder do so because of their own failings. As late twentieth and early twenty-first century neoliberal political philosophies took hold, rhetoric extolling self-sufficiency grew especially strong. Those philosophies reinforced and necessitated personal efficacy by asserting that spending on social services stifles capitalism and the free market, thus producing sluggish workers and economies.[17] As a consequence, funding for family support services experienced cuts and now fall well short of demand.[18] Other institutions and policies benefitting families have also receded. Labor unions and guaranteed "family wages" have declined, as well as civic institutions that connect families to nongovernmental community supports.[19] Unfortunately, neoliberal doctrines extolling the virtues of bootstraps ignore the inconvenient fact that not everyone owns the requisite boots and cannot possibly acquire them if the government remains wary of handing them out.

Compared to other countries, America ranks last in the supports it offers families.[20] It is one of only three countries worldwide that does not guarantee paid maternity leave after childbirth; it is one of the few advanced nations that does not provide universal, high-quality, and affordable child care; it mandates less flexibility for parents in terms of hours worked, overtime, and vacations; it offers no guaranteed affordable housing options; and, in general, the overall financial help and benefits it provides to support children and families are stingier and less assured than in other high-income countries. America's skimpy policies towards families explain part of the reason for the country's ongoing stratification, economic stress on families, and the unequal burden placed on parents of different means.

As America idles in an age of particularly high inequality and low mobility, strapped parents find themselves increasingly handicapped. With the engines of social change accelerating and the country's in-

Parents Under Pressure

dustrial base transitioning into an economy powered by technology, service-based industries, and globalization, parents once again find themselves faced with unforeseen challenges.

The newer and less stable workplace favors those with a distinct skill base: knowledge, flexibility, self-advocacy, and collaborative ability.[21] Cultivating these traits in children falls to parents, whether or not they have the necessary resources. Pressure is exerted to raise children in enriched environments, to stimulate them from an early age, and to teach them numerous emotional and social skills. In this costly and time-consuming parenting culture, well-resourced families once again start from a highly-advantaged position. While some families are thriving in the new economy, others can barely stay afloat. Nonetheless, overall expectations and ideologies about parents' abilities to toil, sacrifice for, and independently raise their children remain unchanged.

The stories in this book challenge common perceptions of what parenting is like for many Americans. Told primarily from the parents' perspectives, each chapter centers on one family and includes accompanying commentaries, research, and interviews that contextualize their experiences:

- Chapter Two, *The System is Down*, recounts the struggles of Victoria and Nathaniel, whose children suffer from multiple disabilities, and delves into the impact of America's social service systems on families' income, isolation, and health.

- Chapter Three, *The Perils of Poverty*, examines Diana's efforts to raise children in a poor community ravaged by the opioid epidemic, and how the country's limited safety net and drug treatment services affect her chances.

- Chapter Four, *Chasing the Ideal*, tells the story of Robin, a mother with a history of trauma, who struggles to create a standard American family, and how the parent guidance industry, popular culture, and psychotherapy shape parenting ideals.

- Chapter Five, *Judgment's Furious Footsteps*, discusses how society and the child welfare systems' judgments about proper parenting, teen parents, poverty, mental illness, and race hinder Angelina and Jacob.

- Chapter Six, *When Race Matters*, looks at how race and income affect Sophia's attempts to procure assistance from schools and courts and the unique challenges parents of color experience.

- Chapter Seven, *Alloparents*, explores the role of communities in helping families through the story of Kim, who adopts two traumatized children from the child welfare system.

- The final chapter, *Getting from Here to There*, suggests ways to improve the supports offered to struggling families.

Although individual chapters highlight specific themes, the subjects they probe course through the other narratives. Each family, in different ways, is stressed by American parenting ideals, economics, judgment, inadequate supports, and the strains of interacting with fractured, overwhelmed, and underfunded helping systems. The vignettes expose the ill-suited expectations and supports with which families contend, and the differences in opportunities that income and race confer.

While the book samples a number of familial hardships and systemic responses, it cannot cover the full spectrum of issues families face, nor adequately represent the diversity of contemporary households. The American family keeps changing in composition and challenges. Contemporary families look increasingly different from families of previous centuries, with more divorced, blended, and same sex parents, more working mothers, single parents, cross-cultural, and adoptive families.[22] Fathers, on average, perform more parenting responsibilities than in previous generations, although mothers still assume the greater share.

Taken together, these stories push us to confront a number of crucial questions about the overall state of parenting and inequality in twenty-first century America. For those not financially comfortable, how possible is it to successfully raise a family? To what extent should parents sacrifice for an ailing child, at the expense of themselves or others? How much judgment gets cast at families, and what are the costs of that judgment? When parents need extra help or struggle with basic survival, when and in what ways should communities and institutions intervene? Tasked with helping, too often systems and services get in the way.

2. Nathaniel and Victoria:
The System Is Down

"MOST PARENTS PUSH THEIR KIDS TOO MUCH," said Victoria. "You have to be proud of them, appreciate that they are walking and breathing." She speaks with the authority of hard-earned experience. Only one of Nathaniel and Victoria's two children walk, and even then, with a limp, although both can now breathe independently. Achieving that outcome has not come easily.

Nathaniel and Victoria live in a small city near Springfield, Massachusetts, in a middling row of simple, sparsely landscaped homes with some of the area's most impoverished neighborhoods beckoning from just a few miles away. They moved there by accident rather than design, at a time of diminishing options, when a roof, any roof, was sorely needed.

The house in which they reside is old and ailing, cluttered with too many demands and too few reserves. The home needs new plumbing. A tree teeters precariously over the roof. Furniture swallows most of the space, paperwork crowds surfaces, untouched art materials fill shelves, and newly delivered medical supplies sit boxed on the porch. Victoria bemoans the lack of storage and her limited ability to organize their belongings. It is only one of the ways that parenthood has forced them to alter their priorities and downsize their expectations.

"Victoria and I followed this vision," said Nathaniel, "that she was going to spend the day working with our child and doing all the motherly things: being creative, going outside, and teaching about the crunchy stuff, gardening, and cooking. It didn't matter if it was a boy or girl, we didn't care. We would have adapted to the child and his or her interests. But when the girls were born, it blew a lot of that out of the water because they were so sick."

After marrying in 1994, Victoria and Nathaniel thought carefully about children and what they could offer. They wanted to be ready. Nathaniel worried about financial stability, about amassing a sufficient nest egg for ongoing needs. He worked in retail at JCPenney and Victoria as a child-care aide, earning them a modest, yet sufficient salary, but adding a child would stretch their resources.

Victoria did not want to wait. The nest egg could not be guaranteed. Four years older than Nathaniel, in her early thirties, she worried that time was running out. She also suffered from polycystic ovary syndrome, a condition that made her menstrual cycle uneven. Getting pregnant might be hard, and would require extra time, planning, and medical care.

A discussion with her doctor persuaded her to take medication to steady ovulation, despite the risk of twins. Soon after treatment started, a pregnancy test, on St. Patrick's Day, confirmed the success of their efforts. Morning sickness, which began later the same day, established a new rhythm and pattern to their lives. "I was vomiting really badly," said Victoria. "Nathaniel ended up bringing me to the hospital, which was a ways away. They checked me out and sent me home. But I got sicker and sicker. They said I might not hold on to the baby. Then all the fun began."

Victoria felt dizzy and ill, tired, day in and day out through the entire pregnancy. Small movements required enormous exertion, setting off rounds of nausea. Everyday tasks turned into ordeals. Wondering about the cause, her doctor ordered blood tests. When the tests detected high hormone levels, he sent her for an ultrasound. As Victoria lay on the table, watching the technician identify their baby's limbs, organs, and beating heart, they discovered the reason for her illness. "The lovely part is that the technician waited until I stood up to get a better look," remembered Nathaniel, "and there is a little white cursor blinking, it's the heart, and I am leaning over her and she says, 'There is another one.' We looked at each other and said, 'What do you mean, there is another one?'"

Nathaniel felt excited. Elated. Victoria experienced shock. The following day, she noticed her heart pounding, her breath constricting, and her body stiffening. Disquieting waves of fear and anxiety welled through her. "I was sitting in a rocking chair and rocking, rocking," she said. "I just felt pure panic about, I don't know what. The hormones and physical changes set me off. I had never had a panic attack before. That was my first of many to come."

As they prepared for two babies instead of one, they realized they needed to make immediate changes. They lived in an old farmhouse in Belchertown, in a home they loved. Although quiet, in the country, and with lots of space, it was not suitable for children. The house needed almost a complete remodel. Exposed wires and unfinished support posts posed dangers. In addition, the well from which they drew water sat near a road and wood treatment facility, raising the risk of water contamination. Victoria was pregnant, with twins, and they could not take chances.

They found a newer, cleaner place to rent in Ludlow, with a freshly installed well. The property's higher cost strained their budget, but they managed. Nathaniel had switched jobs, working at Mass Mutual in Springfield as an insurance analyst, and the move would ease his commute.

The new location did nothing to halt Victoria's slide into ill health. She felt sicker and sicker, with more and more complaints. In her fourth month, she developed gestational diabetes, which required careful monitoring. She also started grumbling about the smell of mold. "It was a cold March," said Nathaniel. "Everything was dormant and then it warmed up and things grew. The landlords had taken the stove and vented the hood into a back porch, which was literally coated with mold. We never went in there because they said it was just storage. I hadn't smelled it at first, but Victoria did. I thought she was psychosomatic. You know—she didn't feel good and was associating things. But the reality is that she was right."

The home also housed snakes. Their white cat kept staring at the foundation, gawking and pawing. They gave the behavior little thought, until Nathaniel discovered one of the creatures in the house. He placed it in a plastic bowl, poked holes in the lid, and took it to the nearby Laughing Brook Wildlife Sanctuary for identification. The naturalist informed them it was a small constrictor milk snake, non-venomous, harmless, but disturbing nonetheless.

"You have to put that back where you found it," he told Nathaniel.

"I don't think so," replied Nathaniel, "I found it in my living room."

In the fall of that year, at week twenty-eight of the pregnancy, too early, Victoria's cervix thinned and contractions began. Finding themselves unable to stop labor, Victoria's doctors at the local hospital transferred her to a facility with advanced capabilities. The new hospital's physicians subdued the contractions, but Victoria felt uncomfortable. She did not know the doctors, and they did not know her. Explaining her symptoms to a rotating set of unfamiliar staff discomfited her. She missed the easy communication, comforting presence, and implicit understanding offered by known and trusted providers.

Only a day later, the contractions still halted, Victoria felt the unexpected gush of her water breaking. Wanting the twins carried for as long as possible, to give more time for their lungs and organs to develop, the doctors continued to suppress her labor. They forestalled the birth for another five days.

Diabetic, in her mid-thirties, and carrying preterm twins, Victoria's pregnancy was high risk, necessitating a high level of care and monitoring. Nurses strapped a tocodynamometer (TOCO) around her waist so that the rise and falls of her contractions could be followed. They tested the amniotic fluid to ensure that bacteria had not entered and infected the twins. Doctors also prescribed steroids that would strengthen the fetuses' lungs, so that they could breathe upon birth. When the transition from labor to birth began, the hospital would need to move quickly, setting up an operating room and assembling two neonatal intensive care units (NICUs), one for each twin, to address any medical needs.

The high level of care and monitoring did little to alleviate Victoria's growing symptoms. Soon after her water broke, she felt a burning sensation accompanied by intense pain. "I told them I thought I had a urinary tract infection," she said. "They didn't check on it. Or clean the room. I would stand by the bed, wait for the amniotic fluid to come out, and then grab my own towel to mop it up because I thought I would fall. It was gross. They weren't cleaning. Nobody seemed to be listening."

Victoria felt the pain spread to her back, where it became harder and harder to bear. A nurse, trying to help, applied a hot compress that scorched rather than soothed. As Victoria's distress billowed, the nurse, searching for a solution, suggested morphine. The attending doctor advised against, explaining that the drug could cause her babies respiratory distress. But he prescribed a small dose, anyway. Even on the medicine, Victoria's pain worsened. She screamed and screamed. The doctor told her to calm down, take a deep breath, she was out of control. Labor and delivery hurts.

Feeling silenced yet apprehensive, she called her childbirth educator, who timed her contractions. They were less than two minutes apart. "Get someone in there," the educator said, "or the twins will be born on the floor." The nurses had set up the TOCO monitor backwards, the peaks of the contractions showing up as plateaus, so that her advancing labor had gone undetected.

"They were treating her like a hysterical first-time mother," said Nathaniel, "when she was in the middle of labor and the kids were in distress. Hospitals have charts about each patient. She had so many risks, hers should have been dipped in red-ink. It should have been glowing."

The hospital organized for an emergency delivery, preparing the operating room and assembling the NICUs, fourteen people in all. Victoria did all she could to curb the pain and birth urge until arrangements were complete. She remembered it as the hardest undertaking she had ever attempted. Nathaniel recalled it as pure chaos.

Victoria was right; she had contracted a urinary tract infection. Her twin daughters slid through the infected birth canal, ingesting the contagion, which entered their lungs. Their first child, Autumn, received an initial Apgar score of three, on a scale of one to ten, in which ten indicates an infant in prime physical condition. She required immediate resuscitation. Her sister, Olivia, received an adequate score of seven. Both suffered oxygen depletion during the birth. Both sustained intraventricular hemorrhages, bleeding in various areas of their brains. Olivia had a grade one hemorrhage, affecting only a small area, that bled into her spinal fluid. Autumn underwent two hemorrhages, one that entered her spinal fluid and another that leached into her brain matter. They both weighed about three pounds eleven ounces.

"It was terrifying," remembered Nathaniel. "Horrible. Basically, we survived the experience. It was traumatic, it was awful."

"All I was thinking," said Victoria, "was, 'Please let them live'."

The girls lived. They remained in the NICU for one month and spent another month in the hospital's critical care nursery. For eight or nine hours a day, one or both parents stayed with them, learning about their care. Then Victoria and Nathaniel would go home, without their babies, feeling disoriented and empty. Nathaniel took a week off work after the birth and when they were released from the hospital, another two. That was all the time he could get.

Caring for the twins took eighteen hours a day, sometimes more. An apnea monitor, which tracked Olivia's breathing and heart rate, necessitated vigilant supervision. Steroids to enhance their lung functioning needed to be sprayed through their reluctant mouths. Each baby required feeding every few hours, and their mouths wiped clean afterwards so that they would not develop thrush. With weak musculature, they found digestion difficult, requiring the administration of medications for gastroesophageal reflux disease. Their tiny diapers needed frequent changing, and their monitors had to be unhooked and refastened before and after bathing. They were undersized and fragile, a constant source of concern.

A home health aide helped a few hours a day, but the majority of the care fell to Victoria and Nathaniel. The incessant attention to medical needs, frequent medical appointments, and endless worries, combined with Victoria's recovery from childbirth, created strain. "I had one experience when we had to bottle feed them," remembered Nathaniel. "You had to support them and hold this tiny little bottle of formula with only about four drops, and they had to suck on the bottle, but you had to position their heads properly. And Autumn was choking. I was terrified. I said, 'I can't do this.' There were all these insane challenges. We were constantly in a state of vigilance over medical issues. We weren't in this happy afterglow."

"It's hard," said Victoria. "These are your babies. You don't want anything to happen." Guarding against happenings, with two delicate infants, seemed almost impossible.

Two weeks after Autumn and Olivia came home, Victoria was changing their diapers when she noticed red streaks in their poop and a terrible smell. Their doctor took a sample, suspecting salmonella, and sent it to the state lab. Nathaniel and Victoria thought the contaminant came from their well, the new, attractive well that drew them into renting the house. The well housing had cracked and the water had absorbed runoff from a nearby farm.

The girls' symptoms introduced a host of agencies and regulations into their lives. The town tested the water, seeking the source of contamination, but only after the errant homeowner poured bleach into the well, eradicating any evidence. A public health nurse warned that if the girls could not shed the infection, they would not be allowed in school. Nathaniel explained that "the girls" were only infants. The Women, Infants, and Children (WIC) nutrition program, noting that no proof of water contamination existed, denied their initial request for premade formula. However, with potentially toxic water coming from their taps, Victoria and Nathaniel could not risk mixing it into baby formula; and they found buying large volumes of bottled water unaffordable.

After a few weeks of exasperating bickering and hardship, the lab agreed the symptoms could have resulted from water-born salmonella. Their doctor wrote a letter in support of formula, and WIC at last approved the request. Around the same time, while Victoria briefly relaxed, she overheard their home health aide screaming at the twins. Hampered by one complication after another, and coupled with the girls' extensive care, Victoria and Nathaniel felt completely overwhelmed.

More than anything, Nathaniel and Victoria craved a pause in the action, a hiatus that could allow the rush of troubles to subside. They needed their overwrought nerves to settle and their exhausted bodies to recuperate. But relaxation and recuperation existed as little more than a threadbare fantasy. They could not remain in a house with contaminated water. Short on cash, with limited choices, and the twins just thirteen months old, they moved in with Nathaniel's mother, who lived in a nearby city. At the time, she suffered from the early stages of

Alzheimer's. When she died a few years later, they inherited the house.

The twin's care consumed the bulk of their time and efforts, but also reaped rewards. In Victoria and Nathaniel's living room hangs a picture of the girls, nine months old and lying on their bellies, both with broad, contagious smiles. Olivia, healthier since birth, pushes her body upward; Autumn struggles to do so. The differences between them would grow starker.

Olivia flourished with the support of a teacher who told her to "bloom where you are planted," a motto that she and her parents repeated in times of frustration and stress. Born with cerebral palsy, she required assistance to learn to walk and move, and participated in ongoing weekly physical therapy for moderate physical delays. She acquired physical and verbal milestones slowly, but development steadily proceeded. Although at continued risk for complications—a pulmonologist followed her for years to ensure that her heart and lungs developed properly—she appeared to be a happy, thriving infant.

Olivia's biggest challenges involved diagnoses of autism, nonverbal learning disability, and a low IQ that led to problems with social cueing and made her an easy victim for school bullies. As a consequence, she found school a miserable experience and performed poorly until the eighth grade. Then a change came. Anger and will coalesced around the sudden recognition of prejudice and injustice. Emboldened, she took matters into her own hands. She threw a dodge ball at one of the bullies, screamed at another, and pinned the arms of a third, holding down her hands so that the girl could not get away. Leaning into the bully's face, Olivia yelled at her to stop the teasing and torment. It stopped. So, too, did some of her remedial functioning. Olivia flourished after that, learning more rapidly, moving from a student destined for vocational employment as a janitor or kitchen aide to an adolescent considering community college and a career that included public speaking.

Autumn presented a bigger challenge. At nine months old, she started banging her head. Victoria and Nathaniel had installed swings for the girls in the doorway of the living room, and Autumn would lean out of the swing in order to whack herself on the posts. They would carefully snuggle her back in, secure her in the swing, and pad

Parents Under Pressure

the posts with pillows, but she continued to bang. Sometimes she banged with such vigor that she scarred herself and shook the house. She also started to rock, vigorously pulsating back and forth. She enjoyed humming, as well, producing a discordant, bitonal, and jarring sound. The banging and cacophonous hum, repeated endless times a day, pelted Nathaniel and Victoria's already brittle nerves.

Encouraging but intermittent signs of progress punctuated Autumn's repetitious behaviors. During her second year, she began to talk and respond. She would sit on the couch and ask for food, videos, or objects, delighting her parents. She progressed to one or two-word commands before her speech completely evaporated. As her skills slipped, so did hopes of a functional childhood. By age three, she had collected a variety of diagnoses: autism, cerebral palsy, gastro-esophageal reflux disease, and chronic idiopathic constipation. When Olivia started walking, Autumn was still tackling independent sitting. She never mastered toilet training. For years, she vomited frequently. She even threw up while sleeping, requiring Nathaniel and Victoria to prop her head while in bed. Even then, they needed to change her sheets up to four times a night. She felt miserable. She arched her back and threw herself around, sleeping restlessly, if at all.

When Autumn was four years old, the neurologist thought her difficulties were behavioral and put her on Risperidone, a powerful antipsychotic drug that aimed to reduce her irritability and aggression. He also prescribed Clonidine to ensure a normal sleep pattern for herself and her family. Further evaluation uncovered a gastro-intestinal cause to her behaviors. She had a very slow small intestine, digesting food in twice the time it took others. As a consequence, she was uncomfortable and suffered severe reflux, which damaged her esophagus. One year, her medical conditions sent her to the hospital seven times.

Twice Autumn tested positive for lead poisoning, for which they treated her with large doses of iron. Upon investigation, they found that the house's interior paint contained lead. Autumn had ingested its poisons by licking the window sills. Needing a solution, Nathaniel and Victoria researched options, but found them limited. The state's de-leading program would not cover the full costs, rendering that route unaffordable. The alternative, they discovered, was to seal the contaminated areas with duct tape. Which they did. Autumn could no longer lick the sills, but they could no longer open their windows. Hot summer days were stifling.

Autumn's numerous medical conditions necessitated so much care and so many appointments that at times Olivia got pushed into the background. Her parents wished they could spend more time talking, coloring, or playing dolls with her. They worried that they did not do enough. "Because Autumn took so much," they said, "we felt like we didn't have time for other things, even our own relationship. And you feel guilty thinking you want that, because you are basically trying to keep your child alive and functioning and trying to push her forward."

"Once you decide to bring these children into the world," Nathaniel said, "you are going to do whatever you can to keep them in the world."

Lack of time interfered with their relationship, but so did the complicated emotions that accompany painful and taxing experiences. The anger Victoria felt about the twins' birth, the way she had been treated by doctors, and the accruing difficulties since then, became directed at Nathaniel. "It was very degrading," she said, remembering her time in the hospital. "I was screaming and Nathaniel was listening to the doctor and I felt he should be listening to me. After that, I put up a wall between myself and everyone else, including him. I was putting up a wall because I was defending my children. It's like, I had to fight for their survival."

The stresses mounted. Victoria found it harder and harder to cope. "I would go to bed and eat," she said. "I like food, I like to eat. When I could go to bed and eat, that was a good moment. You have to survive. Everyone has their drug."

"That's what it became," said Nathaniel, "surviving. It was about making it to the next day."

Survival, and the cost of that survival, is the subject of Ruth Levy Guyer's book, *Baby at Risk*, which details the experiences of infants like Autumn and their families.[1] A writer and medical ethicist, Guyer was interested in decision-making in the NICU, in how and when decisions are made to save imperiled lives. *Baby at Risk* grapples with the various ethical, medical, social, economic, and political factors that hamper infants born suffering and with severe disabilities, as well as the effects on their parents. It documents a medical establishment more skilled at saving lives than enhancing them, a society more willing to pump money into advanced medical technologies than the daily care of sick children and their families.

"Even though we are willing to have the NICU rescue these children," Guyer said during a conversation through Skype, "we don't prepare for them in our communities." Some of the families Dr. Guyer interviewed recounted strenuous challenges obtaining adequate educational, medical, and social supports. They felt isolated and ostracized, and often suffered physical, psychological, and financial damage. Marriages burst from the strain. "Some families got stronger," she said, "but most were broken apart. Some of the situations were impossible. Most of them did not end well."

Other researchers have documented similar findings.[2] Mothers of children with disabilities are two to three times as likely to suffer from anxiety, depression, and stress than the general population. The 2009/10 National Survey of Children with Special Health Care Needs reports that 22 percent of families claimed that their child's health conditions create financial problems and 25 percent indicated that family members needed to cut back hours or stop working to care for an ill child. When the number and severity of a child's impairments rose, families' financial and work-related difficulties surged.

Lower income families felt the impact more than higher income ones. Canadian researchers David McConnell, Amber Savage, and Rhonda Breitkreuz found that families with financial hardship and few social supports paid an especially high price. Faced with challenging child behaviors, one in three financially-secure families, with substantial social supports, fared well. Families lacking both struggled mightily, with only one in one hundred respondents reporting a high quality of life. The odds tilt strongly against families like Victoria and Nathaniel.

Despite the daily pressures, Nathaniel and Victoria wanted the girls to experience and do as much as possible. There were moments of joy. They took them to fairs, like the Eastern States Exposition, the largest in the area. Nathaniel would carry Autumn's forty-pound frame up the stairs of the giant slide so that they could glide down together. She loved it. They went to Cape Cod, swam in lakes and pools, and enrolled the girls in the Special Olympics.

Victoria arranged a family trip to Disney World through the Sunshine Foundation, a charity that funds the dreams of chronically ill or challenged children. The foundation paid for everything, including an aide. While at Disney World, the girls swam at the Dolphin Experience. Autumn squealed happily, emitting a high-pitched noise that resembled a dolphin's whistle. The dolphins responded by trailing her in the water. The family also went out to eat, in restaurants, when money allowed. Autumn would grunt loudly, catching the attention of other customers. Victoria and Nathaniel did not care; it was worth it. "Our kids are our joys," said Victoria. "We treat them well. We raised Olivia to be caring and wonderful. But it's getting from one day to the next that's hard."

As the children aged, the toll on Victoria increased. She experienced panic attacks, depression, and fatigue. For the first three years, she had functioned as their primary caretaker. Nathaniel would help out as much as he could, sprinting into the fray and the care as soon as he returned from work, before he even caught his breath or took off his coat. It helped.

However, as Autumn got older, so did the caretaking demands. Autumn became too big to carry up slides or into swimming pools, so many of the family outings halted. She also continued to require a high degree of daily care. Even at the time of this interview, at age eighteen, she was not able to perform any Activities of Daily Living (ADLs) independently. She could feed herself some foods, with her thumb and forefinger, but was unable to effectively use utensils without making a mess. When not maneuvering in a wheelchair, she walked on her knees, thumping and rocking the house with her large body. Incontinent and still wearing diapers, she gestured, but did not speak, and could only understand and follow a one-step direction about 70 percent of the time, if she was familiar with it. She would cooperate when she understood. For instance, if shown her clothing, she would lie down to be changed.

Along with the daily demands of Autumn's care, a constant flow of unpredictable difficulties cascaded through the family's life, threatening to overrun its banks. Taking the girls anywhere involved a massive production of assembling and carrying equipment: wheelchairs, medicines, special foods, and large diapers and wipes, even when Autumn was full-grown. The equipment itself was vulnerable to malfunction. Autumn rocked so violently that she broke more than one of her wheelchairs. Without it, she could not attend school. In addition, as Autumn grew and put on weight, she became more difficult to manage and Victoria could no longer lift her. Victoria threw out her back in one attempt, from which she never fully recovered. After the first few years, it thus became clear that Nathaniel's full-time presence at home was sorely needed.

The pressing issue was not just Nathaniel's time and labor, but also how his job affected family finances and services. His income, as well as their limited nest egg, turned out to be a hindrance, pricing them out of certain benefits. When he worked, the girls did not qualify for subsidized state health insurance or for Supplemental Security Income (SSI), the federal income supplement program started in 1975 to help low-income individuals with disabilities. SSI only allowed $3,000 in family savings and cut awards if families owned more. Other services, such as Personal Care Attendants (PCAs), which they sorely needed for Autumn, were only available to those with state health insurance.

Sorting out and applying for benefits took time. A labyrinth of bureaucracies confronted them, agencies and programs with their own twists, turns, obstructions, and dead-ends. Each required a suffocating amount of research, applications, coordination, and, all too often, battles. "It's constant," said Nathaniel, "it's been one challenge after another. You need to do the research on services, become the experts, and try not to make an enormous mistake at the same time." Working had become a liability.

When Nathaniel left his job to care for his family, they managed by strapping together a rudimentary income through disability and food stamps and relying on the kindness of friends. One gave them his used car. Neighbors shoveled their walk in the winter. But apart from those helpers, they felt isolated, with no family or friends nearby who could provide substantial aid. They hoped that their low income, lack of savings, and minimal supports would not decimate them in the event of an emergency.

They had reason to worry. They lived in an old house with built-in hazards. On their limited income, sufficiently maintaining the house was impossible and paying property taxes a ludicrous extravagance. They owed thousands of dollars in arrears.

The previous fall, they discovered a hole in their roof and made a claim to their home insurance. When the claim came through, it was initially denied due to unpaid taxes. Nathaniel negotiated with the city and insurance company to allow the funds, despite the tax debt, arguing that not fixing the problem would ultimately cost the city more. Without a solid covering, the house would deteriorate and become uninhabitable and unsellable. The town and insurance company demurred. While Nathaniel successfully plugged that leak, future floods menaced. The rest of the roof was deteriorating, but cost $50,000 to fix. A tree overhanging the house needed to be cut, lest it fall, but that came with a $5,000 price tag. The heat and plumbing worked poorly. Their house threatened to break down and thrust them into homelessness.

Victoria and Nathanial looked into getting a new house through Habitat for Humanity, but their income fell short of the minimum requirement by $200 a month.[3] They wanted to move into Treehouse, a nearby multigenerational, supportive community, but found it only accepted foster and adoptive families.[4] They researched grants that assist the handicapped by providing money to refigure their homes to make them more accessible, but their house was too old, with too many needs, and they did not qualify, anyway, because they owed back taxes.[5] "There are lots of systems," said Nathaniel. "There are little bits and pieces that come together, but there is always this wall. It's like you are in this world of mountains. Every time you crest one, there is another one."

"There's always some crack we fall through," agreed Victoria, "programs you don't qualify for because of this or that. I don't have enough money, but you want to cut my food stamps because I got an extra $2."

"What happened," explained Nathaniel, "was the girls would get a COLA (cost of living adjustment) increase through disability, which should reflect the rising cost of goods. It's not just, 'here's more money.' But that COLA increase cut food stamps by more than the increase we got. So, you'd never make it forward, you'd always struggle with something. It is insane."

COLA increases are linked to inflation to ensure that families receiving benefits do not suffer decreases in spending power as prices rise. As services and benefits calculate eligibility based on income, changes to one can affect another. Timing also plays a role. SSI delivers COLAs in January of each year, while food stamps utilize an October 1 date.[6] In that ten month gap, eligibility can be recalculated and lead to cutbacks.

Managing the systemic requirements, and their fallouts, required a tremendous amount of time and energy. The school used food as a reinforcer for Autumn, rewarding her with treats when she attempted a desired task. Autumn would swat the food with her hand, not wanting to eat, but the staff misunderstood her cues. With her slow intestine and gastrointestinal problems, Autumn could not handle even the low volume of snacks they gave her. Her vomiting and esophageal damage increased to the extent that, for a few months, she required a feeding tube. At home, she risked dislodging the tube while she moved and rocked. Nathaniel and Victoria spent their afternoons holding the tube and following her around the house.

The school also seemed unsure how best to synchronize her services. Autumn qualified for physical therapy (PT), occupational therapy (OT), and speech and communication skills. Each specialist worked in a silo, setting up a unique time and agenda. The end result was an uncoordinated matrix of services with limited effectiveness. Autumn could not integrate each independently learned skill into larger tasks, so she made poor use of the training.

Nathaniel and Victoria worked with the school to revamp the program. They organized the specialists to work together on a single goal, broken down into multiple, interlapping elements. For instance, when teaching Autumn to pick up a crayon, PT would work on the arm and body motion, OT would work on the finger grip, and speech would work on the signaling. Nathaniel and Victoria soon found that their direction was similarly required in all aspects of Autumn's care and services.

Autumn's school program did not cover all her needs and in particular, offered only a short half day summer program and no coverage during vacations. For a child who required twenty-four hour care and needed a lot of skill training, much of the burden fell on the family. Once Nathaniel stopped working and earning, the doctor secured Personal Care Assistant (PCA) services for her, which helped, but also came with its own ups and downs.

Families needed to hire their own PCAs and finding qualified ones was hard. Sometimes finding anyone at all was hard. Not everyone they selected could work the hours they needed. As a consequence, they would go months without assistance. The reliability of attendants also varied. One PCA stole from them. Victoria, suspecting she had done so, set up a camera, caught her, and turned her in.

Autumn qualified for help through the Department of Developmental Services (DDS) and acquired a case manager who attended school meetings and helped locate additional services, but not without Nathaniel and Victoria digging and probing for what might be available. They were never offered a menu of services or list of possible sources of assistance. Instead, they needed to scrupulously figure out what they needed, where it might be available, who to ask for it, and how to coordinate the particulars.

Ruth Levy Guyer, when given a summary of Victoria and Nathaniel's experiences, remarked that they are typical, mirroring the ordeals of the families she studied. "These families are spending 100 percent of their time caring for the child," she said, "and yet they also have to go out and find special schools, special equipment, and special medicine. For instance, children need new wheelchairs every year because they grow. Every one of those requests involves paperwork and phone calls. You need a guide through this, but that's rare. Agencies don't have that, they ask you to show what you need. But you're so busy with your child, how can you? That's why it is so draining."

With school and PCAs services loosely in place, some pieces of Autumn's care puzzle fit together, while other gaps remained. Nathaniel and Victoria badgered DDS for additional options. It was not until Autumn was seventeen years old that their worker, acquiescing to the pressure, finally told them about a grant program, only available to a limited number of children with the most severe disabilities, which offers funds for in-home services as well as reimbursement for otherwise non-covered supplies.[7] While the grant allows families to choose the services they want, it also makes them responsible for hiring and managing the professionals. Victoria and Nathaniel used the funds to provide Autumn with in-home music and speech therapy and gave themselves regular consultations with an autism specialist.

Through another grant from United Cerebral Palsy, Nathaniel and Victoria purchased iPads with specialized speech software installed. Autumn can now touch buttons on the iPad to indicate her choices and preferences, which are then spoken out loud for her. They have provided the school with the same software to create a program that works home to school, bringing continuity to her life and allowing for enhanced skill practice. Nathaniel and Victoria are convinced that, given the right tools and opportunities, their daughter can and will communicate. But they realize that goal will take ongoing efforts and interagency cooperation.

"The systems have to be more interconnected," said Nathaniel. "While one system is helping, you are locked out of others through economics. Obtaining different programs or services is seen as double-dipping, but really, they cover different things. People on the receiving end don't want to screw the system, they just want services."

Unfortunately, services are often in short supply and hard to procure. A lack of adequate funding perpetuates the problem, reflecting America's confusion about how much the care of distressed families should exist as a private, household concern or a public responsibility, whether individuals with handicaps are valued as assets or demonized as drains on society's coffers.

Linda Blum, a professor of sociology at Northeastern University, addresses such questions in her study of mothers raising children with invisible disorders like attention deficit disorder (ADD) and attention deficit hyperactivity disorder (ADHD).[8] Blum grounds her research on contemporary families in the effects of neoliberal economic policies favoring the free market and private sector over government programs.

Earlier in the twentieth century, as the country faced the devastation of the Great Depression, the government, backed by broad public support, showed greater interest in buttressing citizens' well-being. The Social Security Act of 1935 established a safety net that grew to aid the elderly, unemployed, poor, disabled, veterans, and others. Public benefits peaked in the 1970s, after which a stalling American economy, and policies tilted towards companies, led to reforms and cuts.[9] By the 1980s, neoliberal philosophies also began drifting into family life, inflating the message that individual choice, rather than social or public benefit, shapes success.

Blum's office at Northeastern University, in a refurbished state building, bears a distinctly corporate feel. She works in one of the small, enclosed, mostly glass cubicles on the ninth floor, with a receptionist prominently located outside the elevator, a carpeted hallway, and a bevy of glass windows overlooking the common area. Blum expresses some discomfort with the setting, perhaps because it surrounds her with the exact motifs that her work critiques.

"Part of the neoliberal belief," she said, "is that it is our responsibility to work on ourselves continuously. We must train our brains and maximize our physical health. When you are talking about kids, those tasks fall on mothers. Individual responsibility for that health maximization is very intense right now. People don't recognize that it's new. And they don't recognize what it is covering up, which is the lack of social and public responsibility. We used to take more public responsibility."

Originally interested in mother-blaming, and how, historically and morally, class and race were used to sort mothers into good and bad parents, Blum's 2015 book, *Raising Generation Rx: Mothering Kids with Invisible Disabilities in an Age of Inequality,* documents new twists on old themes. The role not only of caring for their children, but also figuring out and securing help for their conditions, fell largely to parents. They needed to navigate what she calls "dense bureaucracies," decentralized, fragmented, and underfunded systems that, as Nathaniel and Victoria found, place responsibility on parents' shoulders.

"What is striking is how relentless it was," she said, "how many different sources of expertise they sought. The mothers might find someone who is helpful, but they couldn't stop, they had to keep going, had to keep thinking there is probably more, another piece, another kind of specialist, or a more accurate diagnosis. They continually wondered, 'Is there more I could be doing? Is there something I am missing?'" She also found that none of the parents escaped the stigma of their children's conditions.

"One of the paradoxes," she explained, "is that you might think that affluent mothers and kids would have better experiences, because we usually think that higher education leads to greater tolerance. What I found, and some of the other literature suggests, is it doesn't really work that way. Disability may be more threatening in affluent communities that fear downward mobility."

Blum's research shows that prosperous families of children with difficulties face social isolation and even ostracism in their neighborhoods and schools, while poorer families and those from racial minorities experience greater acceptance in their communities, but are more likely to encounter judgment and surveillance from institutions and professionals. In both cases, the message is the same: families must struggle virtually alone, and are faulted if they cannot.

Blum found that judgment and surveillance took many forms. School personnel and psychiatric professionals sometimes blamed mothers for their children's troubles, and even more often, for not doing enough to address them. Single parents, particularly those of low income and racial minorities, were more likely to come under the scrutiny of child protective services and lose custody of their children. Even when state intervention led to helpful services, mothers found themselves angered and disparaged by the intrusion and punitiveness of the system. The cumulative demands took a toll on many of Blum's mothers, with almost half reporting that emotional stress led them to take antidepressants or other psychotropic medication. Blum concludes that the solution for those families, and for society, in general, is less mother-blame and more public accountability, resources, and support.

Nathaniel and Victoria's experiences mirrored many of Blum's findings. A white family from a middle-class background, they avoided the scrutiny of child protective services, but suffered from social isolation and the judgments of others. Their large burden of care left them little time to nurture and reciprocate friendships, and engendered strong reactions from relatives. Although some of Nathaniel's siblings and cousins lived nearby, and Victoria's brother resided within a few hours' drive, they provided more criticism than support.

"Why can't she stay home and take care of the kids by herself?" Nathaniel's siblings would ask. "Why can't he hold down a job?"

"You make your bed, you lie in it," Victoria's brother told her. "It's your choice, you should have known what you were getting into."

The disjointed bureaucracies, lack of social supports, and assorted stresses that Blum describes, and Victoria and Nathaniel experienced, are also familiar to Jason Litto, the child and adolescent service coordinator for the Holyoke and Chicopee office of the Department of Developmental Services (DDS).

Housed in a reconditioned mill-building in what used to be the industrial hub of Holyoke, the area office of DDS perches on a pockmarked street and across from a low-income housing complex, its back facing one of the city's three power canals, originally built for the mills and still used to generate hydroelectricity. The building's location, historical relevance, and scantily equipped interior all but announce that its solid intentions receive limited backing.

Litto is a veteran of the disability field, with over twenty years of experience working with children and adults in respite support, group homes, public and private schools, and at a nonprofit that helps those on the autistic spectrum. Now at DDS, he carries a caseload of four hundred and fifty children whom he approves for services and connects to the department's contracted service centers. His high caseload reflects repeated budget cuts at the state level for service coordinators.

During his tenure in the field, Litto has witnessed the highs and lows of the system. He applauds the dedicated workers, generally underpaid, who labor to improve the lives of children and families; the determined parents who struggle daily to provide care to their children; and the way the field has grown to create improved strategies, resources, and curricula. But he also acknowledges the frustrating inaccessibility of many services. Waitlists for therapeutic help are long, sometimes eight months or more, and finding psychiatrists or psychotherapists with a solid understanding of children with special needs is challenging. Low pay leads to a high turnover of workers, which in, turn, affects the quality of services. A decentralized system provides different avenues of support, each with a separate point of entry.

"This sums it up," he said, "for this, you've got to apply in this avenue, and apply here, and apply here. As opposed to, 'Here are all your needs.' A lot of what DDS does is to help families navigate the system, assist them with getting applications, and letting them know about different opportunities, but it's still a complicated process. Who is funding what, and providing what, is confusing for families."

Karen Franklin, Vice President of Outpatient Services for ServiceNet, headquartered in downtown Northampton, describes similar difficulties in the community mental health system.[10] ServiceNet provides services to over twelve thousand people each year in programs that include counseling and psychiatry, vocational services, homeless programs, and residential and day treatment. Franklin, a clinical social worker who has worked in the field for over thirty years, oversees the agency's five outpatient clinics, which employ one hundred and seventy clinicians and service two-thirds of the agency's clientele. Located accessibly near the main intersection of the downtown, the Northampton clinic's slight, recessed entranceway appears dwarfed by the large brick building and voluminous awning under which it is tucked, as though simultaneously asserting and protecting its presence.

"In the mental health system," said Franklin, "there is no system for coordination amongst agencies to ensure that all needs and specialties are covered. We can coordinate well within our agency, but outside is harder. We don't always know what other agencies are doing or where to send people for problems we don't cover. And because there is little integration across agencies, there are lots of gaps in services or a family could be getting services from different places, which can be difficult for them."

Even when families breach the gaps and locate services, approval is not guaranteed. "All these resources are limited," said Litto. "Just think about numbers. There is only so much availability. So, often, we rely on families reaching out to us. Families are not always offered services because we can't fund everyone and everything. Sometimes we don't share information, if we feel that the family won't qualify for, or be prioritized for, that service. That's hard for us, as professionals. The answer is more funding across the human services systems which comes from a higher value placed on people with disabilities and for people working in the field. There's just not enough."[11]

Franklin's agency contends with similar shortages. "We need more child and family therapists. But people do not want to work for a clinic if they can do private practice and make more money."

At ServiceNet, starting salaries for therapists with graduate degrees are $35,000 and licensed psychotherapists earn $40,000. "We try to compensate by offering good benefits, trainings, consultation teams, and a nice work environment," said Franklin, "but if you have to take loans to go to school, and then you get that low a salary, why would you do it? I wish we had a system that valued the work and paid more." One of the biggest problems ServiceNet and the mental health field faces is a shortage of psychiatrists.[12] "We are exploring every possible avenue we can," said Franklin, "but there's nobody available. Nothing."

When it comes to disability and mental health services, "not enough" may at least be more than there used to be. In previous centuries, with little value placed on people with mental illness or disabilities, and stigma directed at the parents who bore them, many professionals pressured families to hide or institutionalize children viewed as compromised. Unfortunately, parents risked placing their children in institutions that were of poor quality or downright abusive. Allegations of sexual abuse and unsanitary conditions, of making residents work without pay, along with the introduction of new drugs that could control psychiatric symptoms, led to lawsuits and the dismantling of those institutions in the 1970s, a process referred to as deinstitutionalization.[13]

Across the country, due to the insistence of parents and advocates filing lawsuits, new service systems began forming that aimed to care for children at home, at school, and in the community.

At the same time, attempts were made to restructure mental health services. In 1963, President Kennedy signed the Community Mental Health Act to finance community-based treatment facilities. However, the Act was never allocated adequate expenditures. In 1980, President Carter, confronting a faltering system, signed the Mental Health Systems Act, which aimed to restructure and improve services. Just one year later, President Reagan repealed the legislation, instead paying for mental health services through block grants to states. An uneven, disorganized, and poorly financed system emerged that rendered service delivery dependent not just on need, but on funding.

"We have data about the ages, socioeconomics, and diagnoses of our clients," said Franklin, Vice President of Outpatient Services for ServiceNet, "and we look at it to help determine what services to provide. But it is hard to start up new programs or treatments. A lot is guided by reimbursement. If the insurance companies won't pay it, we can't afford to do it. We eat some costs and do things, anyway. But all our outpatient clinics lose money. There is very little other funding besides insurance. Insurance drives policy and services."

Deinstitutionalization and community services have improved many lives, but overall the attempts to restructure mental health services have been considered a failure.[14] Adequate treatments and facilities were never established, so that numerous individuals needing services ended up incarcerated or homeless. When it comes to children, most of whom have families to care for them, deinstitutionalization proved more humane than institutionalization, but the policies ended up shifting more and more tasks onto parents' shoulders.

"Having a child with a disability is intense," said Jason Litto, child and adolescent service coordinator for the Department of Developmental Services. "No matter how much support a family is getting, there is still a lot 24/7 that they have to deal with. It's life-long. Sometimes I think what families need is respite support, someone to provide childcare who is knowledgeable about their child and can let them take care of other things and themselves."

The same exigencies exist amongst the population Franklin serves. "We see families with intensive needs," she said. "They need a lot more support. In-home therapy is great, and I value what they do, but families sometimes need basic things. Like they could use someone in there who could be a parent advocate, or a nurse, or a PCA, or just help them go food shopping. Basic needs. But their difficulties need to be very severe to get that kind of help."

Ruth Levy Guyer has come to a similar conclusion. "Society does nothing for the parents," she said. "If a child has a disease, someone forms a foundation and raises money for that disease. But the parents? Nobody does a thing for supporting them. Real help would be having someone say, 'How can I help you today and tomorrow and every day, physically help you? Can I sit with your child so that you can take a shower?' That's what they need. Every day."

In an era that valorizes intensive, selfless parenting and the maximization of a child's individual development, caring for a child with severe disabilities or mental health difficulties tests the limits of those propositions. Children may receive better care at home than in institutions, but parents often fare worse.

The strains accumulated for Nathaniel and Victoria, and so did Victoria's weight. It climbed to four hundred pounds. She underwent weight loss surgery and for a while ate through a feeding tube. She could not eat much, only small bits of food several times a day. Yet even when consuming morsels, she vomited uncomfortably. Her low intake of food led to dehydration, and once she entered a state of starvation. Victoria lost one hundred and eighty pounds, but her body was wracked with constant pain. The physical pain caused mental distress. She could not do much. Walking and breathing felt burdensome.

A psychiatrist treated her for depression, but the medication only made her feel worse. Surveying the wreckage of her body and hearing her tales of daily life, the psychiatrist told her that her condition had no fix. "I have no hope for you," she said. It was the last straw.

"Two years ago, I asked Nathaniel to help me commit suicide," Victoria said. "Of course, he said no. I was suffering with that stupid feeding tube. I decided to take it into my own hands. I put liquor in my feeding tube. Next thing I know, I woke up in the hospital."

"There is a limit," said Nathaniel. "There really is a limit. I don't believe she wanted that, she just needed to get to the other side, to survive it."

When she regained consciousness, Victoria found herself in Intensive Care, her arms tied to her side and a breathing mask covering her mouth and nose. She realized she was still alive, which terrified her. It took months, and a change of psychiatrists, to restore her belief in life. "I am grateful I survived," she said, "and got to continue to raise the girls. I realize how much damage I could have done to this family. I always wanted to be a mom. I don't regret it. I would never wish that I wasn't a mom."

Nathaniel also loves his parental role, but he, too, shows signs of wear and tear. He lives in a constant state of anxiety, which has driven his blood pressure to dangerous levels. Medication has thus far failed to lower it to a safe limit. He would like to go back to work, perhaps back to school to become a therapist, finish a children's book he started, and patent the special diaper extenders he created, but he wonders how much time he has left for that.

They live precariously, always on the edge of a disaster that their vigilance and resourcefulness might not deter. Bills pile up and homelessness threatens. With two children with disabilities, one in a wheelchair, and Nathaniel the primary caretaker, the thought scares them. There are no local emergency housing services or shelters for families like them. If something happened, what would they do? "I can't imagine anyone who could manage this alone," said Victoria. "If Nathaniel got sick and went into the hospital, I'd have to give Autumn up."

"It's the way the system is built," agreed Nathaniel. "I envision our lives this way: It's like being on a really wide, high-speed river with lots of jagged rocks. On this river, there is white water and we are on a raft and we zip down the river and we have no control and we have nothing at this point. It's dodging the rocks. We've hit medium rocks, but not the ones that will pop the raft."

They persevere. "We love each other," said Nathaniel. "I can't imagine my life without Victoria. We try to give each other the stuff we need, even when we can't." Most of all, he and Victoria would like to give each other a new beginning, a fresh start for the second half of their lives.

They have finally landed in a small body of still water that makes dreaming of stability a possibility. Six months ago, they discovered Autumn's prolactin levels had risen precariously, the hormonal rise apparently triggered by her long-term ingestion of Risperidone. Now off the medicine, her behavior has improved: she is less restless, her humming has diminished, and her head banging appears less severe. She can sit long enough to watch a video or manipulate a slinky.

The atmosphere in the house has changed. Victoria and Nathaniel can sneak in time for their own conversations. A two-hour educational meeting also resulted in the school agreeing to an out of district school placement for Autumn, in a school that is full day, full year, and more geared towards her needs. She can attend until she is twenty-two. In addition, at age eighteen, the girls' disability payments are no longer tied to family income and Nathaniel can once again think about working and earning more.

Victoria and Nathaniel anticipate that the lull is temporary, as future challenges portend. At age twenty-two, Autumn will transfer into adult DDS services, requiring a new round of research, coordination, and jockeying. They also acknowledge that at some point Autumn's needs will outgrow them. What will happen when their own bodies and minds decline, when the physical and mental tasks of caring for her outpace their abilities, and they can no longer organize or supervise her care? At the thought of Autumn's future, Victoria's eyes well into tears.

For now, the children are growing up, moving on, finishing high school, even if not moving out or assuming independence. Olivia's prom dress, a low-cut, purple taffeta gown, hangs in the living room.

Autumn's dangles in the closet. Olivia procured a prom date for herself, and Autumn attended, as well, accompanied by an aide. Nathaniel and Victoria, watching their children become adults, are beginning to imagine the next phase of their lives.

"We want to be able to wake up in the morning and not worry about what bill is paid. Or about who is going to take the house from us. Whether or not the car will start. Will the PCA come in? Will we have a day when we don't have to worry about the girls' school, or their health? We just want peace, somewhere."

3. Diana: The Perils of Poverty

MOTHERHOOD GREETED DIANA before she had time to plan for it. She had imagined a different future: joining the Navy, traveling the world, getting away. But she found herself pregnant at fifteen. "I didn't want to be pregnant," she remembered, sitting in her neatly manicured living room with aquariums of fish, a bearded dragon, a chirping bird, and swaths of family photographs lining the walls, "but it was the 1970s and I didn't believe in abortion. So, it was meant to be."

Getting away would have meant escaping Athol, once a thriving manufacturing town in rural Massachusetts, but now a faltering municipality, its best jobs lured elsewhere. It would have meant fleeing her mother, a recovering alcoholic, a dry drunk and aging matriarch who had a penchant for cruelty. It would have meant rearing her children in more favorable conditions, in which hopes, careers, and lives could more easily thrive. She could have exposed herself to new people, new experiences, new opportunities. Instead, she was pregnant, filled with the responsibility of raising a young son and ushering him through an uncertain world. At least, this would not be her first experience with caretaking.

The summer before she became pregnant she had worked as a babysitter for a neighbor with five children, laboring from 6 a.m. to 6 p.m., doing housework, laundry, and cooking, as well as bathing and dressing the children. She enjoyed the job: the smiles on her charges' faces, the activities, knowing that she had taught them something. Before that, she spent years looking out for herself and her mother. Her father abandoned the family during her preschool years and her sisters, nineteen and twenty years older, had already left, leaving Diana the sole remaining child at home. She cleaned, cooked, and ensured that her mother's Coca-Cola stayed alcohol-free. The doctor warned that if her mother ever took another drink, she would drop dead or lose her mind for the rest of her life.

Her mother worked in a boarding house with nine rooms in exchange for the family's room and board. Diana lived there, along with her grandmother and uncle, and later on, a stepfather. At the boarding house, her uncle ran the front desk, her mother cooked, cleaned, and laundered for the residents, and her grandmother reigned supreme. Diana has warm memories of playing cards with her grandmother, sharing a room with her, and listening while her royal majesty dispelled the consequences and punishments her mother and uncle tried to impose.

"My grandmother was always my savior; she was the law," said Diana. "She wore purple, like royalty. She was the queen. I was the princess. My uncle was the king, and my mother was the maid. My mother did a lot of work. She was a miserable person. She didn't have a happy life. When she was in second grade, she suffered a nervous breakdown and was taken out of school. Then, after nineteen years of marriage, her first husband walked out. They had not had a fight or anything. He said, 'You're a good wife, a good mother, but I'm leaving.' That's when she really started drinking."

The boarding house had benefits. Diana met interesting people. Traveling salesman came through and told stories. Families moved into the cottage out back. She gravitated towards them, helping with the dishes and cooking, playing with the children, forming relationships. When her grandmother died, Diana, just ten years old, sought the companionship of her fellow boarders.

Pregnant with her first child, she hoped to create her own family differently. She wanted what she called a "Beaver Cleaver" family, referencing the 1950s sitcom about a two parent, middle class family that wrestles with the minor worries and squabbles of a stable life. She wanted her children to grow up with married parents, financial stability, siblings, and the experience of close family relationships. Also, a clean, orderly house. Family dinners and activities. Open communication and discussions. Most of all, she did not want to repeat the mistakes of her parents. Young, poor, and living in Athol made attaining such an ideal a tall order.

A small rural town of just over 11,000 residents, Athol sits seventy miles west and slightly north of Boston. Despite its quaint New England architecture, it is a community subsisting beyond its heyday. Current per capita income hovers in the lowest 10 percent of Massachusetts's municipalities and 15.8 percent of its population lives below poverty. Athol's schools rank amongst the lowest 12 percent in the state, its teen pregnancy rate amongst the highest.[1]

A tour through Athol reveals numerous abandoned mill buildings, their windows broken, their brick exteriors chipped, their interiors empty, remnants of a more prosperous past. Intersected by two rivers, Athol thrived as a mill town during the Industrial Revolution when manufacturers provided plenty of employment at good wages, and railroad and highway transportation routes led directly to larger cities.[2] In 1811, L.S. Starrett Company began producing high-quality tools in the downtown area, quickly becoming the town's major employer. The Union Twist Drill Company followed, adding an additional eight hundred jobs at its peak. Textile, boot, wood, paper, furniture, and toy manufacturers also set up shop. Until the mid-twentieth century, its manufacturing core and steady employment opportunities conferred regional prominence upon Athol. Its population, residential areas, and downtown grew alongside its industries as it became a flourishing commercial center. However, that was not the Athol in which Diana or her children would grow up.

Industrial decline struck in the second half of the twentieth century.[3] Starting in the 1930s, in an effort to provide increased water supplies to the growing Boston area, the state changed the contours of Athol's southern border. Engineers dammed the adjoining Quabbin Lake and Swift River Valley, diverted their contents, and constructed a reservoir to hold and redirect water to the east. Over a period of seven years, the Quabbin Reservoir slowly filled, submerging four towns, numerous roads, approximately sixty hills and mountains, and with them all, much of the region's economic prospects.

Miles of railroad and transportation routes linking Athol with southern Massachusetts's cities and towns were truncated and abandoned, while the new roadways bypassed the town's economic center. The diversion of commercial byways combined with the lure of cheap-

Parents Under Pressure

er labor and tax benefits elsewhere led to the scaling back and shuttering of many local enterprises. Growth slowed and economic languor set in. Boston's gains proved to be Athol's losses.

Whereas in earlier eras a worker could quit a job in the morning and find another by the afternoon, jobs, particularly good paying ones, became scarce. Retailers, such as Walmart and Market Basket moved in, picking up part of the slack, but providing much lower wages. In the nineteenth century, manufacturing accounted for a vast percentage of Athol's jobs, but starting in the latter twentieth century, the economy sharply shifted. By 2015, 27.5 percent of local employment came from the education and healthcare sector, only 19.7 percent remained in manufacturing, and 12.5 percent existed in retail.[4] Getting ahead and making ends meet became harder and harder.

Diana's Beaver Cleaver ideal encountered difficulties from the start. Her baby's father ran on the wild side so she wanted nothing to do with him. She also wanted little to do with her own mother, but she could not avoid her. Without sufficient income of her own, she moved from apartment to apartment in the boarding home and then into the cottage out back, attempting to create some semblance of distance and privacy for herself and her healthy, newborn son. Her attempts to separate did not work.

One night, Diana awoke to find her mother had entered her apartment, lured by her six-month old son's soft whimpering. He had soiled himself while sleeping. Enraged, her mother removed his diaper, wiping the dirty nappy in Diana's face. On other occasions, when Diana reprimanded her son for infractions, her mother barged in and smacked her for doing so. She constantly hovered and interfered. She did not allow Diana to parent the way she wanted.

Pregnant for the second time and with her son now three, Diana snatched her first opportunity to move out. She married the new baby's father, only to miscarry on their honeymoon. Her husband was not there when it happened: he'd left on a drinking spree. A little while later she became pregnant with a daughter, Mackenzie, a planned pregnancy. Then came another son, two and a half years after. With a husband and three children aged seven, two and a half, and a newborn, Diana's family finally resembled the Cleavers, at least in its shape.

Her husband was an alcoholic, unpredictable, erratic, irresponsible. She knew that before they married, but, desperate to get away and not wanting to have another child out of wedlock, she overlooked it. He had been in the military and drank his way through, garnering a stack of Article 14's for misconduct and alcohol abuse, which resulted in his dishonorable discharge. [5] In civilian life as well, he could neither hold a job nor stay sober.

"This guy did some really dumb things," said Diana. "He was so drunk once that he got up in the middle of the night and started peeing in Mackenzie's crib. I was in there catching it with a Tupperware pitcher. Another time, he peed on the kitchen floor. He was the idiot of every party. First one to pass out. And he always had to drive that first mile, no matter how drunk he was. He wouldn't be seen with me driving."

Her husband drank, broke into cars, and came home with bundles of unwanted CDs. He would leave to buy a gallon of milk and disappear for three days. Once he went out with her oldest son and returned alone, unable to remember where he left him. And one time, he broke into a monastery and stole some machinery. He had no idea what it did or how to use it, but he took it anyway. Diana convinced him to return the goods. He did. The monks thanked him and blessed him for the gesture. Somehow, he always dodged disaster.

The trade-off between a domineering mother and an unruly husband was uneasy. Diana had gotten away at least, and for a short time family life proceeded smoothly. Surprisingly, her husband procured good employment, they lived in a nice apartment, and she dedicated herself to her children. However, neither the work nor the apartment lasted long. They moved nine times because of job losses and financial troubles. In one location, in exchange for rent, she babysat the landlord's children. The landlord later evicted them after Diana and her husband fought loudly over whether or not he should drive drunk. Unexpected problems constantly arose; she never knew what he would do or what would come next.

Diana did her best to keep the family afloat and hold everything together. She maintained a meticulous house, scrubbing the floors daily on her hands and knees. When her children were aged two, five, and ten, she would drive them to day care and school, work for five hours at McDonald's for $2.18 an hour, and then pick them up and go home. She paid the bills, cared for the children, and tried her best to protect them and herself.

He laid hands on her only once, when, in a drunken rage, he banged her head on the floor. She waited for him to get completely inebriated and pass out. Then she pounded him. "I just kept punching him and slapping him," she said. "Everywhere. He was so drunk he never knew."

He woke up black and blue and asked what happened. She told him, "Don't you ever put your hands on me again." He never did. "It was a game of survival," she remembered.

He also put his hands on the children only once. It happened while they were entertaining guests, the children playing upstairs, the adults talking and eating below. Diana's two older children, aged three and eight, were cavorting with friends, slamming the bedroom door with childish glee. One pushed the door from the inside, one from the outside. Diana worried. Little fingers easily get stuck and smashed in banging doors. As she served the food, she sent her husband to calm the game. He went upstairs, took off his belt, and hit his daughter and Diana's older son. The assault left welts on their arms.

Diana disagreed with his actions. She saw no need to strike a child. Instead, she applied her own methods of discipline. She kept a spoon, a small, orange plastic spoon, near her and the children. When infractions occurred, she slowly and deliberately picked up the spoon, its brightness catching her children's attention, and then carefully laid it down again. It sufficed. They got the message. But that one time, her husband used a belt, not a spoon, and daycare workers noticed the marks and filed a child abuse report. That brought the Department of Children and Families (DCF) to their house, the agency that investigates child abuse, and an introduction to Bette Jenks.[6]

At the time of their first meeting, Jenks was the social worker at the Little Tots day care, where DCF provided Diana a paid slot for her infant son and three-year-old daughter. A small, robust woman, Jenks has lived and worked in the community for decades, giving her a good glimpse of the district and its needs. She is considered the "go-to person" by Diana and others, someone who knows the local resources, the important players, and how to get things done. Her career spans stints at residential schools for troubled youth, programs for individuals with developmental disabilities, and private boarding schools. She has worked for DCF and in elder services. Currently, she serves as the Coordinator of the North Quabbin Patch Program of Valuing Our Children, located in Athol, a program that aims to integrate services into the community in response to local needs.[7]

In keeping with its mission, the Patch office is located in the center of Athol, on Main Street, in an aging building, its entrance inconspicuous from the other storefronts surrounding it. On one side sits an empty shop, a driving school, and sporting goods store, on the other, an eye care center. Copious flyers, announcing resources and events, lie on a table in the entry and are posted in the windows. Free standing partitions divide the large, open interior into smaller work and meeting spaces, giving the sense that the agency must cram a lot into a little, and be ready to change on demand, allowing limited opportunity for neat and comprehensive planning.

During the five years that one or both of Diana's children attended the day care, Jenks and Diana met frequently. Jenks helped her handle the difficulties in her life and get the resources she needed. She found herself particularly drawn to Diana: "She was strong. She was funny, caring, intelligent, and had goals. She had a great sense of humor. It was very easy to talk with Diana. And the way the kids were with her, you could see the bond. They would run up to her and give her a hug. The kids were confident in her home. When they were around Diana, they were happy. There was a connection."

Jenks also observed Diana's hardships and how she strove to compensate and cope. "The struggle was between what Diana wanted and what she had," said Jenks, "and always feeling that she was the person who must fix it. She was maintaining everything for the kids, trying to make it all right and safe. She kept the apartment well maintained. The children were always well dressed and clean; and she was always attractively attired. And this guy really brought her down. Everything she tried to achieve would be undone. He was very manipulative. It was emotional abuse."

For years, Diana struggled through, thinking she had few options but to make the best of it. Her husband told her, if she left, she'd never get anybody. "Who's going to want you with a bunch of kids?" he pressed. She believed him. "I figured I could fix it," Diana said. "I thought I could fix him."

A few times, she almost succeeded. She would get him to leave for a treatment center and he would detox, move into a halfway house, and clean up his act. He would start ironing his shirts, pressing his jeans, and wearing vests; and then he would get a job and move back in. After two or three months, his efforts dwindled and he returned to his old ways.

Diana kicked him out numerous times. She realized he was too much trouble and too little help. Getting him to stay out proved harder. Their daughter was a "daddy's girl" who suffered from asthma. She would get sick, cry for him, and Diana would let him back, hoping his presence would help her daughter stay happy and well. Other times, Diana would take the children and leave him, a gesture that incurred his wrath and spite. One time, after she left to get a restraining order and regain access to the apartment, he intentionally ran all the oil out of the furnace so that there would be no heat. Another time, he blocked her from taking food that she had purchased. Yet another time, he nailed a 2x4 inside the front door so that she could not enter. They finally divorced when Diana's oldest son was twelve, Mackenzie seven, and their youngest son four.

The divorce brought Diana into contact with the legal system for the first time. With no money in her pocket, and a High School Equivalency for education, she needed to figure out and wade through the process largely on her own, with occasional advice from a court advocate. The judge ordered her husband to pay child support, but he never did. He quit jobs rather than pay, forcing her to rely on welfare to make ends meet.

Then there was the question of custody. Her daughter wanted to live with her father. Diana knew his faults, but felt she had little say, and so allowed Mackenzie to move without fighting. Her sons remained with her, as her ex-husband wanted only minimal contact with either boy. Somehow, he convinced the judge that the children should visit their noncustodial parents only one day a month. As a consequence, she never got to be as close to her daughter as she wanted. The arrangement also left her with limited ability to protect her daughter from the wiles of her ex-husband. She has worried ever since about what Mackenzie experienced in his care.

Diana now found herself a single mother caring full-time for two sons, aged twelve and four, and part-time for her seven-year-old daughter. She struggled to make ends meet through low-income jobs and welfare. After leaving the job at McDonald's, she managed the cafe at the local Walmart, made extra money baking cakes and through yard work, and did her best to ensure that her children grew up with structure and limits. "I tried to keep things going however I could," she said. "I had my kids' friends come over here to play, so I could keep an eye on them, because when they went elsewhere, they got into trouble."

She hosted social events for the basketball team, the wrestling team, and other groups to which her children belonged. She held family meals every day. She took her children on hikes. Her goal was to compensate for what she could not provide materially. "I was involved in school stuff," she said, "but I didn't have the money to do all the things and go all the places that would have broadened their horizons. If you don't have money to keep your kids occupied, there is nothing for them except peer pressure. You need money to afford to take the kids to the Y or go out of town."

Not having money left children stagnating in Athol's economic morass, especially as they got older and started to stumble out into the world, looking for stimulation and vocational opportunities. "They were good kids, could be trusted until they went to middle school," said Pat, Diana's current husband. "That's when they became liars and thieves." Middle school was when kids in Athol started drinking and smoking and getting into trouble. There was nothing else to do. No teen center, no skate park, few after school activities, especially for those with no money.

Diana finally secured economic stability and cultural capital when she married Pat. He was a man of many trades: a carpenter, mechanic, and musician who earned good money driving a trailer-truck out of Boston where the pay was $15 an hour instead of the $10 he could get in Athol.

He owned property, a number of acres, in a rural and isolated area a little out of town, tucked amongst hills and woods. The land had been a wedding gift from his parents, for a previous marriage. Pat logged some of the wood, sold a few acres, and kept a parcel for himself and his new wife to live on. Together, they built a home. Purchasing a modular house out of a magazine, she coordinated the particulars: the excavating, plumbers, electrician, and installation of the foundation and septic tank. They removed the brush and put in landscaping and a hot tub. That was almost thirty years ago, and the two have remained ever since, proud of their home and secluded location, as though a closer association with the town in which they both grew up might indelibly taint them.

The land anchored them, physically and financially. Allowed the possibility of a Beaver Cleaver family. But stability may have come too late for Diana's children. At the time of the move, her oldest children were entering their teenage years and facing the travails and pressures of middle school. Trouble kept descending; Diana could never quite know what her children would do or what might come next. Her oldest son, at thirteen, joy rode a car and shoplifted. When they were fourteen, both he and Mackenzie fought with peers, and were charged with assault and battery. Her youngest son, when he reached his early teens, was indicted for breaking and entering after he misappropriated a boat and sank it on the lake. "For a few years, I thought I had my own bench at the courthouse," she recalled.

Her children's troubles made their adolescent years a trying time, worrisome and humiliating for Diana. She wondered what she had done to invite such torment. She felt the sting of society's judgment. One of her son's lawyers told her she was a poor excuse for a parent. "People always judge you," she said. "If your kids are getting into trouble, obviously, you are doing something wrong. It doesn't matter how many times you drill them. And I would drill them and drill them and drill them. Before they went out the door, I'd say, 'Pretend like I am standing on your shoulder. Would you do that if I was standing on your shoulder?' We had all kinds of mottos in our house: 'Always be sure your brain is in gear before engaging your mouth.' 'Stop before you speak.' 'Think before you talk.'"

Even though Diana's first husband, the father of two of her children, was no longer in the picture, they seemed to have inherited his traits, or his genes. "Her kids went down the wrong path," said Bette Jenks. "We are all susceptible to that. Part of it is being raised around an alcoholic. It makes kids more vulnerable. It was also a tough time in this community; everyone was misbehaving back then. Even though she had a good bond with her children, once they got to be teenagers, that bond was pushed by all those other factors."

"All those other factors," which include poverty, divorce, a struggling community, and the volatility of an alcoholic parent, continuously conspired against Diana and her children. A close connection between adversity and escalating hardships has now been confirmed by a substantial number of researchers. The implications of their research also suggest that the most common ways society tries to help families cope may not sufficiently target root causes.

Dr. Vincent Felitti, chief of the Kaiser Permanente Department of Preventive Medicine in San Diego, California, first discovered the far-reaching implications of adverse childhood experiences (ACEs) in 1985. Dr. Felitti ran a successful obesity clinic, but felt stymied when he discovered that half the patients withdrew each year, despite making progress. Interviewing those who had left, he discovered that many had experienced childhood sexual abuse. He speculated that they dropped out because they were not ready to shed their weight. They wore the extra pounds as protective armor against their fears, anxieties, and vulnerabilities.

Wondering what other experiences lay beneath the ailments, he and Dr. Robert Anda from the Centers for Disease Control and Prevention (CDC) began the ACE study in 1995.[8] The study surveyed over 17,000 adults about their experiences with ten types of childhood trauma and family dysfunction. Following the group longitudinally, they compared the number of ACEs each person reported against health outcomes. The results were startling. Even amongst the mostly white, middle class sample, adverse events were more common and more harmful than anticipated. Sixty-seven percent reported one traumatic experience, 40 percent two or more, and 12.5 percent at least four. Accumulating ACEs, they found, is a lot like piling bricks on a person's back, one heavy load after another. The more ACEs amassed, the greater the subsequent likelihood of disease, substance abuse, mental illnesses, prison terms, broken marriages, joblessness, and poverty.

Once the number of ACEs equals or exceeds four, the weight becomes almost too much to bear, causing the victim to falter and fall. Compared to individuals reporting no adversity, people with high ACEs were seven times more likely to be alcoholic, ten times more likely to use street drugs, twelve times more likely to attempt suicide, and two to four times more likely to suffer physical ailments.

The initial study fueled more research. Included in the data collection for the 2011/12 National Survey of Children's Health were nine adverse experiences, amongst them frequent economic hardship.[9] Child Trends, a nonpartisan research center, analyzed the data and found that in the United States, economic hardship is the most common ACE (26 percent occurrence rate), and also that poor and near-poor children have double the likelihood of experiencing three or more ACEs than their well-off peers.[10] Deeper and more persistent poverty correlates with even higher ACE scores. Like dominos precariously perched in a line, poverty could ripple through a child's life and topple the stack.

Income appears to affect both parenting and children's exposure to a range of adverse experiences.[11] Poorer children are more likely to witness neighborhood violence, attend substandard schools, and suffer from poor nutrition. They are more often subject to household and housing instability and troubled peers. Given that many poor parents also lay claim to their own set of ACEs, and, because of their limited income, have fewer resources at their disposal, the stresses mount, the dominos tip and are hard to straighten.

A Pew Research Center: Social and Demographic Trends (2015) survey of 1,807 U.S. parents with children younger than eighteen found that while both high and low-income parents worry about the impact of depression, anxiety, bullying, and drugs on children, lower income parents are much more likely to worry about their children's safety or getting into trouble with the law.[12] Low-income parents also note difficulty securing high-quality, affordable, extra-curricular activities. Due to their economic location, poorer parents must make a much greater effort, do more with less, in harsher circumstances. As sociologist Frank Furstenberg writes:

> The middle class need only to be motivated, while the poor need to be super-motivated to rise above their circumstances. Ordinary levels of talent and motivation will not suffice for the disadvantaged, as it does for the more affluent. A stratification system that requires more of those with fewer assets is manifestly unjust, but that is precisely what is required of low-income families in American society.[13]

Parents can buffer their children from some ACEs, but they have a way of seeping through the porous barriers of poverty. Studies on attachment show that a close, supportive relationship with a parent offsets some of trauma's impact and helps instill resilience.[14] But even a secure attachment cannot erase every side effect of cumulative adversity or environmental influences. Resilience cannot be measured on the same scale as survival. When recovery from one adverse episode merely brings a person face to face with another, and fortitude wields insufficient power to lift daily life to tolerable levels, tenacity can hurt as well as help. Researchers have found that amongst African American youth from low-income backgrounds, psychosocial resilience comes at the expense of physical health.[15]

Poorer parents are also handicapped in other ways. Like Diana, they cannot pay for activities and accessories that might expose their children to new interests, vocational and leisure skills, or role models. They find it more difficult to move into neighborhoods or school districts that might better serve them. And they often find it hard to distance themselves from the negative influences of partners on whom they depend for financial and other supports.

They are also more dependent on public systems and institutions, a route Nathaniel, Victoria, and Diana found provides headaches as well as help. Procuring services from agencies takes time, persistence, and paperwork, and exposes parents to increased scrutiny and demands.[16] When the goal is survival, physical, emotional, and monetary outlays towards other enterprises feels excessive.

Just as Jason Litto of DDS encountered systemic limitations to helping those with disabilities, so, too, Dan Phillips, a supervisor with DCF in San Francisco, California notes the constraints of the public welfare system in confronting and mitigating poverty. "As a worker," he said, "there aren't ever enough resources, so you are always making these very tough decisions, because you can't really do as much as you want. We can't actually get someone a house, but we can afford to get them therapy to adjust to the idea of not having a house. So that's what you get. The underlying belief is that if you actually gave people resources, it would encourage them to behave irresponsibly. If you gave this person a house, then what about all those hardworking chums out there that don't get the house? You can't make it that easy to give people what they need."

Americans' ambivalence about helping is demonstrated in a Reuters/Ipsos 2012 poll that found that while 52 percent of respondents believed the government did not do enough to help poor people, 40 percent also expressed that most people receiving aid did not deserve it.[17] Although the government continues to spend on public aid, policies have made it harder and harder for poor families to get what they need.

When Diana raised her children in the 1970s and 1980s, living an impoverished life was difficult, but at least she encountered a stronger safety net than currently exists. Families facing Athol's declining opportunities could gain some financial relief from Aid to Families with Dependent Children (AFDC), a federal welfare program created in 1935 that gave cash assistance to poor families. AFDC was created with the goal of allowing women, especially white women impoverished by the Great Depression, to stay home and raise their children. In the following decades the program increased considerably, its rolls growing to include more and more families. As America prospered through the 1960s and President Johnson declared war on poverty, the government also created and expanded numerous other programs: school lunches, job training, Headstart, healthcare, and social security.[18] Official poverty rates subsequently dropped from a high of 22.4 percent in 1959 to 11.1 percent in 1973.[19]

The rhetoric began to shift during Reagan's presidency. Growing costs, wasteful spending, and distrust of government led to fears that the programs created disincentives for people to work. Opportunities to prosper, available to the privileged, were erroneously believed to extend to everyone. Political rhetoric popularized the idea that people who were poor had only themselves to blame for faulty choices and lack of income. No longer did the state hold a moral duty to help. Social problems were viewed as personal failures and governmental interference an extravagant trap that encouraged a cycle of dependency.

In 1996, Congress passed the Personal Responsibility and Work Opportunity Act, which, as President Bill Clinton claimed, "ended welfare as we know it." The bill eradicated AFDC and replaced it with a new welfare program, the Temporary Assistance for Needy Families (TANF), a time-limited program that aimed to promote work and get families off welfare. While the initiative succeeded in moving many families off the rolls, it has not lifted them out of poverty. Low-wage jobs pay too little, and do not provide security or predictability in terms of hours and shifts worked, thus keeping poor families poor. Benefits have shifted away from cash hand-outs towards food stamps and tax credits that do not provide flexibility for paying bills, which also limits families' abilities to make ends meet. Thus, while Diana found her situation quite trying, parents in similar positions today face grimmer circumstances.

As the safety net withers, and stresses accrue, the most commonly employed remedies focus on reducing the health and mental health byproducts of adversity. Psychotherapeutic trends reveal a proliferation of approaches aimed at helping people increase coping and resilience,[20] as though the responsibility for avoiding and enduring a stressful life belongs to the individual or, in the case of a child, the parent. As Professor Linda Blum noted, discourses about individual obligation absolve society from public accountability. They blame parents for inadequate childrearing. While current practices thus focus on skill-building and individual transformation as propelling escapes from adversity, research suggests the opposite. A little material help aimed at easing the strains of poverty goes a longer way.

In the 1990s, the United States Department of Housing and Urban Development (HUD) initiated a social experiment called Moving to Opportunity for Fair Housing.[21] As part of the program, a few thousand of the most impoverished families were given vouchers to live in low-poverty neighborhoods. In 2015, in a long-term follow-up, three Harvard economists, Raj Chetty, Nathaniel Hendren, and Lawrence Katz compared the children who moved to those who stayed in poor neighborhoods.[22] They found that youngsters who moved prior to turning thirteen years old, the age in which Mackenzie would return home to Diana, were likelier to attend college and earned 31 percent more as adults than their less fortunate counterparts. As adults, girls married and stay married more often, settling in better neighborhoods. A second study tracking the careers and earnings of five million subjects over seventeen years found similar results.[23] The younger the age of the child when a move to a better neighborhood occurred, the better the child's outcome. Studies investigating the role of income on children lend additional support to those findings. When the incomes of poor families rise, ACEs decline and children's achievements increase.[24]

Nonetheless, programs that substantially reduce familial poverty hardly exist and those that do have been reduced, even when found by researchers to be effective. Welfare benefits given to poor families are anything but generous, often failing to cover even basic expenses.[25] Affordable housing, especially in better neighborhoods, remains scarce.[26] Even psychotherapeutic services can be hard to access or mismatched to a family's needs.[27] Parents thus remain primarily responsible for shouldering the bricks, no matter how uneven the surface on which they try to stand or how large the load they carry. For many, including parents like Diana, who struggled through her first marriage, that expectation is untenable.

Mackenzie remained with her father for six years, until he left for Florida when she turned thirteen. She then moved back to Diana's home. Diana was pleased. Mackenzie appeared to be adjusting well. She formed a nice set of friends, attended birthday parties, invited classmates to sleep over, and involved herself in cheerleading. At age fourteen, she accepted an opportunity to work as a live-in babysitter in Cape Cod for the summer. There she met a guy, an athlete, who dealt in crack and got her hooked. She came home soon after.

Alarmed, Diana immediately took her to counseling. Mackenzie straightened out. She ceased smoking, earned her High School Equivalency, and obtained certification as a preschool teacher. At age twenty, she became pregnant with her first child and moved in with the father. He came from a reliable family, maintained stable employment, and had inherited a large house with ample acreage and a built-in pool. "From the outside," said Diana, "it looked like everything you would want."

Her daughter found employment at a preschool and enjoyed the work. When the program closed three years later, she took a job in a restaurant. She earned decent money and found the owner personable and supportive. At the end of the last shift, while everyone cleaned, he offered his workers six-packs of beer. Mackenzie drank, and drank some more, and then began drinking just a little too much. Simultaneously, she underwent minor surgeries for a rotator cuff and bunions. Her doctor put her on Percocet to control the pain. She quickly became addicted. When the prescriptions ran out, she started using tip money to buy other drugs and substances. She overused them all. One time she overdosed on caffeine pills, another time on Motrin. Her boyfriend also bought drugs for her, using them to smooth out the wrinkles in their relationship. She continued to drink, downing schnapps and beers alongside the drugs.

Mackenzie's addiction wreaked havoc on the family life Diana had so painstakingly constructed. Diana's daughter could not care adequately for her young child and the father took custody, but Mackenzie was allowed to remain in their joint home as long as her time with the child was supervised. Diana did her best to help out and often stayed with them. She also cared for her granddaughter a few hours each day while both parents worked. On weekends, the girl would stay at Diana's.

But the addiction, and worries about it, dominated Diana's days. She monitored Mackenzie, took her to appointments, and tried to help her stay clean. It was an uphill battle, a game of survival, with Diana as one of the prime casualties. Mackenzie, trapped by her addiction and cravings, routinely circumvented Diana's efforts. "I went to stay at her house," recalled Diana. "She stole my shoes and took off to get drugs while I was asleep on the couch. It was crazy."

In an effort to sober up Mackenzie, Diana, in conjunction with others, arranged for her to enter one detoxification center after another: The Brattleboro Retreat in Vermont, Spectrum Detox in Westborough, and AdCare in Worcester. One of the facilities would only admit her if intoxicated, so Diana stopped on the way, allowing Mackenzie to buy drugs and get high for the intake. At these venues, Mackenzie met dealers and heard about new drugs. She discovered heroin, a cheap, readily available, and potent narcotic.

An uneasy pattern ensued. Mackenzie would get high and then cry, rage, carry on, say she wanted to die, that she was sorry, she needed help, she did not know what to do. Diana would try to obtain help, shuffling her from place to place, emergency room to emergency room, seeking some way to quell the addiction's power.

"We would spend all night in the emergency room," Diana said, "and in the emergency room, she would say, 'I am going to kill myself'. They would give her something to calm her down, she'd sleep, and then she'd wake and say, 'No, I'm not.' By the time they found her a bed, she was fine, and they would release her. But I hadn't slept. I was dragging because I was not getting any sleep. I was a wreck."

Diana did what she could to cope. "It was horrible, horrible," she said. "I tried taking notes, writing down my feelings. I have notebook after notebook after notebook. For some reason, I'd start writing at the back and work my way to the front. And then I'd try reading it afterwards and I couldn't figure out the mess I had scribbled. I was too tired. But I had written down every time we sat in the emergency room all night. Once I was so tired on the way home, I started to doze off. I tried to cut a corner on a sharp road and suddenly a truck was there. Almost got us killed. I was, like, 'I can't keep doing this'."

Mackenzie was prescribed methadone with the hopes that the drug would suppress her heroin use. Diana took her to a clinic in Greenfield, a forty-five-minute drive each way. The methadone did not hold her, did not control the cravings, and the clinic, in response to Mackenzie's complaints, kept upping the amount. Eventually she received such a high dose that she would nod off on the drive home. Now, she was overdosing on methadone. But Diana could not intervene. The clinic kept a strict confidentiality protocol, interacting only with the patient, not with the family. A policeman guarded the locked entrance, blocking entry. Calls from family members received no response.

"It's a ridiculous situation," said Diana. "To get services or help, you can't call. The addict has to, and then you have to stand over them to make sure that they do. People who are too sick to help themselves are in charge of getting treatment. People who are watching from the outside and agonizing are cut off."

Mackenzie complied spottily with services. She would go to short term detoxification, sober up, flash her alluring smile, and charm her way out the door, leaving before the program's end. In a small town, the pattern was noticed and influenced her ability to obtain treatment. "Getting services was horrible," said Diana. "We would be dealing with the same people. After she blew them off a couple of times, they didn't really do anything. I even went to the courthouse to involuntarily hospitalize her. I thought it would give me permission to force her to get help, hopefully long-term. But I found out that it only meant she would be evaluated by the same people I had been dealing with, the ones who were throwing in the towel over and over. There are so many holes in the system. With one hand, they say, 'We are going to help you,' and while helping, they drop you in another hole."

The holes into which Diana and Mackenzie had fallen were too steep to climb out without a much longer ladder than either of them owned. Without sufficient income to travel to distant facilities or pay for private treatment, the family had to rely on locally available services, the same people whom Diana deemed ineffective, unreliable, and even disdainful.

Opioid addiction is a growing problem in Athol, as well as across the nation, which public systems struggle to combat. In the greater Athol region, the fatality rate in 2015 reached 19.7 percent, compared to 9.7 percent statewide. The number of addicts has grown over the years, in combination with wage stagnation, underemployment, and the availability of cheap drugs. Treatment options are scarce. The area lacks a comprehensive care system that extends from detoxification through full recovery, and it has no long-term residential facilities.

Bette Jenks, as coordinator of the PATCH program, has watched families wrenched apart by the opioid crisis, and seen the community's difficulty in responding. She believes that Athol's limited response derives, in part, from a state bureaucracy that sets general policies that do not necessarily match the needs of the specific locality.

"This is a poor community that lost its major employers," she observed. "Drugs are a cottage industry. We have no treatment facilities right in the community, they are not close by, and buses take a long time. People go to detox, but then wait for longer term treatment and often relapse in the span."

Diana blames the opioid crisis partly on doctors who liberally write prescriptions for painkillers, despite their known danger, and a local medical system that lacks highly trained personnel and facilities. She has had to advocate for fewer and less potent drugs for herself, to control the pain from previous back injuries.

"For a while, with my back, they had me on fentanyl patches and I said, "This is ridiculous, I am not doing this. So, I can see how the medical profession can push that on you. I went to my doctor and said I need to get off these patches. I look like an addict. He put me on OxyContin. Because of what I know, I don't want to take more than I have to."

Statistics show that most people requiring help for substance abuse do not receive it. In 2015, only 13.6 percent of users in Massachusetts received treatment for illicit drug use, a statistic close to the national average.[28] Reasons vary from reluctance to pursue help to lack of available options. Not all insurances cover the cost of treatment, are accepted by treatment facilities, or pay for the full span of needed services. As Diana and her daughter further found, qualified providers may be hard to find, and addiction and mental health services may not be coordinated, leading to less effective treatment. To redress these gaps, Massachusetts invested, beginning in 2018, in a five-year plan to increase the span and availability of substance abuse treatment.[29] Whether or not these efforts prove sufficient remains to be seen.

According to Jenks, improving services would help, but may not be enough to quash the problem: "We need to understand that when someone in this community recovers, they are still not in middle class America. They are still poor. They still lack jobs and opportunities. They still face all the difficulties that lead to the addiction in the first place. Problems build up and they can't get out from all of them. They can only handle so much."

The larger the load of ACEs people carry, combined with the fewer resources at their disposal, the more complicated the remedy. When long-term, comprehensive solutions do not exist, individuals like Mackenzie, suffering from physical and mental despair, and abbreviated expectations of getting ahead, find the relief offered by drugs too compelling and addictive to turn down.

Once, after receiving methadone, Mackenzie went home and fell asleep on the couch. When her partner returned, he could not rouse her. He immediately took her to the hospital, where the attending doctor, who had seen Mackenzie multiple times, refused to admit her. "I know what you did, you know what you did," he said. "Go home."

The hospital reversed the decision soon after, calling and telling her to come back. She was admitted with kidney and liver failure, the result of years of heavy substance use. While undergoing dialysis, she fell into a coma, in which she remained for a full three weeks. Diana stayed with her at the hospital, pacing the hallways, living on coffee and no sleep. She walked off twenty-five pounds in those three weeks.

When Mackenzie regained consciousness, the doctor informed her that she should no longer drink or use drugs. Her liver and kidney were so fragile that further use would kill her. The news did not go over well. "She said she was fucking twenty-eight years old and if she wanted to drink, she would drink. No one could tell her what to do," Diana remembered.

Thoroughly exhausted, consumed with worry, and encountering the futility of her efforts, Diana had reached her limit. "I couldn't do it anymore. I couldn't watch this anymore. I couldn't watch her kill herself," she said. Diana stepped away. She severed contact with her daughter for almost two years.

Not watching entailed its own anguish. Diana wondered what was going on. She heard bits and pieces of news. Mackenzie had moved to Gardner. Then closer. She had moved in with a drug addict. She was getting treatment and receiving Suboxone, a drug that reduces withdrawal symptoms and cravings. Even with distance, Diana could not banish anxiety. She wanted to help, to rescue Mackenzie from her demons. She wondered if there was anything she could do, if there was anything anyone could do.

They met next during a chance encounter outside a Subway restaurant in Orange, the town abutting Athol. Spotting Mackenzie from afar, Diana felt a surge of concern and desire. She yelled Mackenzie's name. Reached out. Talked with her. Mackenzie had another child, a young daughter, whom Diana met for the first time. As she scanned Mackenzie's demeanor, saw the bounce in her step, the brightness in her voice, and the healthy infant in her arms, Diana felt relieved. Mackenzie and the baby appeared well.

Diana took her granddaughter home, and Mackenzie and her new boyfriend moved in a few days later. Within days, Diana's optimism waned. Mackenzie had been selling her Suboxone and buying heroin. Since heroin leaves the body within three days, she would spend most of the month high, stop using a little before her drug test, take Suboxone for a few days, and sell the remaining pills. The practice was common and enabled addicts to falsify tests and earn income. When the ploy failed and Mackenzie was caught with a dirty screen, the Suboxone program expelled her. Another failed treatment. Diana told Mackenzie to move out, and she did, leaving her daughter behind.

Diana had found psychotherapy helpful and for years had relied on its support. When she attended her next session, she took her granddaughter with her. The little girl played with the therapist's dollhouse. She enacted fights between the mother and father dolls, bitter, loud, drug-induced rages. Diana felt dismayed.

The counselor, a mandated reporter of child abuse and neglect, suggested she call DCF. Diana agreed. For three months, while DCF opened a case and began services, the little girl remained with Diana. Then, after Mackenzie agreed to stay off drugs and submit to drug screens, the agency let the child return home. Diana disagreed with the decision. She knew Mackenzie actively used and evaded the screens. She later learned that, after moving back with her mother, her granddaughter cried frequently for her.

Just a few months later, Mackenzie fell grievously ill. She vomited severely and persistently, and could not keep anything down. The illness progressed, but she avoided seeking help, fearing that her mother, doctors, or DCF might suspect she had partied, treat her derisively, or take her child. As Mackenzie grew sicker, her neighbor's brother intervened and took her to the hospital. At 4:20 a.m., Diana found out that Mackenzie was hospitalized and unresponsive. She drove to the facility, and upon arrival, discovered that her daughter had died.

A hospital spokesman explained that Mackenzie died from sepsis, caused by the virulent spread of a urinary tract infection. With her kidneys and immune system compromised by drugs and alcohol, and the symptoms of infection mimicking those of an overdose, the illness had at first gone undetected and then spread rapidly. The end came suddenly.

A nurse told Diana, "She had been doing her hair and texting a guy and the next thing you know, she had undergone respiratory arrest and died." Diana found the explanation unsatisfactory. She asked the attending doctor, "What happened?"

"I was treating her for a urinary tract infection," he answered. "It never killed anyone before." His cavalier manner angered her. "It was all I could do," she said, "not to jump over the counter to throttle that man. It was, like, how cruel can you be?"

She was upset that she was called so late and disheartened that her daughter died alone. The medical records she received were confusing and contradictory. The time, place, and cause of death were recorded differently in various documents. Neither she nor her husband trusted the hospital's actions or assessment. Year after year, system after system had let her down, had sunk her in hole after onerous hole.

Mackenzie's death continued to inject social systems into Diana's life. Despite the three months she previously spent caring for her granddaughter, DCF would not give Diana custody. The day Mackenzie died, she begged them to let her see the youngster. Instead, they placed her in foster care. "DCF went out of their way to place her with strangers," she said. "It was ridiculous. I had to bury my daughter and I didn't know where my granddaughter was. The day after Mackenzie died, I went to the courthouse and thought I would get her back. The baby's father was allowed in the court, but not me. He had never been on the birth certificate. Mackenzie did not want him on. He was an addict."

Years later, Diana learned that DCF blocked her bids because the father claimed Mackenzie disapproved of her as a guardian. She wonders at his ability to convince the department of that lie, particularly after she had previously cared well for the girl, with Mackenzie's consent, for three months. However, as a grandmother, Diana held no legal rights to custody or visitation without parental permission or court order.

Her granddaughter attended the daycare run by the sister of Mackenzie's prior partner. She was the aunt of Mackenzie's first daughter who remained with her father. When Diana failed to get custody, the aunt adopted her. "It was good because I knew where she was," said Diana. "It was bad because I couldn't take her. I needed to have supervised visitation. It wasn't until DCF got out of the picture that I could take my granddaughter again." She now sees her regularly on weekends.

"She's in a good place," she said. "She's adopted. She's been to Florida, Disney, the Bahamas, doing stuff I couldn't afford to do. But this is her favorite place." Her other granddaughter, now a teenager, has also landed in a good spot, with her father, in a family with money, that can access resources, pay for activities, keep her busy and out of trouble, and help her look into college. Diana visits regularly with her, as well.

Being a grandmother has brought Diana closest to the Beaver Cleaver family she always wanted. Without the struggles to keep afloat, pay the bills, and hold everything together, she finds the relationships easier and more satisfying. But they cannot erase the decades of struggle that she endured.

Describing herself as rail thin and exceptionally active when younger, the years have added bulk to her frame and impeded her movements. Disabled from numerous falls and injuries that led to five back surgeries, she can walk only haltingly and cannot rise without aid when seated. Arthritis has attacked her joints, back, and hips, further compromising agility. She has been diagnosed with Fibromyalgia, likely the byproduct of a stressful life, and struggles with anxiety and depression. Pain, both mental and physical, accompanies her as constant companions, with medication only partially relieving their burdens. She needs knee surgery, but the doctor wants her to lose weight first, and losing weight is nearly impossible when her ability to move is so compromised.

The loss of her daughter sits particularly heavily with her: "You never get over it. It's been six years and the loss doesn't get easier over time. There is an empty spot that never gets filled." She struggles through the pain, keeping life as vibrant as possible.

"I have depression and anxiety," she said, "but I still keep going. You do what you have to do. I wake up and pray every day. I still love my grandchildren. I still love all my children."

4. Robin: Chasing the Ideal

"THEY WERE COSY and comfortable in their little house made of logs," writes Laura Ingalls Wilder in *Little House in the Big Woods*, "with the snow drifted around it and the wind crying because it could not get in by the fire."[1] The cover pictures a young Laura Ingalls standing in a cabin with a hunting rifle on the wall and a cooking pot on the stove. She cradles a doll, her Christmas gift, gazing at it lovingly as her parents and siblings look on. Laura lives in a tight-knit family. Pa, an impeccable provider and protector, plays the fiddle with blue eyes that snap and sparkle. Ma, the ultimate homemaker with smooth, shining hair, can scrub corn clean without allowing a speck of water to soil her pretty dress.

Little House captivated six-year-old Robin's imagination. She devoured each and every book in the series. Written in the 1930s and transformed into a popular television series in the 1970s, the books fictionalize the childhood of Laura Ingalls Wilder (1867–1957). Through industry and hard work, the Ingalls move to the prairie, laboriously build their own homes, farm crops, and cope with accidents, disease, and natural disasters. No problem is too big for them to handle. No concern too small. Parents protect and care for their children, emphasizing cooperation and hard work. Robin craved that so badly that, like Laura, she started calling her own parents "Ma" and "Pa."

In reality, Robin's family was nothing like the Ingalls. A lesbian, who was raised by a white, Protestant family in a wealthy suburb of Boston during the 1960s and 1970s, she grew up in a war zone of physical and emotional abuse. Her father brutally beat the dog, belittled his wife and children, and vilely yelled at them. In fits of rage, he punched Robin's older sisters and threw them across the room. On one occasion, when Robin told him she loved him, he replied, "I hate your guts and I never want to see you again." At age eleven, after being sexually molested at a party that she and her mother attended together, she started drinking. She spent the next decades chasing sobriety, coping with the aftermath of trauma, and attempting to create a modern version of *Little House*.

"I wanted a family," she said. "2.4 kids and a car in the garage and the whole bit, the family I always dreamed about as a kid." Thus, in her thirties, with a successful career in hand, unable to find a fitting lesbian community, and leery of parenting on her own, she pushed aside her lesbianism and professional ambitions to marry a man and give birth. She opted to make her family constellation mainstream. Acceptable. The norm.

Robin lives near Northampton, a small, vibrant city that serves as the county seat in a rural area dotted with small towns. Nestled into a quiet valley carved out by the Connecticut River and surrounded by hills, the city and its environs has earned a strong reputation as amiable to families, the arts, and outdoor activities. Home to Smith College, Northampton boasts a well-educated, liberal-leaning population with a vibrant gay and lesbian community and a large number of same-sex families. While not a wealthy area, it is also not poor, with median incomes slightly higher than state means, and poverty and crime rates lower than average.[2] The Northampton area is very different from Laura Ingalls's prairie or big woods, but it has special appeal for Robin. "There is something about the valley that I really like," she said. "I like the mountains and the river. It's defined. It helps me feel contained. I feel safe."

Lacking safety and stability in childhood, Robin strove to form herself out of the rocky clay of her upbringing. In fifth and sixth grades, she fed and took herself to school each morning, and then spent afternoons in her bedroom, in lonely isolation, eating junk food. She tried to detach from the overflowing anger of her home, and the inattentiveness of parents wrapped in its grip. But her father's criticism and temper infected her desires and feelings, until she cast them, misshapen, into the corners of her life. She transformed fear into deference, sadness into irritation, and doubt into determination. Whatever she said or did, it needed to be right, because wrongness amounted to the deadliest of sins.

Her mother offered a lifeline in the form of learning. She valued intellect, encouraged reading, and took Robin to museums and other enriching activities. At the suggestion of Robin's sixth grade teacher, she sent her to a private middle school. When it came time for high school, however, her mother pushed for a public education, fearing Robin would get entrapped by the elitism of the private academies. Used to fending for herself, Robin applied to and won a scholarship to a top private school about an hour from her home. Her mother agreed to let her go.

Despite the daily commute, Robin loved the school and grasped the offered opportunities. The school gave her structure and purpose, as well as access to reasonable adults. She spent long days there, enjoying the curricular and extra-curricular offerings and the tight community of students. But school could not shelter her from the conflicts and confusions at her now divorced parents' homes. As high school progressed, and after a particularly brutal exchange with her father at age seventeen, Robin felt increasingly dazed and numb, even desperate. Focusing on schoolwork was difficult. She drank, relishing the escapes alcohol offered.

When Robin graduated, she felt lost without the supports of the school. After a semester in college, she dropped out, taking some time to travel and work. Her attraction to women crystallized during those years. She fell in love and experienced her first kiss. When she eventually returned to the Boston area for another attempt at college, she encountered an active lesbian community.

"I came out in Cambridge in the early 1980s," she said. "I embraced it. I had very short hair, looked androgynous, and wore loads of buttons. There was a lot going on. I went to Lesbian Liberation at the Cambridge Women's Center every Thursday night, after which a group of us went out drinking at a lesbian bar. But I had a hard time with it all. Many people were very angry and anti-men."

The separatist aspects of the community made her uneasy, forcing her to stand out when she desired to fit in. She liked men, although they terrified her. Was she truly lesbian, she wondered, or just afraid? "I didn't always feel accepted for who I was," she said. "I had this idea that we were all lesbians, so we would be best friends. It just wasn't true."

Robin drowned her questions and discomfort in beer. Every Thursday night at the lesbian bar. Continuing a pattern that she began as a teenager, she consumed so much she blacked out. At first, she thought it normal. Didn't everybody who drank pass out? "I chased the blackout," she said. "I didn't want to feel my feelings. They were too painful."

When she returned to college, she moved in with a woman she had been dating. After earning a B.A., and leaving for graduate school in New York, she and her girlfriend continued the relationship long distance. "We were talking about having a kid," she said, "and finding a donor. My cohorts were getting married and starting families." The relationship ended soon after, but not Robin's wish for a family.

She finished her professional program at age twenty-eight and landed a good job in her field. She had drunk steadily throughout graduate school, in increasing amounts, and regularly blacked out. After embarrassing herself at parties with unsteady, inebriated behavior, she realized she was making a fool of herself and could ruin her career. So, she quit, quelling her cravings by exercising vigorously.

Life felt a little steadier after that, although she continued to find solace in food. She moved into her own place, dated, worked, and took care of herself. Then she set her sights on finding a partner. Frustrated with the women's community, she decided she would try men. "I tried really hard to switch over and find a man," she said. "To say all right, I am going to be straight. And since straight women wear skirts and make-up, I am going to do that, too."

She spent a year experimenting with sleazy men. The first had an arrangement with his wife that allowed for extra-marital affairs. He wanted phone sex, even when she was at work. The second sent her a six-page letter about his penis. The third claimed to be getting a divorce, but still lived with his wife. The fourth bragged of dangerous exploits he attempted with dates, and tried to lure her into one of them. None appealed.

"I was very specific in what I was looking for," she said. "I wanted someone funny, smart, and kind. And I wanted him to like his mother." Soon after, she met Adam, a computer programmer who was raised in a Jewish family outside of New York City. "I heard that clock ticking," she said, "but I also knew I wanted to be with him. He really liked me. We had a lot of fun together. Someone told me, 'Just make sure you marry someone you can be divorced from,' which I took to mean, divorced from without too much drama."

Adam met the criteria, despite some cultural differences. He was a sweet, mild-mannered guy with a funny sense of humor who got along with his mother and delighted in Robin's promising career. He knew Robin had dated women, but gave it little consideration once assured of her love. Robin, in turn, found she liked the company of men and the balance and normality of heterosexual double dating. It felt good to hold Adam's hand while they walked down the street and feel the safety that conventionality imparted.

They spent a few pleasant years together, living in New York City on two professional incomes. They attended the theater and dance performances, heard live music, watched movies, and went out with friends. They traveled to Greece and London. But the thought of a child tugged at the back of Robin's mind. After buying a condominium and watching her friends have babies, Robin started contemplating the nuts and bolts of parenthood.

"I was thinking about how to be a good mom," she said. "Because of the way that I was parented, I was worried about what type of parent I would be. I had to start eating right. And I had to swim, so I was in shape. After my child was born, I read that yoga and walking and swimming were the best things you could do. They help babies come out very calm, because they have oxygen-rich blood."

When she became pregnant, she made sure to take care of herself and her unborn child. She exercised, did regular yoga, and went weekly to a masseuse who helped her decompress and learn about her body. Still, doubts hovered. Could she, like Laura Ingalls's mother, make the required concessions?

One day, during the sixth month of her pregnancy, a fire engine drove by, its sirens screeching. The sound drove Robin to grab her bulging stomach. She felt thrilled by the reflex, relieved. She had displayed maternal instincts. "Part of me thought, 'I am going to be a great mom,'" she said. "I knew I had it in places. But I also knew I was volatile and a bit of a loose cannon."

Robin had a short fuse and a sharp edge, whetted by years of tension and trauma. Decades of trying, and failing, to form a relationship with her difficult father had braided yearning with frustration, love with disappointment, and past into present, bundling them together into an indistinguishable mass. She related to others as though they resembled her father. Striving to please authority figures, she simultaneously resented them. When conflicts arose, she protected herself through capitulation or resistance, causing her to agree with a statement in one instance and argue incessantly the next. While attempting to satisfy the requests of friends, family, or co-workers, her own fears and unmet needs kept slipping out. Unsure of her feelings and motivations, she searched for a definition of motherhood that could guide and direct her.

"What *is* a good mom?" she wondered. "What does it look like? How do I do it? What books should I read? Who should I talk to or model myself after? Am I up to the task? There was such an enormity to it. And so many books, all of which you need to sort through to weed out contradictory advice. It's challenging to be a mom if you think you have to do it right, and everybody else thinks you have to do it right, and you don't know what right is."

She picked up tips as best she could, trying to thresh the most effective techniques from the proffered advice. She talked with friends and her sisters, and watched how they raised their children. One friend favored attachment parenting, which recommended creating a strong parent-child bond through holding and sleeping with the baby, and through calibrated responsiveness to children's needs.[3] Another bragged that her two-year-old already knew Spanish and could read. Robin wondered if she could live up to their ambitious standards. Her mother reassured her that children, and parents, should not be judged by two-year olds' accomplishments. Learning and imagination develop over the long-term.

Robin liked the perspectives of Laura Davis, author of *Becoming the Parent You Want to Be* and Penelope Leach, who wrote *Your Baby and Child: From Birth to Age Five*.[4] Davis talked about creating a personalized family vision, finding balance, growing as a parent, and accepting imperfection. Leach focused on children's needs and feelings, but also acknowledged that every child and family is different. They both gave practical advice on day-to-day tasks and activities. Their suggestions felt more doable than the intensive and competitive philosophies espoused by her peer group, although she continued to feel befuddled by the array of childrearing opinions and lack of role models providing hands-on instruction.

Davis and Leach's books have enjoyed widespread popularity, but, as Robin found, they share space on the parenting bookshelves with a dizzying assortment of competitors. As of this writing, Amazon returns 56,978 results for "parenting advice book," and Google shows 13,600,000 entries for "parenting advice blog."

Expert advice has been a staple of the parenting field for a long time. In 1914, the U.S. Children's Bureau, seeking to counteract high rates of newborn sickness, published *Infant Care*, a 127-page manual that covers babies' development, health, physical care, sleep, play, and discipline.[5] After its publication, the Bureau received up to 125,000 letters a year from mothers seeking advice.[6] *Parents' Magazine* began dispensing childrearing guidance in the 1920s, as did other magazines, newspapers, and radio programs.[7] Dr. Benjamin Spock's *The Common Sense of Baby and Childcare*, published in 1946, became an all-time top seller.[8] Modern parents gravitate towards guidance and the market appears more than happy to oblige.

What is less clear is why parents seek information and what they do with it. Like Robin, some distrust their instincts, and/or want to stay abreast of current recommendations, to cull interesting or helpful tidbits. The proliferation of advice, however, also bespeaks other trends. Historically, as recommendations about childrearing increase, so does parental anxiety, each likely boosting the other.[9]

Parental angst and consumption of advice does not mean that recommendations will, or can, be followed. Parents pick and choose amongst available ideas, retaining some and discarding others.[10] Sometimes, even with the best of intentions, implementation proves hard or conflicts with other priorities. Following expert recommendations is a lot like New Year's resolutions: easy to contemplate, harder to enact.

Parenting advice also tends to shift, complicating the passage of knowledge from person to person and generation to generation. Over time, suggestions have tilted in various and contradictory directions, depending on whether cultural concerns favor health, morality, achievement, or other outcomes. *Infant Care*, written in the early twentieth century during a time of high mortality, pays a lot of attention to babies' physical care and does not ask parents to be as solicitous towards other developmental tasks. The authors advocate the strict training of habits and the parceling of parental attention, lest babies form unrealistic expectations. As the century progressed and worries about childhood sickness declined, and as technological advances allowed parents to spend less time tending to housework, interest in other aspects of children's development spiked. The door opened to Spock, Davis, and Leach, whose philosophies diverge from those expounded in *Infant Care*.

While the three experts differ in many ways, they converge on key points that have now become the dominant, child-centered doctrine that Robin encountered. Parents should show children affection and take interest in their thoughts, feelings, and play. They should follow their children's leads in order to encourage individuality and exploration. Limit-setting should be accomplished through clear, gentle instructions combined with consequences and rewards, and in conjunction with reasoning and explanations.[11] Authors of parenting advice books tend to outline various ways of implementing those ideas.

Research ratifies that when parents are sensitive and responsive, and stimulate their children, cognitive and emotional development accelerate. As Margot Sunderland writes in the foreword to *The Science of Parenting*, "There was a moment of shock when I first realized how much impact the everyday interactions between parent and child can have on a child's developing brain."[12] Ideal parenting is now fully associated with scientific parenting, implemented through moment by moment teaching and learning that is designed to help children reach their "full potential." However, for a variety of reasons, that goal remains impractical for many.

Researchers have reported that mothers who are both affluent and educated show the most affinity with parenting styles focused on fostering individual development.[13] Middle and upper class parents define mothering as a sensitive and responsive endeavor. Like Robin, they also view the product of parenting as intellectual and emotional growth, not just for their children, but for themselves. In contrast, mothers with less financial and educational resources, and those from some immigrant populations, characterize parenting in more behavioral terms: the provision of material care, good communication, and correct interactions. Emotional and intellectual growth, reaching one's full potential, is, and always has been, secondary to survival.

Whereas in traditional, pre-modern societies, children achieve adult competencies by the age of ten to fourteen, with minimal direct teaching from parents,[14] in contemporary America, the estimated age at which youth fully mature, and master necessary adult skills, keeps creeping upward, with the latest projections falling into the mid-twenties.[15] Modern parenting has transformed into a long-term, high-stakes enterprise where cognitive competence, college degrees, reasoning, negotiation, and emotional understanding are considered more crucial than ever for occupational and financial prosperity, causing parenting strategies and advice to shift in sync.

It was in that intricate, ardent parenting environment that Robin found herself looking for guidance. Although her childhood experiences limited her knowledge and confidence, at least she had the time, finances, and contacts to figure out what she needed and try to get it.

At age thirty-seven, Robin gave birth to a daughter, Rose, by Caesarean section. She stopped working a week before the due date. "People were surprised I didn't go back to work," she said. "I was offered some big jobs, but this felt more important. I was fortunate that we were wealthy enough that I could stay home."

Even with Leach and Davis's books by her side, and Adam helping out, the dilemmas of parenting quickly presented themselves. The very first night in the hospital, she wondered whether or not her daughter should sleep with her? The decision felt momentous. Breastfeeding also proved difficult. Rose would not latch on, and Robin did not know what to do. The nurses at the hospital provided no help. She requested to see a lactation expert, but none came.

On the second day after the birth, a crowd of friends and relatives visited her at the hospital. Rose fussed the whole time. The pediatrician explained that her baby's agitation meant that she felt overwhelmed. Robin and Adam accepted the explanation and sent the visitors away. "I didn't know," said Robin. "I had no idea why she would fuss like that. I didn't understand what she was feeling or experiencing."

Rose continued to show problems with nursing. She made meager attempts, and drank only a dash of milk before crying and falling asleep. Robin called the pediatrician and again asked for a lactation expert. The referral did not go through, but Robin did not want to push. Eight days later, when she brought Rose in for a well-baby check, the doctor told her that the baby was not gaining weight. Robin was not feeding her enough. "When that happened," she said, "I got scared about nursing. I got scared about a lot of things about parenting. What was the right thing to do?"

Her mother gave her the number of a friend who worked for a lactation firm. The friend told her the baby was crying because she was hungry and that the hunger made her fall asleep at the breast. "You are not a terrible mom," she told her, "but you need to feed her. Tickle her and keep her awake. Make sure she stays on each breast for ten minutes."

"I felt like an idiot," said Robin. "I should have known. I should have known to ask and keep asking."

Rose also developed asthma, which required months of consults with numerous doctors, most of them useless. Only after conferring with a practitioner of Chinese medicine did Robin find a combination of acupressure, herbs, and dietary changes that assuaged the symptoms.

Parenting settled down once Rose started to eat and baby and mother got into the swing of things. The hormones released during pregnancy and nursing softened Robin's edge and intoxicated her towards her child. "When she was seven or eight months old," she said, "I would pack up the stroller with food, books, toys, and a blanket and go to the park and find a tree and just lie there. She'd nurse and gurgle, and then sleep. And I'd read and nap along with her. It was lovely. I was devoted. I knew what to do. I was a fabulous mom and completely patient."

After weaning Rose at fifteen months, Robin's experience of parenting changed. Rose's growing needs and willfulness got harder to figure out and manage. How much should Robin force her picky daughter to eat? Where lay the line between childhood exploration and safety? What behaviors should she allow and what deny? Handling Rose's feelings felt even trickier. When anger or sadness welled, they threatened to inundate Robin's already brimming reservoir.

One evening, while Robin walked home with two-year-old Rose perched in a backpack, Rose cried inconsolably. Robin talked to her, sang to her, checked to see if she was hurt or uncomfortable, but to no avail. As the darkness thickened and air turned colder, Rose's wails amplified, and Robin's anxiety rose in concert. Her daughter's anguish became her own, flooding her with deep waves of childhood pain. Overwhelmed, and worried that Rose could suffer an asthma attack, she dialed 911 as soon as they reached home. By the time the ambulance arrived, Rose was playing happily.

Frictions between her husband and daughter made Robin particularly uncomfortable. She tried to quash the troubles or resolve them quickly, afraid of allowing them to run their course. Instead, her interference protracted the conflicts.

"Time to brush your teeth," Adam would prompt Rose.

"Not now," Rose whined.

"Rose," Adam would respond in a firm and slightly raised tone, "you need to go and brush your teeth. Now."

Adam never yelled, but when the timbre of his voice deepened and intensified, Robin's heart raced, her throat turned dry, and her neck tensed. Sometimes she felt nauseous. Entering a dissociative state that hijacked her body and mind, and severed awareness from experience, she reacted as though Adam were her father. "Stop picking on Rose," she would demand, her voice frenzied and tight. "Leave her alone."

Adam's protests only served to draw Robin's formidable ire. She condemned his words, actions, and misguided priorities, until he gave up and withdrew. Rose, confused and alarmed by the storm blowing through, kept her distance.

As a survivor of multiple forms of trauma, Robin ventured through life encumbered by ACEs (Adverse Childhood Experiences, see Chapter Three). They infused her responses to people and events, and sparked her urges to drink and eat excessively. Neurobiological research elucidates how trauma causes those outcomes by disrupting the regulation of stress and emotions.[16] Under recurrent assault, the mind and body learns to prioritize self-protection by improving the efficiency of the stress response system. Even slight signs of danger are reacted to with the same alarm as extreme duress. Reminders of traumatic events, whether they be sensual cues such as sights, sounds, and smells, painful feelings, or situations that are reminiscent of the original ordeal, also trigger a stress response. When the accompanying emotional arousal becomes overwhelming, as happened with Robin, a person may dissociate, thus reducing distress.

Other events also ignited Robin's traumatic reactions and stretched her patience. When Rose was almost three, the 9/11 terrorist attack struck the World Trade Center. Robin did not see the planes hit or watch as the buildings fell, but she lived close enough to feel the blasts' emotional tremors. The imploding towers toppled the fragile security she had built, terrifying and devastating her. At the same time, her father-in-law, diagnosed the year before with a debilitating illness, started sliding into death. His plight consumed Adam, who could offer her little consolation.

"I was really pissed," she said, shamefully remembering her self-absorption. "I wanted to have another baby and Adam was too distracted. Everything was interfering with my plans. And I was, like, this is really inconvenient."

Also inexpedient was that Robin found parenting one child difficult, let alone contemplating a second. Starting when Rose was ten months old, she enrolled Rose in childcare for three hours a day. Then, picking up part-time work for a nonprofit, she increased her attendance to six. Rose adored the program, but Robin felt guilty, even though her mother stressed the importance of early daycare. "I am supposed to want to be with my kid," she explained. "I am supposed to hang out with her most of the day. Play blocks, take her to the playground. I did not want to do that all day long."

She missed the stimulation of her previous, high-powered jobs, but did not think she could balance the deadlines and travel with familial aspirations. Yet without work's structure and status, she struggled to feel competent.

As time wore on, Robin felt less and less like the mother she thought she should be. Less and less like the parents championed on television or the parenting manuals. Rather than encouraging her daughter's physical and intellectual prowess and attending to her emotional needs, Robin would pick Rose up from day care, come home, park her in front of the television, and continue her professional work. Rose cried for attention, or asked for a drink, and Robin barely and briefly responded before succumbing to preoccupation.

Stressed and moody, Robin slept fitfully. At 4 o'clock in the morning, her internal critic echoed her father and bellowed that she was an idiot. A failure. She yearned for a drink, thirsting for something that would douse her unrelenting judgments and feelings. She staved off the cravings by eating, downing a whole bag of tortillas in one sitting, and putting on substantial weight in the process.

Robin did not return to drinking, but she acted like she did. She was a dry drunk who got into fights with everyone. Over anything. From the bus driver to the neighbors to the condominium board. No one could talk to her without risking a backlash.

"Pass me the salt," her husband would request.

"Jesus, get your own salt," she retorted.

Robin called her daughter "a pain in the ass" and emitted loud, telling sighs when Rose made requests. She noticed Adam and Rose pulling away, shutting down. She felt fearful and lonely, a reality reinforced and aggravated by her own behavior. At age three, her daughter called her on her conduct.

"Mama, that was mean!" she said.

"You're right," Robin replied. The comment jolted her. She knew she needed help.

She had gone to psychotherapy for years, engaging numerous providers. The choice to seek therapeutic help was not difficult; her family approved of it. In fact, just about everyone saw somebody. Her father had gone to psychoanalysis. Her mother worked with a gestalt practitioner. Her sister attended couples' counseling with a boyfriend. In her childhood home, discussions abounded on what makes a good therapist and who fits with whom.

She first saw a therapist in high school when a school counselor pulled her through a wobbly senior year. A few years later, in Boston, she worked with a clinician who taught her to recognize her feelings. The woman also suggested she get her driver's license and go back to college, advice that she appreciated. A stint in group counseling revealed her strengths, reflected in the words and camaraderie of others. For a time in New York, she saw a therapist twice a week who helped her structure her life and feelings. When she later worked with someone who combined talk with body-work, she felt the pieces of her life and history start to meld together. "With her, I started to feel my body and understand more deeply," she said. "She validated me and showed me that my reactions came from trauma. I learned to recognize bodily signals of stress and fear, and how I lashed out to protect myself. I did not understand that before. I felt heard, developed skills on how to be with people, and put a narrative to my story."

Adam supported her ongoing therapy, or at least did not balk at the considerable time and expense. Robin felt lucky that their income and flexible schedules could accommodate her needs. She also found her education and contacts critical when researching and selecting psychotherapeutic methods and practitioners.

Not every therapist worked well. One kindly older woman neglected to probe important issues, like her drinking, so Robin quit after a few sessions. Another forgot two sessions and required her to lay on the couch, causing her to plunge into a panicked and dissociative state. Robin ended that therapy quickly as well. Over the years, Robin developed an instinct for professionals who would connect with and challenge her, sticking with those who did, and moving on from those who did not.

In choosing psychotherapy as a mode of help and understanding, Robin marched in step with contemporary trends. Psychotherapy landed in Massachusetts when Freud introduced its precursor, psychoanalysis, to America during his visit to Clark University in 1909. In the country's fertile ground, the new treatment quickly took root. Emotional distress had swelled when workers left their communities for cities, traditional and religious ways of life eroded, families and individuals became more isolated, and urban poverty spread. Concerns about health and happiness proliferated.

Known as the "talking cure," psychoanalysis involved a patient speaking freely to release unconscious conflicts and desires, which an analyst interpreted. The treatment fit well with Progressive Era ideas and cultural aspirations. Rationality and understanding could tame unruly passions. Knowledge could improve the self and society. Freud planted the hope that by analyzing the unconscious and changing the individual, the nation could rise above society's ills.

Psychoanalysis, which was time-consuming and expensive, appealed mainly to the elite. In 1940, 4 percent of the population had partaken.[17] However, in the 1950s and 1960s, as communities struggled with delinquency, alcoholism, and the reintegration of World War II veterans, the field adapted by sprouting less arduous methods. Hundreds of different psychotherapies now exist, mostly understudied and of variable quality, making practice dependent on a given therapist's skills and training. Focuses range from gaining insight, to enhancing relationships, to changing thoughts or behaviors, to learning to manage distress. Interventions are implemented with individuals, families, and groups, although most of the modalities retain an emphasis on personal change.

Popularized by novelists, academics, and television shows, psychotherapy has met growing acceptance. According to *A Survey about Mental Health and Suicide in the United States*, conducted by the Harris Poll in 2015,[18] 40 percent of young adults in America have utilized some type of psychotherapy compared, to 27 percent of adults twenty-six years old and above. Following Benjamin Spock, an M.D. who studied psychoanalysis, and Penelope Leach, a psychologist, dispensing parenting advice has become one of the field's roles. Another message is that raising well-adjusted children requires parents first to resolve their own issues.[19] By improving themselves, they can better perceive and meet the needs of their offspring. Robin wholeheartedly embraced those ideas.

As community networks shrink, demands grow, and parents like Robin find they must either rely on themselves and/or locate sources of knowledge and support,[20] psychotherapy becomes an ever more inviting option. However, it remains an undertaking better suited to those like Robin with time, means, and cultural compatibility. About one-third of the respondents in the 2015 Harris Poll indicated that psychotherapy is inaccessible and just under half found it unaffordable. Approximately half of adolescents and adults with depression or mental illness did not receive counseling.[21] The numbers of people who derive benefit are also reduced when race and class are considered. Numerous researchers have found that low-income participants, and those from racial and ethnic minority groups, enter psychotherapy less often, drop out more quickly and frequently, and reap fewer benefits than their white or middle-class counterparts.[22]

Impediments to care derive both from practical considerations and inherent biases. Diagnoses and treatments rarely reflect diverse sociocultural presentations and needs, which can lead to poorly tailored services.[23] For low-income clients, attending sessions requires not just time and money, but transportation, and sometimes childcare. Participants must commit emotional and cognitive resources, which may already be strained by day-to-day demands.[24] Partaking in psychotherapy also means subscribing to the belief that by changing the self, people can overcome their problems, even ones created by the environments and neighborhoods in which they live.[25] Individuals who hold privileged status in the majority culture, and who have more choices and control over their circumstances, tend to agree more readily with that proposition.

After all, psychotherapy cannot be separated from the culture that produced it.[26] The field's theories and methods, continuously updated as times change, reflect the concerns and assumptions of the dominant classes. Recent treatments replaced Freud's initial focus on the unconscious with interventions that build skills for adapting to a quickly changing, decentralized culture with loosely knit social networks.[27] Isolation is combated through developing deeper interpersonal connections. A demanding culture is counteracted by mastering coping and stress management. Complex occupational, familial, and social arenas are navigated through learning to problem-solve and control the self.

In helping people acquire the skills necessary to live in an individualistic society, psychotherapy provides a public service. But in picking up the slack left by insufficient community and government supports, the interventions inadvertently reinforce cultural trends. The message conferred is that it is a person's responsibility to manage, rather than the public's job to make life manageable. Individuals who fare best in this environment are those, like Robin, who have the income, knowledge, and leisure to find the best help and piece together their own treatment plan from the confusing array of options available.

Although Robin had pursued many different psychotherapies and read many parenting guides, she discovered that they could not solve every problem. When her daughter called her "mean," she knew she needed something else. "I was afraid I'd end up a fat, old, angry woman," she said. "I knew I was out of control. I was alone in my marriage, alienated from my kid, and I had lost my professional identity. I didn't trust myself as a parent. I was in despair about how heavy I was getting. I'd already tried therapy, exercise, acupuncture. So, I decided I'd try a nutritionist."

The nutritionist heard her history and suggested she consider Alcoholics Anonymous (AA). Years earlier, Robin went for about six months. She had also gone a few times more recently, but she ran into people she knew, so she stopped, uncomfortable with being recognized. This time, she considered the prospect more seriously.

"Do you think I should go?" she asked an old friend who went to meetings. "I haven't had a drink in years."

Her friend told her that drinking was just a symptom, not the real problem. "Go," she told her. "But if you go, don't start off too big. Just go to two or three meetings a week. And if they ask you to do something, just say yes."

"What I liked," said Robin, "is that she didn't do a hard sell. I started going a little bit. And then it was Christmas, and I said, 'I'll get through the holidays and then go regularly.' So that's what I did. And I knew I needed a sponsor because of my previous time in AA."

Robin found a sponsor at the first meeting, a twenty-something black lesbian with dreadlocks who was not a parent. Her sponsor gave her a long list of things to do: meetings to attend, books to read. She told her to pray. Robin replied she was an atheist. "Pray anyway," her sponsor said.

"I took every suggestion," said Robin. "It helped me feel better within days. I wasn't alone, and I wasn't crazy. There was a community. It gave me a purpose, a focus, and a reason to be. An understanding and a solution. It explained so much. If that hadn't happened, I would have gone back to drinking."

Her sponsor told her she could not talk to people the way she did. She was firm that Rose had to be her priority, that she had a responsibility to her husband and child. Robin took the instructions seriously, committing herself to the 12-Step program, and quickly working her way through. The Steps ask alcoholics to recognize their lack of control over addiction, accept strength from belief in a higher power, examine past errors and what led to them, make amends to those they have hurt, and begin to live differently. When the time came, Robin made seventy-five amends.

"I needed AA to tell me what was appropriate behavior, and what was not," she said. "I needed AA to teach me how to live. A lot of what I've had to do is look at my behavior with empathy. I didn't like that I chose to stick my daughter in front of the TV and be neglectful. It's sad that someone has that much disconnect and stress that they act like that."

Attending regular AA meetings was hard, but Robin managed. She was not employed full time and could make her own work hours. Rose had just started preschool, which gave her flexibility. "That first year," she said, "I went to meetings every day. I went to lunch afterwards for the fellowship, which is also encouraged. I was lucky that I had the money to do it all, so I could be held by the AA community. I also saw a therapist during the day so I could preserve my evenings for my family."

Together, AA and therapy helped Robin gain control of her feelings and behavior. Therapy lent her self-esteem and explanations for why she behaved the way she did. AA directed her to act differently and gave her community. Neither, however, could consistently help with the myriad, instantaneous decisions that accompanied parenting. The challenges slipped through unexpectedly.

When Rose was six years old, she wanted a push on the swing, and Robin refused, insisting she learn to pump her legs and propel herself. Rose sobbed, and Robin did not understand why. She reported the incident to her therapist, who explained that Robin was trying to teach independence, which was what she, herself, had needed to survive. But Rose had different needs and priorities.

"What does it mean when you can't escape your own subjectivity?" Robin asked. "When you can't step back and say, 'It's okay, you don't have to teach her that at six, and even if you push her at fifteen, it won't stop her from being independent.' You feel guilty about what you did, but you find your way back, and keep trying to be a good parent."

What Robin discovered is that reading parenting manuals and seeking suggestions is one thing, implementing ideas, another. Science and expert advice may expand understanding of what is possible, but not necessarily what is feasible. Impediments frequently exist. Meeting a child's needs means recognizing them, not in the abstract, but concretely, in the moment, even in the midst of competing demands and the pull of the past. It also means putting aside one's own needs, or at least balancing and postponing them, something that Robin, teetering on the rim of confusion and despair, could not always afford to do. When Rose grew older and Robin resumed full-time work, AA meetings took her away from the family multiple evenings a week. Yet without them, she felt lost, her doubts and emotions threatening to tip her, and sometimes her family, into turmoil.

Robin is not alone in finding the demands of parenthood both fulfilling and exhausting, both attainable and impossible. Unlike the one-dimensional characters in *Little House*, public dialogues and media portrayals increasingly represent parents as multi-faceted people who wrestle with their own dilemmas, desires, and doubts. Recent sitcoms, such as *Modern Family, Parenthood, Black-ish* and *This is Us,* depict diverse families and family structures (although they focus primarily on middle class households) and show more interest in parents' feelings and struggles. Disease, addiction, interpersonal conflicts, and emotional difficulties interject, with not all problems neatly wrapping up in half-hour segments. Parents strive to do right, but often make mistakes. However, while erring may be recognized as human, forgiveness comes only after conceding to judgment and self-blame. In one episode of *This is Us,* a mother accompanies her daughter to a consultation for weight loss surgery and learns of her bingeing and depression.[28]

"Did I do this?" she asks. "I did, didn't I?"

The ethos of personal responsibility means parents must hold themselves accountable for the growth, development, and flaws of their children. They must make the right choices about discipline, stimulation, and daily habits. To meet expectations, parents must work incessantly to become better people and caregivers, with guilt or exhaustion the prominent outcomes.

Robin and Adam entered couples' therapy when Rose was six and Robin had achieved a modicum of emotional stability through AA. Although they liked each other and wanted to stay together, they lacked physical attraction and intimacy. Parenting decisions also continued to cause arguments. Adam, a dedicated father with a good relationship with his daughter, had grown up as the youngest in his family, and had no experience taking care of children. "Adam wanted to be a really good parent," said Robin. "And he was, he is. But he wouldn't say, 'Let's get a plan, let's talk about this.' I felt like I was figuring things out alone."

Rose noticed the conflicts. She was sure her mother and father were separating, just like the parents of a boy in her class. She suggested that, if they lived apart, she could spend alternate days at each of their houses. Robin assured her they were not divorcing and were working on getting along better.

Counseling helped the marriage stay intact. The therapeutic work also opened the door to new feelings and understandings, and ultimately, Robin's desire to leave New York. "I was in post 9/11 shock and stressed all the time," she said. "Driving home from a trip out of the city one rainy night, I saw a flashing light at the airport and thought we were being bombed. I knew we weren't actually being bombed, but I realized then that we had to get out of New York. I felt trapped. I was just waiting for the shoe to fall."

Robin sensed that Adam would feel happier elsewhere, as well. Two of his closest friends lived near Northampton, and Robin, Adam, and Rose had visited a number of times, growing to like the region. In November, three months after Robin first proposed the idea, they moved.

For eight-year-old Rose, abruptly leaving friends and school was difficult. She found settling in and connecting with classmates hard. After a brief stint at a public school, and at the urging of Robin's mother who thought Rose's school was not challenging her, Adam and Robin moved her to a private school. They agreed that Rose was bored and, felt that, like Robin, she would thrive in a private setting. Without confidence in her own intuitions, Robin depended on her mother's impetus. She felt flattered that her mother thought Rose was smart, and wanted maternal approval. Most of all, she wanted to do things right.

Definitude, however, remained fleeting. Each time Robin mastered a move in her parental playbook, new challenges would emerge. Over and over again, she found herself bewildered by how to understand and address Rose's emotions and needs. She was unsure when to take Rose to the doctor for physical ailments. How to handle bullying episodes at Rose's school. What to do when Rose did not like private school and came home hungry and cranky. Having spent her own childhood and teenage years managing by herself, and regulating stress and feelings through food and alcohol, Robin had to learn alternate ways of supporting her child.

She sought help wherever she could find it: from therapists, acquaintances, and even Rose's improvisational acting teacher. Following many of her friends in AA, she started to go to Al-Anon, a companion program for those affected by others' drinking, and found a sponsor there. Her sponsor insisted she find Rose a therapist, as she was showing mild signs of depression. She did. "I had to teach myself," she said, "and understand with a lot of different teachers and in a lot of different ways, what it looks like to parent and be taken care of."

As sobriety, 12-Step programs, and therapy clarified Robin's feelings and priorities, the differences between her and Adam grew more apparent. They drifted further apart, living in parallel worlds. On weekends, he went hiking while she went to meetings. She returned to graduate school, increased her involvement in AA and Al-Anon, and started intensive therapeutic work, attending sessions with two different psychotherapists, one body-based, the other trauma-based. Talk of divorce sporadically flickered, and they tried another stint in couples' counseling. But neither took the prospect of separation seriously.

While Robin's life grew fuller, Rose's mood slipped. She started her freshman year in high school cheerfully enough, but by October, her bright outlook dimmed. Her grades dropped. She lost confidence in herself and her future. She started cutting herself. "It was really stressful," remembered Robin. "I felt fearful and helpless. I was not sure how to behave, what to say. I did not know how to fix my kid. I thought, 'there's a right answer, and I'm the mother. I should know. So, it's all my fault.'"

Part of finding the right answer lay in a comprehensive eye evaluation for Rose. She had shown early signs of vision problems, such as difficulties riding a bike on the street and other activities that required spatial sense. A cursory evaluation five years prior showed no apparent problems, and Robin had let the matter drop, despite her instincts to the contrary. Now, a developmental optometrist discovered that Rose had, in essence, only 10 percent vision in one eye and other difficulties that caused her to over-rely on peripheral vision. No wonder bike riding was challenging. Even more, school and reading had become more and more difficult, as texts became denser with more information crammed on each page.

Glasses and eye exercises improved Rose's eyesight and lifted her reading and school performance. Therapy also helped, and the crisis and cutting abated. But stresses and difficulties continued. One of Rose's friends committed suicide. Rose and Robin felt shaken, the enormity of the tragedy upsetting Robin's stability.

"I was getting into a trauma vortex," she said. "I kept running into people in meetings who knew the youngster who died and they would talk about the incident. That would trigger my trauma, and I would spiral down. I was out of it, dissociating, so consumed by fear and panic that I stopped paying attention to my surroundings. I almost got into car accidents, and I started fighting with people at work, whose statements I misconstrued as critical and attacking. My sponsor insisted that I stay away from meetings and the people who triggered me. Then, after a week of staying away, I got the distance I needed."

During that week, as Robin sought to understand her traumatic reactions, she saw her life flash before her eyes. She recalled images of her childhood, her father's anger, and stories she heard about how he punched her mother who said, "not in front of the kids." She recalled her fears of the household battles, and how they led her to alcohol, blacking out, and overeating. Making a fool of herself. Being sharp, judgmental, and mean. Dropping out of three colleges before finally completing her B.A. She remembered how she sought therapy and finally quit drinking, and how, in her hunger for stability and normalcy, she married Adam. And then, when Rose came, how the difficulties of parenthood rattled her until she found AA. She recognized that AA gave her the grounding, belonging, and acceptance that she ached for.

"I saw it all in a flash," she said, "and I realized I needed to get a divorce. Because I understood why I was with Adam, that he was a lovely, sweet, kind man, but I just didn't love him anymore. I understood how I had given myself up in order to find safety. I had let go of my deepest sense of who I was to get societal approval. Now, I was strong enough that I didn't need to do that anymore. After a twenty-year marriage, decades of therapy, and years of AA and Al-Anon, I more deeply understood that my childhood was traumatic and that I had always been a lesbian."

The present disentangled itself from the past. Motherhood had forced the journey, as well as the sacrifices. "I gave up my career," she said. "I gave up romance. I gave up myself as a sexual being."

Adam took the news well enough. Although surprised at first, he recognized the marriage's limitations, and they ways he and Robin had grown apart. He was, after all, a decent guy, someone who accepted divorce without too much drama.

There were also sacrifices that Robin did not make. "Rose hasn't always been my top priority," she said. "I have wanted to go off and do my thing. Sometimes I would bitch about driving her somewhere, and Rose would say, 'I'm sorry that you have to be a parent. Sorry it's so hard for you.' And it's kind of funny, because I don't want to be a parent some of the time. But I love her unconditionally. I love her."

When Rose graduated high school, Robin started dating again. Through an online site, she met a woman in another state who exuded stability and nurturance. The woman's family has lived in the same village for two hundred and fifty years. She helped raise her ex-partner's children, who, when they were still in their teens, promised they would care for her when she grew old. Fifty-six-year-old Robin still craved that promise of security.

"I like being with her," she said. "I can be myself. She's worked in a warehouse for almost forty years. She never went past high school. At first, I had to work through my judgment about that. But she's traveled extensively, reads voraciously, owns her own house, and has saved a sizeable retirement. She just wants to be with the people she loves, and do what she likes doing."

Robin's family accepted the relationship. "You finally got the family you always wanted," remarked her mother. "Maybe I did get *Little House*," said Robin. She credits parenthood with helping her get there.

"If I didn't have Rose," she said, "I would have started drinking again. Being a parent got me to AA. Being a parent forced me to find myself. It's a challenge. Especially in this country. They don't make it easy. But it forced me to ask, what are my true values, and what do I want to pass on? I would have been very angry if I didn't have a child. I wanted that family, that idealized family. I really wanted it."

As her daughter entered young adulthood, Robin continued to sort through competing messages in order to figure out her role and responsibilities: "Do it right. Pay attention. Don't be a helicopter parent. Let kids fly. But don't neglect them. You can only read so many books or Facebook articles before you pull your hair out," she said.

She has also had to accept her inability to reconstruct *Little House* in her own family. "I wanted to be the earth mama that everybody loved," she said, "and have all the kids come to my house. In Laura

Davis's book, there is a story about a parent who said yes to her kids all the time. As adults, her kids had these rich, wonderful lives. But I couldn't be that person who gave all the time. I would have loved to have been a foster parent, for instance, and I would have loved to have had another kid. But Rose is an amazing person: kind, smart, empathic, funny, very personable, very friendly. It's painful, there's loss, but also a lot of unfair dreaming that you put on yourself and your kid. I had to give up being the parent I imagined I would be, in order to become the parent that I am."

5. Angelina and Jacob: Judgment's Furious Footsteps

WHEN ANGELINA, AGED SIXTEEN, discovered she was pregnant, she felt sure of two sentiments: she wanted the baby, and she would raise her child oppositely from how she had been reared. Her own childhood had been fractured and unhappy. She was an only child, split between different households in the United States and Puerto Rico, bereft of her parents, feeling lonely, blamed, and isolated. At age twenty-one, proud of her two children and the family she assiduously created, she nonetheless found criticism's furious footsteps doggedly trailing her into adulthood.

Angelina was just five years old and living in Boston when her mother died from prolonged alcohol and drug abuse. Apart from a picture and video recording, she retains few early memories. The loss was soon followed by her father's descent into depression and binge drinking, along with his sudden remarriage to a woman he met online and his departure to Puerto Rico.

Angelina remained in the United States for a year and a half, living with her mother's best friend, her new foster mother, until abruptly, once again, her father reappeared when she was seven years old. He met her one day after camp, picking her up from the program, to inform her that she was moving to Puerto Rico to join his wife and himself.

She liked him and her stepmother well enough, but their lifestyle left little room for children. They lived in a one bedroom apartment, worked long hours, and spent their excess money on travel and leisure. Seven-year-old Angelina attended private school in Puerto Rico, where her father expected her to earn good grades and handle the school's high expectations largely on her own.

Lonely and unhappy, Angelina returned to the United States and her former foster mother's home for high school, attending a leadership academy in Boston. Although a conscientious student who spurned drugs, alcohol, and delinquency, her foster mother chastised her mercilessly. When Angelina expressed disappointment at her father's lack of contact and caring, her foster mother admonished her for becoming upset. When Angelina formed friendships, and started socializing, her foster mother castigated her for going out. And when Angelina and her foster mother argued, Angelina was accused of starting the conflict. Arguments veered into physical altercations, leaving Angelina, on more than one occasion, with a cracked nose and bruised cheeks. The harshness and alienation of her childhood consumed her, stunting her self-confidence.

"I was really afraid as a teenager to say anything," said Angelina. "I was so quiet. Everyone always told me, 'Why don't you talk more?' and I was like, 'Cause nobody wants to hear what I have to say.' My ideas were different, my experiences of family and cultures were different, which is why I grew up so isolated. Most kids were walking around listening to rap music and learning how to twerk, and I was in my room on the computer. It sucked growing up so different that nobody wanted to talk with you."

Feeling outcast, she left the academy to finish her schooling through the Job Corps in Maine, where she could also pick up vocational skills.[1] Her foster mother insisted she train as a paralegal or receptionist, hoping to put her on a stable and lucrative career path. She obligingly studied medical administration, completing the program in a year, but found the work utterly uninteresting.

At Job Corps, Angelina met her baby's father, Jacob, a seventeen-year-old with whom she grew close. He came from a different background, and she admired his assertiveness and initiative. Growing up in a white, working class family in Gardner, Massachusetts, a small town, in many ways similar to Athol, Jacob was reared with a strict doctrine and early push towards independence. "I was raised with, if you ate cement, you were on your own," he said.

His parents expected him, from a young age, to cry it out when upset, and bear the brunt of his own actions. He also had to bear the brunt of their actions. They divorced when he was twelve years old, delivering a jarring shock, after which he spiraled into adolescence. By age sixteen, he was a young man on hyperdrive, a party kid, drinking, on the streets, getting into trouble, eating cement.

He would go on binges for days or weeks, barely sleeping, before crashing in exhaustion. A suicide attempt that year led to a psychiatric hospitalization and diagnosis of bipolar disorder. Medication, Lithium and Abilify, stabilized him, but he took it irregularly. His parents disagreed with the diagnosis and drugs, leaving him without the medication that subdued his cycles of manic and depressive episodes.

Knowing about his history and struggles, Angelina did not want to pressure him into caring for their child. "I gave him the choice to stay or go," she said, "it didn't matter to me. I was going to have someone to look after. I wanted the baby even if it was a big surprise and I was young. I wanted a family because my goal was to have a family and treat them how I wanted to be treated."

Jacob found the decision an easy one. "She gave me the option to leave. I said no, absolutely not. It was not really a reaction that most men give. But I was kind of raised like you take responsibility for your actions." He, too, felt ready to step up to the challenge.

Angelina and Jacob ran into hurdles from the outset. Without savings or jobs, they could not rent an apartment. Living with each other's families proved impossible. When Jacob's parents broke up, the family tumbled into disarray, his older brother living with his grandmother, his sister moving in with her boyfriend, his younger brother bouncing back and forth between his mother and father, feeling cramped and unwelcome in both places, and Jacob stagnating, going nowhere. Angelina and Jacob had once stayed with his mother during a two-week break from Job Corps. They squeezed awkwardly into a narrow stretch of her dwelling, feeling in the way. The option was not viable long-term.

Desperate for a place to stay, Angelina moved back to Boston, living once again with her mercurial foster mother. Jacob also moved to Boston, wanting to be close, but could not stay with Angelina because her foster mother disapproved of him. He found residence at the Pine Street Inn, a homeless shelter.

Parents Under Pressure

The decision provoked the foster mother's ire. She told Jacob to 'Take a hike.' She said a homeless shelter was beneath him, no place for a young man with family in Gardner. Buying him a bus ticket, she sent him home.

Pushed out and running out of choices, Jacob returned to Gardner. With no car or easy transit, and short on cash, the sixty-mile gap between Gardner and Boston proved exasperatingly difficult. Angelina and Jacob could only visit each other infrequently.

"My foster mother's family didn't very much agree with me staying in a relationship with him," said Angelina. "They thought I should just move on, because they see white and Hispanic interracial families as the white person being dominant and they did not want me in that situation." They tried to pair Angelina with a Hispanic man in their Church, hoping the match would stick. Angelina had no interest. They questioned her bond to Jacob, told her that the situation was his fault, he came from another culture, took advantage of her, messed with her. They berated her for having a child so young, too young, risking her future, and suggested she put the baby up for adoption or relinquish her to her foster mother. Angelina absorbed their messages, felt their barbs, and held firm.

Angelina's relatives are not alone in expressing concern about the prudence of teenage pregnancy. Popular images of adolescents paint them as too immature and feckless to raise their young responsibly.

The CDC, on its website, professes: "Teen pregnancy and child-bearing bring substantial social and economic costs through immediate and long-term impacts on teen parents and their children."[2] The costs include billions of dollars spent for increased health care, foster care, and incarceration rates, as well as lost tax revenue due to teen parents' higher school dropouts, and lower employment rates. Longitudinal researchers, such as Frank Furstenberg, suggest that such claims may draw lopsided conclusions, often confounding cause and effect.

Furstenberg, a sociologist at the University of Pennsylvania, spent decades studying teen parenthood.[3] Starting in the 1960s, he followed a sample of four hundred low-income teens in Baltimore, mostly African American, who had become pregnant before the age of eighteen. When they conceived, half of the mothers were sixteen or younger, three quarters had not completed tenth grade, and three quarters had no intention of marrying before giving birth.

By middle age, perhaps unsurprisingly, the women in Furstenberg's study had indeed suffered the pernicious effects of adversity, leading to various health and mental health problems and negative life events. Their offspring also faced difficult circumstances. However, the women demonstrated substantial resilience. Many returned to school, entered the labor force, and greatly improved their economic prospects. Perhaps most surprisingly, the outcomes of the group largely resembled those of others in their neighborhood and economic cohort who had delayed childbearing. Teen parenthood, Furstenberg decided, was not the culprit. It was poverty. Several other national samples, as well as professionals who work with teen parents, reach similar conclusions.[4]

"So often these girls get typecast," said Anne Teschner, the Executive Director of The Care Center, an alternative education program for teenage mothers in Holyoke, Massachusetts, aimed at helping students earn their High School Equivalency and attend college.[5] "They're told 'You're irresponsible,' or 'This is really hard for you because all you want to do is party.' That's not what we see. We actually see pretty grounded, sobered young women who are, like, 'holy cow, I've got this on my plate. Alright, I am taking this seriously.'"

Anne Teschner has worked at the Care Center for the past twenty years, alongside Ana Rodriguez, the Education Director, transforming it into a hub of arts, culture, and education that achieves a 75 percent college enrollment rate amongst its low-income students, most of whom are women of color and the first in their families to pursue higher education. Teschner and Rodriguez decided that the best way to help students succeed was to make school a rich, vibrant experience. They modeled the program on private preparatory schools that offer art, music, athletics, humanities, and the expectation of success and college enrollment. The center also provides onsite day care, health and dental care, mental health counseling, and college counseling, as well as transportation and meals for students and their children. Located on a residential street, in a three-story, symmetric brick house with gambrel roofs, the building was once owned and lived in by Elizabeth Towne (1865–1960), a suffragist and publisher, herself a teen parent, and a fitting exemplar for the aspirations of the program.[6]

"The link that we see clearly," said Teschner, "is school failure first, then teen pregnancy.[7] Schools and policy makers hate hearing that. What they really like is the narrative of teen pregnancy leads to failure. If I were in these girls' shoes, I probably would have done the exact same thing, which is drop out of school, see that there are no other options available, that this is the most positive thing I could do, so, I guess I'll be a mom. There's nothing else ahead for me because all those other doors have been closed."

For some adolescents, parenthood becomes a way to gain entry to new experiences and satisfactions. At least that is the view of the seven young women aged seventeen to twenty-one, and of different racial backgrounds, who sat in the basement of The Care Center to discuss parenting and the ways it has altered their lives. "I love being a parent," a twenty-year-old mother of two stated emphatically. "I love everything about it—even the sleepless nights. It's a struggle, but who else is going to stay up with my child? It makes me happy that I can do it."

Her peers agreed. Being mothers changed them, taught them responsibility, gave them a purpose. Prior to motherhood, many lived in violent neighborhoods and attended inadequate schools. They were failing academically, partying, and getting into fights. Now they went to school regularly and were preparing for college. "If I hadn't become a mom, I'd be in jail," said one. Severa; others echoed the sentiment. Parenthood afforded them a lucky break.

Investigations of low-income, teen parents find them, by and large, just as motivated, responsible, and willing to sacrifice and work hard for their children as those in older age groups or with higher incomes. Young women with few prospects often find motherhood a source of pride and satisfaction, one that propels them to grow up, become serious, and find direction. Contrary to American mythmaking, the majority of low-income adolescent parents, even if they had not borne children early, would not have managed to wade into the middle class or enjoy improved destinies.[8]

"The reality is," said Ana Rodriguez, "that if you put systems and supports in place, these young people can succeed. It's not over for them, but there has to be a mentality in the community that supports young mothers. Alone, they can't do it."

Unfortunately, stereotyping dissuades policy makers from putting supports in place, lest they inadvertently encourage wanton behavior. Amidst the judgments of family and society, teens like Angelina and Jacob often find themselves alone, forging their own paths, and heading straight into one wall after another.

Pregnant and committed to her unborn child, Angelina did as much as she could to prepare. She joined a parent group aimed at promoting breastfeeding, which discussed numerous other topics as well. Parents in the group shared articles and she voraciously read each. She felt particularly drawn to attachment parenting, the type of parenting Robin, described in Chapter Four, found intensive, which promoted empathy, responsiveness, and close physical contact between the parent and infant. She went online and read all she could find.

"I thought, this is what I need," Angelina said. "I liked the connection. I believe that a baby that is held all the time isn't spoiled, it is loved. It feels secure. I liked some of the science that backs it. It seemed more sensible to me than any article I read, and I read about everything. I tried talking with Jacob's family, too, but what they recommended, the cry it out stuff, didn't sound right to me. Babies should not be left to cry without getting comfort. Nope, I can't do that. I like attachment. I like my baby being with me, being attuned with me. I also believe that if you give kids choices now, they'll realize that their choices matter. I didn't feel that anything I said mattered as a kid. I want my kids to know I am listening, and they do not need to go behind my back and make a mistake. Studies show that kids raised that way turn out pretty darn decent."

Angelina put her research to the test after their first daughter was born and, then again, after the birth of their second daughter, four years later. She cuddled her babies, co-slept, nursed on demand, responded to their cries, gestures, and statements. She liked the results. "When she cries," she said about her second child, a year-old infant, "if you let her cry it out, she cries for hours. But if you pick her up and rub her back, she falls asleep."

She felt confident that she knew how her children felt, and what they wanted. When her baby leaned into her, she snuggled her. When she grunted or gestured, she followed her gaze or outstretched arm and helped retrieve a wanted object. She could tell when her children felt hungry, when they were tired, bothered, or needed a change of pace. She marveled at her children's development, how they hit milestones early, crawling at six months, walking at ten, and communicating by gesture or words by nine months. She liked the calmness of their temperaments, their ease in communicating. Her older daughter had received an award in preschool for being kind. Her teachers called her a model student.

Jacob largely accepted and supported Angelina's childrearing, and followed her lead. They talked about when to be lenient and when to be strict. Angelina observed him becoming increasingly nurturing with the children, but not without some of his own doubts and growing pains. "I am not saying that it is a bad thing," he said, "it's just that my mom taught me to cry it out. I am not all for that, but there is a time and place for you to put them to bed, do their routine, read them a book, give them a kiss, and it's like, they can come out once, totally, but after the second or third time, it's no, you're done. Go to bed. That's it."

Jacob at first found parenting strenuous, one of the hardest jobs he had attempted. "With working," he said, "you have one or a few tasks and you know how to do it. Same thing over and over. With parenting, every day there is a new lesson, something different, you don't know what's going to happen." He also discovered that parenting bestowed rewards. "Kids think you are the coolest person ever when you do something normal," he said.

Others were less supportive. Angelina's foster mother disagreed rigorously with her parenting methods. She told Angelina to put her baby in the bouncy seat and not to touch her unless she was hungry or soiled. Angelina refused. She had read and researched and knew what she wanted. "I had to fight my foster mother to let me do it," she said. "It ended up costing me a home with her."

As Angelina and Jacob discovered, parenting methods are far from universal, yet they invoke strong beliefs and reactions about right and wrong approaches. Since parents socialize their children to survive and thrive in a particular cultural and economic condition, different circumstances lead to distinctly different parenting strategies. Parenting varies by necessity, adapting itself to an environment's most pressing demands.

Patricia Greenfield, a professor of psychology at University of California, Los Angeles, studies social change and how parenting and human development evolve as countries and communities become more urban, commercial, educated, technological, and wealthy.[9] Greenfield found that as the United States became more urban, between the late nineteenth and throughout the twentieth centuries, family size diminished, communal ideals declined, and individualism rose. She discovered the same trends as China developed a market economy in the late twentieth century and when, in the twenty-first, communities in Chiapas, Mexico based their economies on money and commerce. Greenfield also traces how parenting practices shift in line with economics. She has developed a model that explains how and why that occurs.

Professor Greenfield's model compares two different settings, one a rural, subsistence community, the other a wealthy, urban, or suburban neighborhood. In the former, limited educational and technological options exist, labor is primarily manual, and resources scarce. To maximize survival, families and community members pool assets and rely upon each other. Parenting methods instill group loyalty and cooperation by creating hierarchical relationships between parent and child. Parents encourage obedience, punish noncompliance, limit choices and identities, and emphasize contributing to others. They initiate interactions so that children follow their parents' leads or explore independently. Annette Lareau, a professor of sociology at the University of Pennsylvania, found those strategies predominated amongst the poor and working class families that she studied in a northeastern U.S. city.[10] Jacob and Angelina experienced comparable values and expectations in the families and communities in which they grew up, although they chose to use disparate methods, more indicative of the middle class.

As the wealth and resources of a family or community ascend, and survival becomes less of a driving concern, both Lareau and Greenfield discovered that parenting shifts. Affluent and middle class families and communities only mildly depend on children for concrete help and thus do not require the same degree of conformity and obedience.[11] Relationships are often more egalitarian, and parenting more child-centered and individualistic. Responding is privileged over initiating, reasoning and negotiating over demanding and punishing, and choice is promoted. Parents follow the lead of their children, encouraging individuation, assertion, and self-advocacy. They also provide opportunities to learn and practice a wide range of social and cognitive skills. This type of parenting is increasingly favored by child development pundits, but it requires a high degree of parental involvement, as well as time, knowledge, and resources to implement, factors more often held by the well-off than the poor.

While most American families and communities likely fall somewhere between those two poles, mixing and matching strategies from each, clashes and confusion can result when they collide. Middle class parents typically encourage children to speak up about their thoughts and feelings, and to negotiate with authorities, traits that serve them well in their interactions with institutions, schools, and higher income jobs.

However, the same skills might serve poor and working class families less well, disadvantaging them in their communities. As Val Gillies, a British sociologist who studied working class mothers, wrote in 2007,

> ... the middle-class focus on equipping children with reasoning and negotiation skills can lead them to challenge or reject the authority of parents. Defiant middle-class children might be viewed as naturally struggling towards independence, but similarly disobedient working-class children...are likely to be constructed as a serious threat to society. This is highly racialized as well as classed and gendered.[12]

None of the advice sites and manuals Angelina consulted would have mentioned how parenting differs by community, or the reasons for those variations, nor would they have prepared her for the backlash her parenting might receive. By donning the trappings of middle class parenting while living in low-income communities, Angelina and Jacob wandered straight into a cultural crossfire.

Angelina stayed with her foster mother during her first pregnancy, but it was not easy, given her separation from Jacob and her foster mother's daily judgments and recriminations. Jacob, living apart, struggled to support his fledging family and stay connected. He landed a job and searched for suitable housing.

"I had just gotten a job at Price Chopper," he said, "and I was trying to make enough money to get an apartment, which was complete crap because I only made $8.20 an hour there." With the cost of renting a one or two-bedroom apartment in Gardner costing $800 or more a month, his small paycheck could not easily stretch, along with the food and other bills a household required. Strapped for money and needing to work as many hours as he could, he only took a day off when Angelina went into labor. He left Boston before she even gave birth.

The circumstances were hard on Angelina. "I just remember bawling my eyes out for days and days afterwards," she said, "because I was doing it by myself."

Angelina stayed with her foster mother another two months before finding the parenting conflicts intractable and the situation intolerable. Contacting her maternal grandmother, she moved in with her and her roommates. Five people resided together in a small three-bedroom apartment, so Angelina had to make do with the unfinished basement. She managed. Her grandmother was supportive, liked Jacob, and provided money for them to see each other once a month. Angelina found the arrangement somewhat compatible.

"People wanted to help," she said, "but they weren't helping in the most important ways. I wouldn't get to shower sometimes for days; I was going without sleep. People would hold the baby for a minute, but it wasn't really like 'Hey, I'll hold the baby, so you can go take a nap and maybe take a shower.' It's like, 'I'll hold the baby because you should clean up after the food you just cooked.' And that was hard because even though you had a kid, they still saw you as a kid, so no one really wanted to treat you like a parent, they just wanted to treat you like a kid in the house."

An apartment finally came through in Gardner, in an affordable housing complex that capped rent according to tenants' income. Getting approved and finding an open unit had taken a year, but Angelina, Jacob, and their nine-month-old baby could at last plant their feet and become a family.

Given long waitlists for subsidized housing, they were lucky to find a place that quickly. In the greater Boston area, waiting lists can range in the thousands, necessitating years and years of patience. At times, the waitlists grow so long that the housing authority closes them to new applicants.[13] In smaller, more isolated towns like Gardner, competition for units is less fierce, one of the reasons Angelina and Jacob located there.

The family moved into a two-bedroom, one bathroom apartment in a quiet corner of the city, remote and sheltered, with a small playground on site and within walking distance of a grocery store. They furnished the apartment sparingly with used furniture, toys, and other necessities, scrimping and scrounging on their limited income. Angelina and Jacob kept the apartment neat and clean, trying to impose order and control over their otherwise unruly circumstances. On a bad day, dishes would pile up in the sink or toys spill into the living room, but they soon straightened those minor messes. They have kept the apartment for the past four years, finding it an important refuge.

Renting an apartment, even a low-income apartment, meant paying bills, which required income. Jacob obtained a factory job at Garlock, a nearby packaging manufacturer, and worked twelve-hour shifts, sometimes adding overtime hours. Angelina procured a job at McDonald's and worked overnights. At times they barely saw each other, overlapping only for the brief moments in between one person coming and the other going. The schedule exhausted Angelina.

"When I worked, I had no energy for anything," she said. "I don't remember most of it—it's a blur. I was just non-functioning. I feel bad because I feel I ditched out on being a parent for a while because I had no energy. I would walk to and from work, leaving at 7 p.m. and returning at 7 a.m. and then come home and pass out until 5 p.m. and then muster enough energy to make dinner." Jacob told her not to cook, but she felt obligated.

They had some support, but not always what they wanted or when they needed it. His family gave furniture. Way too much. "It's funny how they'll help you when you need something nonessential," Angelina said, "but when you're on your last living, they don't show up."

A friend gave her hand-me-downs for her children, a one year supply of clothes. Although constrained by limited resources, Angelina learned to take care of herself, drinking heaps of coffee and tea, crocheting, and taking time alone. She even started college, enrolling in classes in sociology and art.

Contending with Jacob's bipolar disorder created stress. His family did not accept the diagnosis and would not admit that some of his behavior was out of his control. His brother insisted nothing was wrong; his manic episodes were simply "doing it just to do it." At first, those episodes occurred infrequently, only once or twice a year, and so were easy to ignore or brush off. But they progressed from semi-yearly to every few months and then to every few weeks.

"The mania is really hard to fight sometimes," he said. "Half the time you don't even know what you are doing. It's like a vicious cycle. I'll be in the best mood for three or four weeks and then, at the end of those four weeks, it's just complete no sleep. Once I had $200 and I went to the store and I didn't come home with anything. I just spent it. I don't even remember what I spent it on. It was just gone. It's completely overwhelming sometimes."

Jacob's limitations left Angelina to take over household tasks and monitor his moods and symptoms. She learned to recognize his warning signs, the aggravation, sleep disturbance, and drinking that preceded an episode, and would try to head it off. She controlled the money and finances, giving him stipends, trying to ensure that an unforeseen manic phase and spending spree would not deplete them. She prepared back-ups and safety plans, in case he deteriorated further and they needed help.

The bipolar symptoms were manageable when episodes occurred months apart, but as the cycles moved closer, it became harder and harder for them both to cope. Angelina came home from work one day to find Jacob sitting on the couch, making no effort to go to his job. His boss called, asking where he was and whether he would make it in. Jacob did not respond. After three days of absence, he was fired from the only good paying job in the area, a job that sometimes brought in as much as $1600 a month. That left them with Angelina's minimum wage earnings from McDonald's.

"Working wasn't really paying the bills," said Angelina, "it was taking time away from my family, and it took so much out of my health. After I worked for six months, I started feeling sick. I was getting dizzy spells and nauseous all the time. I didn't know I was pregnant yet, but it turned out it wasn't just pregnancy, I had a gallbladder infection and I couldn't do anything about it because I was pregnant. My anemia was also at an all-time high because we couldn't always afford the right foods and I would sometimes go without eating three full meals a day. My family needed to eat first. I was losing weight."

When Angelina went to a funeral in Boston for three days following the death of an uncle, McDonald's fired her, even though she had been granted leave. She decided not to look for another job. "When I got laid off, it was with mixed feelings," she said. "I wasn't going to have money, which made me feel awful, but at the same time, I needed to take care of my health because I was carrying another child. So, I made the choice to get back on welfare and lay low."

Not everyone approved. "I get judged because people tell me I should be working," she said, "because I am poor. They basically say, if you can't afford it, don't do it. I had one person tell me I was a burden on society because I wasn't going back to work. The baby was only a month old at the time. I feel like, when you have a new baby, you should stay home with it for a bit. I know that it is financially tolling. It is also tolling on society, apparently. It's tolling on society when they see someone outside of the box."

Angelina incited further reproach when she explained the importance of staying home and being present for her child. "People would say, 'Huh? I never heard of that. Carry her around, breastfeed, spend time with her?' One of my friends told me, 'That's rich people stuff. Yeah, you see suburban moms do those things. Do you do yoga, too, and drink smoothies?' I just hate it when you are trying to be the best mom and dad you can be, and people moan, 'Oh, well, you're breast-feeding your kids past three months, you're not working, your kids are too far apart, too close together."

Jacob felt less bothered by the comments. "No matter what you're doing, there's going to be something," he said. "There's always going to be those people." The problem, however, was that with every denunciation, Angelina watched her circle of trusted confidants and helpers grow smaller and smaller, at a time when companions and assistance were sorely needed.

Angelina became increasingly concerned about Jacob. His manic cycles took a toll on the family, financially and emotionally. She and he were arguing more often and she worried about her daughter witnessing the conflict or seeing her father manic. At three years old, the girl was old enough to notice his mood changes and behavior. After one fight became physical—Jacob hit Angelina once and she pushed him back— she took out a restraining order and gave an ultimatum. Seek treatment and improve, or leave. He moved out and agreed to treatment. Angelina offered to help him find doctors and programs. Jacob's mother and sister assisted by watching their daughter while she and Jacob investigated options.

Angelina had reason to feel concerned. An estimated five million children have a parent with a mental illness, which places those children at risk for adverse outcomes, especially if the parent exhibits volatile and disturbing behavior or does not fulfill parental responsibilities.[14] Mental illness in a parent is associated with higher incidences of abuse and neglect of children, as well as that parent's lower educational, vocational, and financial achievement.

Children of parents with mental illness show higher rates of difficulties and mental illness themselves, both because of their genetic inheritance, and because of the potential adversities, or Adverse Childhood Experiences (ACEs), a mentally ill parent can introduce.[15] Affected families struggle to manage extra demands, while facing discrimination and ostracization, which doubles or triples their challenges. Clearly, however, many parents with mental disorders handle parental responsibilities well, do not inflict ACEs on their children, or doom them to dysfunction. What helps keep adverse outcomes at bay, as Angelina intuited, is treatment and stabilization of the disorder and sensitive, open, and understanding relationships that support children and help them cope.[16]

One day, after consulting with a psychiatrist, Jacob and Angelina returned to the apartment, planning to make dinner and talk. They were tired, with a lot on their minds. Sorting out what steps to take, what would work best, took thought and planning. Settling in around 4 p.m., they heard their buzzer ring unexpectedly. Answering it, they found a policeman and DCF worker at the door. The policeman, expressing regret for the actions the law required, arrested Jacob for violating the restraining order. The DCF worker, stating concern for their three-year-old daughter, declared she could not remain at home. She told Angelina to dress the girl, put on her shoes, and tell the worker where to take her. They sent her to Jacob's sister.

"I questioned it all for a moment," said Angelina. "I was like, wait a minute, you can't just tell me I need to send my kid somewhere else, and they're like, no, this is how it's going to go, and I was scared because they had a police officer at my door. So, I thought, I am just going to do whatever you say because I don't want to get arrested."

After lifting the restraining order and releasing Jacob from custody, the couple struggled to make sense of what happened. They learned later that evening that Jacob's sister, out of concern for their plight, called DCF to request financial and therapeutic help. The agency, hearing the particulars, grew concerned and a 51A report of suspected child abuse or neglect was filed. After all, Jacob and Angelina's lives were rife with risk factors: teen parenthood, low income, low education, parental unemployment, mental illness, and now a hint that the parents' relationship could be violent.

Risk factors are those characteristics of the individual, family, or community that increase the probability of adverse outcomes. They are the ACEs waiting to happen, the ingredients in a child's life most likely to lead to disease, mental illness, and low performance. Angelina and

Jacob's lives had many red flags, but problems arise when risk factors are considered in isolation, when liability is confused with certainty, and the weight of an experience is not balanced or calibrated with offsetting protective factors. A mentally ill parent or even a singular episode of violence may, at face value, look like an ACE, but not jeopardize a child's care or safety. Angelina and Jacob's lives were replete not only with potential hazards, but also numerous protective factors: family supports, secure attachments, intelligence, willingness to seek help, parental monitoring of children, and competence. When Jacob and Angelina came to the attention of DCF, it fell to the workers to sort through the risk and protective factors and decide an appropriate course of action.[17]

"Schools and other reporters often believe that if they refer a family to DCF, they will get help," said Vicky Kelly, during a lengthy conversation. Kelly served as the Director of the Delaware Division of Family Services from 2011 to 2016 (the equivalent agency to DCF in Massachusetts) and has over thirty years of experience working in child welfare and mental health. She currently provides consultation to child welfare agencies across the country through the Annie E. Casey Foundation Child Welfare Strategy Group. "But the system is a child protection system, built around investigation and foster care. It doesn't fund the types of preventative services families need. Efforts to reform child welfare funding to move it to those other services have been continually blocked. What happens is you have families who are poor, using public services, and that brings them under the surveillance of public agencies. Their fundamental problem is not child abuse or neglect, but so often poverty and everything that means.[18] The system is ill-equipped to handle those families because it does not have much cash and other assistance."

DCF evolved in the same era and roughly along the same timeline as other governmental agencies assisting children and families, although the focus differed from the start.[19] The welfare imparted is safety, and the target is children. However, like America's other public welfare agencies, DCF is primarily a twentieth-century construction.

Before the nineteenth century, American courts and local officials sporadically stepped in to rescue children from abusive parents, but no widespread mandate led the state to investigate or intervene, nor did government allocate resources for such actions. A trickle of changes began in the late nineteenth and early twentieth centuries, as cities grew, and Progressive Era reformers became more and more alarmed at the conditions of poor urban families. Reformers worried, in part, that those conditions would compel youngsters to grow up delinquent. They began setting up charities and helping organizations. In 1875, Henry Bergh and Elbridge Gerry founded the New York Society for the Prevention of Cruelty to Children (NYSPCC), a nongovernmental agency, which sought to protect maltreated children. Other nongovernmental, preventative agencies spread around the country, but with uneven coverage and quality.

The Social Security Act of 1935 helped expand and strengthen child protection efforts through government, but not until the 1960s, and the publication of influential articles on child abuse, did concern consolidate. In 1974, Congress passed The Child Abuse Prevention and Treatment Act, which funded reporting, investigation, and intervention of child abuse and neglect. The child protection system (CPS), now known in Massachusetts as DCF, was born.

New organizations often struggle to find their footing, and child protection has been no exception. Mandated reporting laws led to an overwhelming onslaught of cases, which the agencies strove to process. Rising numbers of children in foster care alarmed Congress and proponents of the family, which led to the passing of the Adoption Assistance and Child Welfare Act of 1980, which favored family preservation and reunification whenever possible. However, critics argued that preserving families failed to adequately protect children and, in 1997, Congress passed The Adoption and Safe Families Act, prioritizing child safety in decision-making. Decades ago, when Diana's husband, as described in Chapter Three, left welts on their children and was reported to DCF, she interacted with a system favoring intact families, and her children remained at home. Angelina and Jacob, years later, encountered a system tilting towards safety, and their child, although less wounded, was compelled to leave.

The fluctuations in government and DCF policies towards families reflect America's ongoing debate about family sanctity and the role of government. America valorizes independence and personal responsibility and disdains public interference. Society thus leaves parents alone to bear the brunt of their circumstances, until natural supports fail, and the family devolves into crisis. Although families like Angelina and Jacob receive aid in the form of housing vouchers and welfare payments, when those prove insufficient, or when emotional crises threaten their stability, they can elicit monitoring and punitive interventions. A national ideology that venerates parenting but distrusts parents leads to society's initial under-involvement in supporting families, as well as its eventual and excessive oversight, to its substituting helping hands for slaps in the face.

"What you have," said Vicky Kelly, the former Director of the Delaware Division of Family Services, "is this incredible tension between the legalistic, forensic side of child welfare, which is what workers are held to in terms of accountability, versus why most of them went into this field, which is to help people. Then you hire workers who, in most states, are not required to be social workers—all they need is a college degree—and you put them in situations where they are called to assess complex situations. Then we treat them terribly and pay them horribly, and they turn over and turn over and turn over. And so, we don't build a workforce that is well-equipped to assess families well. And depending on the politics locally, depending on whether there has been a recent high profile child death, a system can be pushed into investigating families instead of helping."

Massachusetts, in fact, had a number of high profile child deaths that pushed it away from family preservation and towards safeguarding children. One occurred in 2013, in Fitchburg, a city thirteen miles west of Gardner and serviced by the same DCF office in which Angelina and Jacob found themselves. At the time, DCF had been involved with five-year-old Jeremiah Oliver's family for over two years due to allegations of neglect, yet failed to notice he had gone missing for almost four months. Jeremiah's body was later discovered in a suitcase, on the side of a highway, and his mother and her boyfriend implicated in his death. DCF had not visited his home in seven months, despite requirement to hold monthly meetings.[20]

Reverberations ricocheted through the entire system. Afraid of future tragedies and liability, DCF started pulling more and more children from their families. By doing so, the agency guarded against one type of harm at the expense of another. In a 2016 publication of The American Professional Society on the Abuse of Children, Ronald Hughes and Frank Vandervort wrote,

> Hell for children served by CPS has two faces: it affects not only children who are inappropriately removed from their homes, causing disruption of family life, assault on parents' rights, and emotional and developmental harm…, but also children inappropriately left in homes at high risk of imminent harm…, who face an almost certain future of injury, neglect, and emotional harm.[21]

Low-income families, more often than the wealthy, live in circumstances that attract the attention of DCF. They interact with more governmental agencies and possess fewer means with which to remedy difficulties.[22] Away from the prying eyes of public scrutiny, wealthier parents can access private resources to address problems. They also have the financial and social capital to challenge dictums with which they disagree. Families like Angelina and Jacob, however, feel powerless to confront DCF. They experience worker's dictums as judgment, coercion, and threat. For them, DCF can feel like a hovering hawk, ready to swoop, take control, and remove a child when the family finally succumbs to its overwhelming pressures. DCF, in turn, stripped of its penetrating eyesight by insufficient resources and an oscillating mandate, labors uneasily to distinguish which families require intervention, and of what type. In the years before Jeremiah's death, the state slashed DCF's budget year after year, about $100 million in all, necessitating sharp increases in worker's caseloads. Since his death, much of the funding has been restored.

"The job is stressful," said someone who works at DCF and asked not to be identified. "Caseloads are sometimes up to double what they

_d the paperwork is extensive. Needed resources for fami-
_always available. So, there is virtually no way for us to
_mands. In addition, workers go into dangerous situations
anu _... _s terrible things, which creates considerable strain. We feel
drained and overworked."

DCF workers manifest vicarious trauma, otherwise known as compassion fatigue, at higher rates than other human service professionals.[23] Their repeated exposures to traumatic events and descriptions of distressing material can produce emotional exhaustion, depression, hyper-arousal, and anger. The end result is burnout, staff attrition, and a less experienced workforce (the median tenure of DCF workers nationwide stands at 1.8 years) which means they are less likely to prioritize, or have the skills for, family casework.[24] While there are many dedicated and experienced DCF workers who provide substantial supports to families, many other workers do not have the backup and resources they need. Organizational supports are key, but when lean budgets, high caseloads, and time pressures prevail, the availability of supervisorial help also declines.

"If we funded the highway department at 60 percent of what is needed to build roads," said Vicky Kelly, "and the roads were crumbling and falling apart, would we be shocked that they weren't doing what we expected them to do? No. Do we fund child welfare to do the things we want it to do? No, we don't. We can pick apart its work, but if we want it done differently, we need to direct and resource it differently. We have significantly gutted the safety net through cuts. When other systems fail, when there is high unemployment or an opioid crisis, the results of those problems fall into child welfare's lap. The child welfare system is then on the hook to pick up the pieces. Things happen in families all the time. Unless we, as a country, deal with the underlying problems, this cycle will continue."

"The system may be imperfect," said the DCF worker, "but it is the only one we have. If families can't make it, for whatever reason, we have no choice but to intervene to try and save the children. Children need a chance at a successful life."

For Angelina and Jacob, the structure and constraints of DCF meant that they were going to encounter a system more likely to inves-

tigate than support, to coerce than cooperate, to censure than understand, to err on the side of family separation than family preservation.
They were also apt to meet inexperienced workers holding their own
ideas about parenting, poverty, and Puerto Ricans. And while Jacob
and Angelina struggled to field judgments flung by friends and family, they found them even more troublesome when cast by institutions
wielding authority.

An investigator from DCF visited Jacob and Angelina's home. She
opened the refrigerator and cupboards, poked her head into the bed-
rooms, asked about a crib for the unborn baby, and questioned how
they would feed their children on their limited income. She disparaged
breastfeeding as difficult and co-sleeping as ill-advised. Then she filed
a report saying that their child had no bed, the household contained
insufficient food, and the apartment appeared filthy and unkempt.

Angelina and Jacob disputed each of those allegations, saying they
were well provisioned, their house clean, and the crib present but
not yet assembled. Nevertheless, at noon, a few days later, a worker
called, telling them to find a longer-term guardian for their child or the
agency would place her in foster care. They had until 5:00 p.m. to sort
it out.

Given the choice between a foster home or a family member, they
chose the only readily available option, Angelina's foster mother in
Boston. They signed their daughter over, granting a three-month temporary guardianship. After a ten-minute farewell inside Walmart, they
tearfully waved good-bye to their three-year-old daughter.

Jacob restarted medications, this time Lamictal and Seroquel, and
stabilized once again. His health insurance demanded he cease working and apply for disability payments. The insurance even paid for an
attorney to help him qualify, an intervention that helped shorten his
approval period to just a few months. Although reluctant, he surren-
dered to the indignity of his position, watching the definition of man-
hood instilled by his parents and community slip through his fingers.

"No, I'm not going to be that guy," he said, "I'm not going to be
that guy. I grew up with a bunch of workers. You work for your money, you work until you are dead. At the time, it was just really hard

because I had to do it the hard way or the smart way. Because I could get a job next week. Yes, with disability, I am supplying money and food for my family, but I would feel more accomplishment if I went out and earned it. That's just the way I was raised, and I feel less of a man to not be doing that."

Angelina, however, supported his leave from work and collection of disability benefits. "He's a great worker," she said, "until a manic episode hits and then he loses the job, and we are stuck with little money for a few months. I would rather have him stay on medication for a while and sort himself out and then be able to work with almost no problems, instead of working unmedicated and getting episodes. Basically, working himself until he goes insane. He used to do that. When he worked at Garlock, he worked almost eighty hours a week."

Angelina called DCF weekly, asking when their child could return home, what they needed to do, whether DCF could provide transportation for them to visit. She called and called, tearful and crying, mourning the loss of her child and worrying about her well-being. Months passed before Jacob and Angelina received answers or a service plan, which detailed the tasks required of them. In the meantime, the sixty-mile divide between Boston and Gardner created a formidable rift, disrupting the close connection between parents and child.

"We never had money to go see her," said Angelina, "because we were on welfare, and we lost some of our benefits because she was not living with us. Jacob's social security had not yet come through so we were living on $160 a month. They expected us to go see her several times a month without helping. And we got chastised every time we said we hadn't seen her. I called her on the phone every day, but my foster mother did not let her talk to us much, and DCF did not intervene to help. I missed Halloween with her, I missed Thanksgiving, I missed Christmas. She missed the birth of her sister. It broke my heart."

Nine months pregnant, and three days before the scheduled C-section birth of her second child, a DCF worker told Angelina to find a new place to stay or she would take the baby upon birth. Then, a day later, the worker told Angelina she could keep both children if Jacob moved out. He left, staying with his sister for two months before DCF allowed him to move back in. The timing made the directive's blow doubly harsh and difficult.

"It's weird how someone can call the shots on your own life," said Jacob, "on your own wellbeing. It's like their word is above the law. It's like your life is spinning out of control and you have no control over it at all. These people come in for a day and tell you what's going to happen."

After three months of living away, their elder daughter returned home, her heart also broken, clingy, nervous about separations, restless, and fearful at night. She worried that she would need to leave again and was jealous of the baby who was born in her absence. She felt terrified of seeing the woman, Angelina's foster mother, who cared for her during the mandated time away, lest she return to live with her. That has, in turn, interfered with Angelina's relationship to her foster mother, whom she has ceased inviting to family events.

Even with the children home, Angelina and Jacob continued to tangle with their DCF workers, who they felt cast one insinuation after another. Jacob and Angelina were accused of not following the service plan, even before they had been given one. The worker told them that because they had not married, Massachusetts did not legally consider Jacob the father, although he lived with the family and was listed on the birth certificate. The characterization was incorrect. State law, in fact, presumes fatherhood when the parent lives in the household and assumes parental duties and responsibilities. A referral for family therapy, sent by their DCF worker to Luk, a local agency, belittled Jacob, claiming that he "thinks he is head of the household and serves as a father of sorts."

"It really hurt my feelings when I read that," said Jacob.

"It broke his heart," said Angelina.

DCF further chastised Angelina and Jacob for having a close relationship, labeling it too close, co-dependent, implying that they cared for each other in destructive ways. Both scoff at that suggestion. "All you have is each other," said Angelina, "especially when you are going through a traumatizing thing like no choice in giving up your kid. Who else are we supposed to depend upon?"

"You already took our kid away," added Jacob, "are you also going to take our love, our relationship, our wellbeing, our sanity?"

Luk provided them weekly couple's counseling. Therapists came to the house and helped them sort out what was happening and ways to cope. The counselors looked at the reports, called DCF, and met with the worker and her supervisor. They told DCF the family was fine, functioning well, the children were nurtured and healthy. The conversation gave Jacob and Angelina the first validation of their efforts and a glimpse of hope that they could escape the yoke of DCF's surveillance. It also taught them what it might take to do so.

"You've got to have a title to get your voice heard," said Jacob.

"You've got to have people on your side," added Angelina.

Luk's intervention, however, failed to convince DCF to close the case. The agency continued to press concerns. The worker claimed that Jacob was an abuser who posed a danger to Angelina and the children, and that she was a battered woman. "The children were never in danger," said Angelina, "and I am very far from a battered woman."

Their first DCF worker told Angelina she cried too much. Another DCF worker sent in a referral for individual psychotherapy for Angelina, stating that she needed to work on aggression. Angelina's assigned therapist was surprised, when he met her, to find a self-contained, thoughtful young woman sitting in his office with no history of belligerence. He thought the worker's statements revealed bias— stereotypical attitudes towards Hispanics, people of color, and the poor—confusing outspokenness with threat and aggression.

As DCF workers investigated the family, they dug into Jacob's past and mental health problems. A worker found an incident that occurred when he was fourteen and used it to stress his volatility and dangerousness. Jacob reminded them that it occurred eight years ago, when he was younger, under the tutelage of his parents, who denied his mental illness. Now twenty-two, he was undergoing treatment, taking medication, and attending therapy. He had matured and changed. DCF asked for proof that he had changed, requesting information about his therapy, what he talked about and worked on. Although he wanted privacy, the right to talk in therapy without

Parents Under Pressure

worrying about what would be divulged, the request scared him into disclosing more information than he wanted or than his service plan required. Jacob and Angelina continually wondered what more they needed to do to prove his stability and their competency.

A setback in Jacob's health prolonged the agency's involvement. Eight months after their daughter returned home, Jacob started drinking, a bit more than usual, a can or two of beer a day. He showed no other signs of impending mania or depression.

Out one night, Angelina came home to find their room a mess: the bed unmade, clothes strewn about, food left out, and dishes uncleaned. The baby was asleep in her crib and her older daughter, now four, away at Jacob's sister's house. Angelina offered to help Jacob straighten up, before his slurred speech and sluggish actions alerted her that he was drunk. She left him in the bedroom and decided to sleep in the living room.

A little while later, Angelina awoke to his questioning why she had not come to bed. She told him that it was because of his drinking. Her mother and father had been alcoholic, and she could not tolerate it. Upset, Jacob went to the kitchen, took a knife, and stabbed himself in the leg. Alarmed, she took the knife from him, threw it in a box, applied pressure to his wound, and called the police.

The police asked her what she had done to instigate trouble. DCF asked her why she had done nothing to prevent the incident. The worker filed another 51A, alleging domestic violence, despite the fact that the only wounds suffered were self-inflicted and no harm was done to the children. Angelina asked herself whether, in the long run, it was better or worse to call authorities and ask for help when troubles arose.

DCF told Jacob to complete a domestic violence program, but it was held in another city, miles away, and cost two-hundred dollars up front to enroll and then thirty dollars per session. The price tag and distant location made the program too costly and time-consuming. "We don't have that kind of leeway," said Angelina. "I am lucky if I have a hundred dollars left after I pay the bills each month. Sometimes we are down to our last glass of milk. And the bus ride would take longer than the class."

In monthly meetings, DCF reviewed their compliance with the treatment plan and interviewed their daughter, checking on her welfare. "Are you safe here?" the worker would ask their now four-year-old child, "do you know what that means?"

"Yes," she answered, "I'm safe."

"How do they punish you?"

"They put me in time out."

"Do you ever get scared?"

"Yes, I get scared."

"Of what?" questioned the worker, fingering her notebook, pen in hand.

"Of the monsters in my closet," she replied. "But daddy gets rid of them."

On days when the worker would come and Jacob would be out, she would speak to Angelina in an inviting, knowing way, asking how Angelina was "really" doing. "Fine," she would answer. Angelina got the impression that DCF believed she hid information to protect her partner. Jacob received the distinct message that DCF preferred he would go away.

DCF also checked regularly with their daughter's preschool and doctor to track her well-being. If the girl came to school with a scrape or eczema, the staff questioned Angelina, wanting to know what happened, and reported back to DCF. Angelina started to fret every time her daughter got sick, scratched, or bumped, regular occurrences for an active four-year-old. She agonized about who might report her and for what. The fear of scrutiny and censure constantly nagged and needled with its power and unpredictability, unnerving her.

"It's so stressful," said Angelina. "The biggest thing with me is that I'm now afraid of everything I do and what will get back to them. I'm afraid of taking my kids to the beach. I'm afraid of my daughter going over to sleep at his sister's house. I am afraid of DCF saying I am not taking care of her. I was never fearful of my parenting. I was always very confident in what I did. Now I question everything I do as a parent and what it will look like to someone else. Like if she throws a tantrum in public, I suddenly don't know what to do, and I will start hyperventilating. It's because people look down at you if you are talking to your kids softly, 'Hey, don't do that,' but they look at you just as worse if you finally snap and say, 'You really can't do that right now.' I don't want someone to look at me or report me. That's the first thing that comes to my head. I am worried about that all the time, in constant terror. I feel like they can change their whim at any time. I don't know how to fight back, because I don't want a worse consequence."

Disturbed at DCF's requests, dictates, and monitoring, she and Jacob looked into a lawyer. The expense was more than they could manage. "I am just taking it," said Angelina. "I wasn't given the option to fight. It's been two years. I've done everything they wanted, and it's not enough."

At home, she continued to parent the way she wanted, following her research and her convictions, but outside of the house she felt paralyzed, unwilling to venture out. She dropped out of college after facing the stresses of DCF's demands and her daughter's absence and owes money for the uncompleted courses. She contemplated returning to school and work, wanting a degree in early childhood education or perhaps to foster other children, but the 51Bs on her record, the substantiated reports of child neglect, could create roadblocks. Watching family videos from 2015 causes fear and panic to gush through her, triggered by memories of her daughter being sent away and her life upturned.

"It's like a horrible cloud hanging overhead and you can't see the sun," she said. "Just a giant cloud that makes our accomplishments seem like nothing. If they just could back up and let me take care of my family, let Jacob and I work on our family, I would not be freaking out."

"There isn't a tool that helps workers weigh out harm versus necessity of child welfare intervention," said Vicky Kelly. "We don't have a way to quantify competing risks so that they can actually do some weighted decision making. You try to assess what is going on, what is the likelihood of imminent harm, but also the protective factors that mitigate that harm. Those are complex decisions. If the risks and harm don't rise to a certain level, then they're just part of what this family struggles with. Families struggle with lots of things and still do right by their kids. The inability to sort these things out is often what keeps a family stuck in the system."

"There's a risk for everything," said Angelina, in response, "everyone has a risk. When you have children, when you're single, there's always a risk for something. There's a risk for cancer. There's a risk of radiation poisoning. There's a risk for everything in life. And they won't leave us alone because there is a risk. I am sure you can ask most people who are with someone with a mental disorder, that risk is going to be there forever, and I am sure DCF doesn't want a forever case. My kids aren't going to end up dead in a river. I am taking care of them. They are first in my life. They are fine. They show no signs of kids who are abused or maltreated."

Feeling judged harshly for the choices she has made, Angelina felt most comfortable retreating to the safety of her home. She spent most days in their apartment, unwilling to go out unless accompanied by the comforting presence of Jacob or her best friend. While the criticisms of others goaded and dispirited her, she stood firm in her identity as a caregiver, calling on internal convictions, online readings, and the unfolding accomplishments of her children to confirm that her efforts and choices paid off.

"I stuck to my guts and got the family I wanted," she said. "I parent how I want and am happy with how my kids are coming out. I like the freedom of expression that comes with being a parent. It is freeing when you can teach a kid it is okay to be different. I am also with the person I want to be with, who makes me comfortable and happy. And I have really smart kids. I guess it's how I parent, how we are, that make the kids what they are. It's nice to say those are my kids, and we helped them come out that way. Yeah, we did this."

6. Sophia: When Race Matters

SOPHIA DID NOT LEARN of her son's special needs until he turned three and entered preschool. At home, Julio was an active boy, slow to talk, interested in dancing and cars, who pointed to make his wishes known. When he was one and a half, she moved with him from Puerto Rico to Springfield, Massachusetts. A little bit after, he uttered his first word. "*Horita*," he said when Sophia told him to bathe, *later*.

At school, Julio's behaviors and delays caused difficulties, and Sophia often found herself at odds with staffs' recommendations. A low-income Latina mother, she encountered numerous barriers when advocating for her son's needs. Endless wrangles erupted with institutions and people, whom she felt showed little regard for her background and circumstances.

Born in Puerto Rico, Sophia grew up in New York and Springfield before her mother moved her and her three siblings back to Arecibo when she was eleven years old. Arecibo is geographically the largest city in Puerto Rico, situated on the north coast. On one side lies the Atlantic Ocean with beaches of soft, golden sand and deep blue water that turns crystal clear as it approaches land. A rocky cliff with caves and wooded hills frame its other borders. Near the coast, the city boasts colorful buildings, painted vibrant tones of blue, pink, orange, and green, and Spanish style churches surrounded by grand plazas. Further inland, the neighborhoods turn poorer, the concrete houses square and pale, as if hope and happiness had been bleached from their exteriors. Sophia lived just outside those neighborhoods.

With rudimentary Spanish, she found school difficult at first, until she mastered the language, integrated, and became an A student. "I liked growing up on the island," she said, "there was a lot to do. We would go to the beach, ride horses, pick fruit from trees. People were friendly. If you went to someone's house, they'd give you food. Everybody took care of everybody's kids. Our family wasn't tight, but the barrio was family, so all the kids grew up together. They hung out. There was a lot more freedom, even in the schools. The school didn't get too involved with families. I didn't see DCF. If you lived in the projects, there was trouble all the time, but we did not live in the projects."

Sophia also did not notice drug use in the city, although the projects were flush in heroin and marijuana. She later discovered that her children's fathers were addicts. "I was a little naïve," she sighed.

Girls from the projects picked fights with her, calling her *gringa*, a foreigner, because she knew English and dressed like an American. Conflicts also arose over boys, whose interest in her stoked wrath and envy. Vengeful girls accosted her as she walked home, inflicting scratches and black eyes. Sophia delivered hard blows in return. She was a good fighter. Her mother knew the value of self-defense and bought a punching bag that she hung from the cement ceiling in their basement. Sophia and her siblings took turns practicing on it.

She met her son's father during high school and gave birth after she graduated. A month after Julio's birth, she went to work, making gyros late night at a sandwich shop. At first her mother helped care for Julio, until her own problems sidelined her. The baby's father provided no assistance. He landed himself in jail for destroying a police car while high on drugs. Sophia was forced to hire a babysitter, which her income barely covered.

Parenting by day and working at night proved exhausting. She worried that she could not give her baby the attention he required and decided to return to the United States, where she had more family support and hoped for better educational and job opportunities. Her siblings, one older and two younger than she, already lived in Springfield, where they were staying with their fathers. Needing money for the trip, Sophia quit the sandwich shop and found work as a bartender. Bartending paid well, especially the tips, and her savings grew.

Within three months, she earned enough to purchase plane tickets for her mother, baby, and herself. Relatives in Springfield took them in, but after a few weeks, conflicts between Sophia and her mother made the arrangement untenable. Sophia applied for low-income housing, living in a homeless shelter for a few months while she awaited an opening. Eager to improve her job prospects, she enrolled in short courses on word processing and computer skills through the Jump Start program at Holyoke Community College. Upon completion, she accepted a position as a receptionist at H & R Block. She managed for about six months until loneliness and the strains of city life overwhelmed her.

The largest city in Western Massachusetts and the third biggest in the state, Springfield serves as the economic headquarters of the region.[1] Major employers include insurance, banking, legal, medical, and manufacturing industries. Despite its size and businesses, Springfield is not a wealthy city. Its medium household income falls below the state and country average. Thirty percent of its residents live in poverty. Springfield's population is also the most racially diverse in the region. Forty-three percent of its population identifies as Latino, 33 percent white, and 21 percent black. Gangs, active in some parts of the city, have lent Springfield a reputation for violence and drug trafficking. Although the crime rate has decreased in recent years, it remains well above state averages.

In Springfield, Sophia felt lonely and scared. Used to fruit trees and beaches, she found herself living in unadorned brick buildings on noisy streets. Drug dealers knocked on her door to ask for water, and gunshots rang out in the dark. Visiting a park required taking the bus. In winter, snow and ice barraged the city, and cold, grey air seeped into homes and bodies. Warm clothes needed to be purchased. Heating and electricity bills rose.

Working at H & R Block felt foreign. Most of Sophia's coworkers were older, and white. The suits she wore hung awkwardly on her body, and speaking English for the first time in a professional setting proved confusing. The agency gave her a script to follow when she answered the phone, but she did not fully understand the legal jargon or questions she dutifully read aloud. She tried to fit in, but differences kept surfacing.

"I couldn't handle it," she said. "I didn't know anyone. I didn't know this city. I didn't know how to live in America by myself. I was missing everything about my youth." She bought a return ticket to Puerto Rico for herself and her son.

In Puerto Rico, she returned to bartending, but it was not the same. Men treated her differently. They spoke crudely to her and slapped her bottom. Needing a place to stay, she rented a small office from her boss, converted into a basement studio apartment, for seventy-five dollars a month. She had a bed, shower, and kitchen area, but the ceiling leaked, requiring her to position buckets across the floor to catch the water. "Reality hit me," she said, "I realized how complicated it is to live alone when lacking money, resources, and babysitters." Once again, she saved money and left after just a few months.

Back in Springfield, she moved into the subsidized apartment shared by her mother and siblings. "My mother was supportive, but my siblings made my life miserable," she said. "My son was the cutest kid ever, and he made me happy. But my siblings would tell him to shut up when he cried. He touched stuff, and they would get really upset. We felt like outsiders."

She found affordable housing for herself and Julio, now almost two years old, but it meant living in the poorest and most troubled neighborhoods. "They weren't really safe," she said. "None of them. In my last apartment, if you didn't want to go out with one of the guys, they would send a girl to come and try to beat you up. The guys would also hang out in front of my house and smoke weed because next to my entryway was a sunroof, connecting to the next house, that protected them. From the street, they weren't visible to the cops. The managers of the complex blamed me for letting them smoke there, but I wasn't involved. And I would have to come home and say, 'Excuse me,' to get to my door."

Fights would break out over trivial slights: a parking space, refusing a social invitation, or looking at someone the wrong way. When attacked, Sophia fought back, which earned her bite and nail marks and a broken finger. One woman kicked her in the face. "This is stupid," she thought, "people are fighting me over stupid stuff." But she did not know where else to go or what else to do.

When Julio entered Headstart at age three, the preschool teachers noticed oddities in his behavior and speech. He spoke in occasional single words, but had not yet mastered short sentences. He mumbled and stared. Restless, he could not sit still or finish a task. And, like

Michael Jackson, he always wore a glove. He refused to go anywhere without it. At home, he seemed calmer. He played and spoke more, but not as much as other children his age.

Sophia was not concerned. She, too, had been a hyper child, and she thought it normal. Plus, she knew bilingual children sometimes spoke late. But she agreed to an evaluation. An early intervention team from the Child Guidance Clinic appraised him and diagnosed autism and ADHD. They put services in place to develop language and social skills and taught him sign language. A therapist was assigned to the family who coached Sophia on how to catch Julio's attention, pair words with sign language, and repeat instructions. Julio also attended day care before and after preschool, with transportation provided between them. The efforts paid off. By age four, Julio spoke in full sentences. He appeared happy in his programs, and Sophia could work full days to support the family.

Working and developing herself was important to Sophia. When not employed, she went to school or pursued trainings. Over the years, she worked at McDonald's, in child care, at factories and warehouses, and at an industrial laundromat, a job that she came to appreciate. "It was quiet," she said, "just folding and washing." She studied business administration at Springfield Technical Community College, and received training as a forklift operator. None of the jobs, however, paid more than minimum wage.

When Julio was four years old, Sophia gave birth to a daughter, whose father had disappeared after she informed him of the pregnancy. At the time, Sophia had no car, and she had to coordinate her work in a factory with her children's different daycares. Each weekday, she rose at 6 a.m. and got herself and her children ready. Around 7 a.m., her daughter's daycare provider picked up the three of them, dropped Julio at his early morning program, and Sophia at a nearby bus stop, and took her daughter to her home-based program. With the daycare provider's help, Sophia made the setup work. "Everything was fine," she said, "until Julio reached kindergarten. But within the first two weeks of starting public school, I got complaints. 'He won't sit down. He's too hyper.'"

Julio found the large class at his elementary school over-stimulating. Bright fluorescent lights assaulted his eyes. The voices of students and teachers, and sounds made by pencils and chairs, bombarded his ears. Red fire alarms mounted on walls, and teachers' smartphones sitting on desks, captured his interest. He asked incessantly about them and remembered staff not by their names, but by their phones. To soothe himself, he rocked in his chair or ran in circles around the class. He stuttered. Sophia called his therapist and reported what was happening. The therapist told her to ask for an Individualized Education Plan (IEP).

Sophia requested the IEP, which would provide Julio special educational goals and services. The school conducted an evaluation and held a meeting, but refused to put him on a plan. His teacher acknowledged that Julio worked best with individual support, but felt the regular classroom could accommodate him.

"Then the suspensions came," Sophia said. "Within the first months. He was suspended for not sitting down, running around, not listening. Screaming. Wearing the glove. An array of stuff." He bit a teacher after she pulled him from the classroom because he refused to take his feet off a chair. His therapist came to meetings, and the school started implementing small changes, such as going for a walk when he could not sit still.

The little changes made little difference. Complaints about Julio's behavior continued, as did the suspensions. "Everything he did was a problem," said Sophia. "He didn't know his colors. He was obsessed with fire alarms and lights. He could not focus." The stuttering also continued.

"I didn't know exactly what he needed," said Sophia. "I didn't understand autism. I didn't understand IEPs. But the therapist was working with him and me regularly, and I trusted her. So, I kept asking for services." Sophia and his therapist advocated for speech therapy, a one on one aide, breaks, accommodations for testing, and a smaller class. The school denied the requests.

When Julio entered first grade, the cycle continued. Sophia would meet with the staff to discuss his lack of progress and ask for additional services. The school would refuse. "Are you taking him to

therapy?" school personnel would ask, in tones ting/
and condescending kindness. "What are you doi/
Frustrations and distrust ballooned.

"Sometimes I would go to work," Sophia said,/
and then the school would call. They'd say, 'You neea ͺͺ ͺͺ
up your child now.' I was constantly needing to leave work to take
him home. And it would take one and a half hours for me to get to his
school on the bus. It got to the point that with all the suspensions, he
would not be in school for weeks. I ended up quitting work because
I was paying a lot of money for daycare, and I wasn't making up the
money. The whole family was struggling."

The principal told her Julio needed medication and could not return to school without it. His therapist said medication was not the
answer. The principal threatened to call DCF, saying Sophia was not
following school recommendations; she was neglecting his medical
needs.

Intimidation rarely deterred Sophia. She preferred to fight and accept the occasional black eye than back down. But this battle involved
her son, and she felt his hurts more acutely than her own. While
she did not want him medicated, she also did not want him to miss
school. And she certainly did not want DCF called. Unfortunately, neither she nor the therapist knew that, under federal law, schools cannot
require medication as a precondition for students' attendance or receiving special services.[2] The principal would, or should, have known,
but seemed to surmise that she could flex her institutional muscle.

"I hate that they threaten you," Sophia said, "if you don't do everything they say. They have the services, why not provide them? He
clearly needed them. They could have saved a lot of trouble by providing them. His trouble, my trouble, their trouble."

In her research comparing middle class families with working class
and poor families in the Northeast, sociologist Annette Lareau found
that one of the skills middle class parents pass down to their children
is institutional knowledge.[3] Parents coach their children from an early
age about how to speak with doctors and teachers and advocate for
themselves. They teach them the "rules of the game," when and how

help. Consequently, as young adults, her middle class subjects ·eeded at procuring bureaucratic accommodations more often than ,outh from working class or poor backgrounds. The imbalance, however, may be multi-determined. As sociologists Val Gillies and Linda Blum found, institutions may also respond less favorably to parents of color and those who are poor, rendering their efforts less effective.[4]

In Sophia's case, both forces seemed at play. When faced with an obdurate school system, she felt impotent. "I thought, 'Wait, the school isn't doing what it needs,'" she said, "but I was young, and I did not know how to express myself." Sensing her hesitancy, as well as limited resources and knowledge, school personnel could also get away with tactics that would have incurred greater repercussions if tried with a more privileged family.

Many families, besides Sophia, find obtaining IEPs a frustrating and perplexing endeavor. The process requires jumping through administrative hoops, whose specific arrangement and level of difficulty differs from school to school and district to district. "The way the special education bureaucracy is set up," said Alison Greene, an educational advocate, "it's easy to keep parents out, despite the good intentions of Congress and educators." Greene has worked as an advocate for over ten years and interacted with numerous school districts throughout Western Massachusetts. Families hire her to help them navigate the steps and rules that govern the IEP process.

Special education services are mandated by federal law and funded through federal, state, and local monies, leading to a complex intermixing of bureaucratic rules and local resources. The Individuals with Disabilities Education Act (IDEA) requires states to provide a free, appropriate public education for children with disabilities in the least restrictive environment.[5] For those children who are not profoundly disabled, Massachusetts' schools tend to apply a three-tiered approach (although this is not the only approach).

First a child receives intervention in a regular classroom, then in a small group, and then in a more intensive small group. Only after exhausting those interventions is special education considered. Student eligibility also relies on showing that the student has a qualifying disability, is not making effective progress, and requires specialized in-struction.

Greene notes that while schools must and should teach children in the least restrictive environments, specialized services are also neces-sary. "General education teachers often do not receive much in the way of special education training," she said. "Trying to teach a child with autism or some other disability how to write can be difficult. If you don't understand how the disability impacts the learning process, you don't know how to differentiate for that child's needs, and that child can be left behind. Often the child is just seen as someone who is obstinate and doesn't want to learn."

One of the reasons that obtaining an IEP can be hard is that school funding and resources are limited. IDEA provides monetary grants to state education agencies, but not enough to cover costs. In 2016, Con-gress appropriated sixteen billion dollars for the grants, which equals less than 10 percent of what states spend on services.[6] The rest of the money comes from a combination of state and local taxes, leading to considerable funding disparities within and across cities and states. Wealthier school districts generally obtain more financing than poorer ones. The end result is that school systems serving low-income popula-tions, especially poor communities of color like Springfield, often do not have the resources they need.[7]

"IDEA is practically an unfunded mandate," said Greene. "Schools are legally obligated to provide whatever services are needed, and they often can't afford to do it. Nor can teachers meet the vast array of needs. They are trying, but they can't. So, it is a constant battle for appropriate services. Parents are forced to push and push and push. And for schools, depending on the size, the wealth of the district, and the population, it can be incredibly difficult. A district like Springfield is inundated with need, massive amounts of need."

According to statistics provided by the Massachusetts Depart-ment of Education, in 2017–2018, 77 percent of the 25,604 students in Springfield's public schools were economically disadvantaged, and 83 percent showed high needs, meaning they were at risk of failure without extra assistance and support. The school district also primar-ily serves students of color. Sixty-five percent of its students are listed as Hispanic, 20 percent African American, and 11 percent white.[8]

Educational advocates often succeed in procuring services where others fail because they know the laws and terminology. "The IEP language is difficult," said Greene. "The process is not transparent, the rules are many, and they change all the time. It is unbelievably hard for a parent to know the existing resources, what specific interventions a child needs, and how to fight for them. There is, more or less, a formula, so parents can get resources, if they know the route. If they don't, they end up in meetings screaming, shouting, and bullying, and sometimes that gets them somewhere."

Psychotherapists, as Sophia relied upon, can also attend meetings and advocate, but few therapists have detailed enough knowledge of the formulas and resources to sway a resistant school district.[9] While hiring an educational advocate can be expensive, the Department of Disability Services provides limited grants to qualifying families, and pro bono services are available through the Federation for Children with Special Needs, a Massachusetts nonprofit.[10] Neither Sophia nor Julio's therapist were aware of those possibilities.

Pamela Plumer and Kelley Knight are key players supporting students with special needs in the Northampton Public Schools, a smaller district north of Springfield. The city serves a student population that is one-tenth the size of Springfield, 71 percent white, 26 percent economically disadvantaged, and 39 percent high needs. Northampton's pupils are more economically stratified than Springfield, with a solid middle class, but even there, budgeting requires careful planning.[11]

Plumer is a licensed school psychologist and Director of Student Services. After serving as a school psychologist for six years, and rising through the managerial ranks, she took over leadership of the district's special education department in 2017. She presents as cheerful and optimistic, someone who approaches challenges by rolling up her sleeves and announcing, "we've got this."

Knight also projects determination. She has been a Social Worker and Supervisor of Attendance in Northampton for the last twelve years, but her titles do not fully describe her roles. She wears many hats, more than most people could fit on their heads. Each year, she consults on a couple hundred of the 2,700 children in the district, reaching out to families in need and connecting them to services. She also functions as a resource for teachers and staff.

"Addressing the wide variety of needs in the district is a real balancing act," said Plumer, "between students, teachers, parents, and taxpayers. Every decision made affects other students and access to services. We have hard conversations about committing resources. But the kids have to come first. We are most successful when we can collaborate around their needs."

Knight and Plumer find that their school district, like others throughout the region, is increasingly asked to meet needs that used to be covered elsewhere. As state agencies such as DCF, the Department of Mental Health, and the Department of Disability Services direct services to those with the most acute hardships, as the opioid crisis ravages some of Massachusetts' communities, (Northampton's opioid overdose rate is much lower than Springfield's or Athol's)[12] as waitlists at mental health clinics grow, and specialized, out of district educational programs diminish because of unaffordable costs, public schools net more and more families' difficulties. Funding has not increased in line with demands.

Plumer and Knight recognize the necessity of schools responding to community needs, as well as the impact on budgets and resources. "Stable families have stable kids," said Knight, "and stable kids can learn. Families might need food, shelter, or outside services. Maybe support on rent, or getting clothing." In 2017, Northampton took in thirty Puerto Rican families displaced by Hurricane Maria, and Knight directed her energies toward them.[13] "For the first six to seven weeks the hurricane refugees were here, we were their sole providers," she said. "As a consequence, other tasks that I would have otherwise done, I did not do."

Despite the greater demands, Plumer feels her department can stretch its budget to meet students' needs (although not every parent would agree). The district's small size allows educators and administrators to get to know each student well and direct funds to areas of most immediate urgency. But if Northampton's budget has proven adequate, it is because it has in part been balanced on the back of its workers. Kelley Knight often works long days and on weekends.

Plumer, along with many teachers, principals, and the superintendent, also works overtime. "We can't add more staff because of fiscal restraints," she said.

While the IEP process involves many obstacles, parents of color often find themselves vaulting the highest hurdles. Chandice, a black mother with a Ph.D. in education, holds both a personal and research interest in how families of color navigate school services. Her son developed a high fever and seizures as a toddler that left him with verbal processing difficulties. Thoughtful and committed to doing well, he struggled to understand directions and performed below his academic abilities. Chandice, as well as the other parents she studied, who lived in small, predominantly white communities similar to Northampton, found it difficult to get schools not just to recognize their children's needs, but also their abilities.

"Children of color flounder in school systems that are not designed to honor who they are and what they are capable of," she said. "Society speaks of children of color as if they are all black, poor, and uneducated, as though the three qualities are packaged. That's also how research presents us. Our kids were much more capable of doing well than they were given credit for."

Researchers document stark disparities in school tracking and discipline along racial lines.[14] Throughout the United States, black and Latino students are underrepresented in gifted and talented programs and overrepresented in disciplinary actions. Teachers recommend black students less often for rigorous study, even when test scores demonstrate their ability. Blacks are almost four times as likely to receive suspensions and expulsions for infractions that bring lesser punishments to their white peers. In 2017, 2.1 percent of white students in Northampton faced school discipline, compared to 8.3 percent of blacks, and 7.1 percent of Latinos. In Springfield, a lesser gap existed because whites were disciplined at a higher rate.[15]

Disparities also occur in how children of different races are assigned special education services. Compared to white students, blacks more often receive labels of Emotionally Disturbed (ED), a designation denoting behavioral problems, rather than Learning Disabled

(LD), which focuses on intellectual needs.[16] Since labeling affects the type of interventions and instruction students receive, it constitutes yet another way students of color get tracked.

"Differential diagnosis along race lines happens a lot," said educational advocate Alison Greene, "especially with ADHD. I have seen parents who are white arguing very strongly that their child's difficulty is ADHD and they have pediatricians, or prescribers, on board to back them up. With families of color, it gets labeled behavior, behavior, behavior."

"The narrative," said Chandice, "is you people don't care. You people aren't good parents. You are not involved enough in your children's lives."

Even when families of color move into majority white communities, as did Chandice, so that their children can attend better schools and live in safer neighborhoods, they experience those subtle expressions of derision and exclusion.[17] Chandice found that when she and her son entered public spaces, such as supermarkets and playgrounds, parents and customers tensed and avoided them. She found remarks that she made in classes or meetings were often ignored, while the same statements made by a white man or woman were acknowledged. Her son also felt ostracized. Peers teased him about his differences, and other children did not want to play with him. On one occasion, after classmates told him he had ugly hair, he tried to snip off his dark curls.

Linn Posey-Maddox, a professor in the Department of Educational Policy Studies at the University of Wisconsin-Madison, found similar experiences amongst the black families she studied from 2013-2014 who lived in a predominantly white Wisconsin suburb.[17] While most of the parents Posey-Maddox interviewed felt positive about the resources and safety of their schools, only two out of the fifty-six recounted no episodes of racial bias. Families were subject to stares and comments about how they looked, found their perspectives unwelcome and overlooked, were assumed to be poor, urban, and uninvolved with their children's education, and seen as threatening and criminal. While they strove to integrate, negative experiences discouraged them from participating.[19]

Parents in Posey-Maddox's study put a lot of energy into monitoring and managing prejudice and helping their children withstand it, a stressor shared by Chandice and the other parents she studied. "At no point," said Chandice, "could we relax our gaze or warrior stance. If you are to remain truly aware and own how difficult this is, you can literally feel the pain in your body. The tension, the headaches, the sleepless nights. The tightening at the base of your belly. Fear. Uncertainty. Lack of confidence. The realization that your presence is not wanted."

Concerned about racial disparities and exclusion, Northampton's school administrators have instituted reforms. The district analyzes student growth and the way current systems maintain gaps in achievement and discipline. All educational staff partake in anti-bias trainings. "We are trying to shift the playing field," said Knight, "so that students are seen for their abilities, so there is not that divergence. But I don't think the time and energy that we work on it is yet demonstrated in the data."

Despite the limited progress, Knight and Plumer express confidence that ongoing efforts and open conversations will bear fruit. "The more that teachers, paraprofessionals, and administrators understand the complexities of peoples' lives," said Plumer, "whether it is class, gender, race, or ability, the more you will have a community that can be responsive, work together, and partner."

Lacking partnership and a detailed understanding of the IEP process, and encountering a high needs school district that considered Julio's difficulties as primarily a behavioral and parenting problem, Sophia felt she had no choice but to capitulate and get him a medication evaluation. "I went to his therapist," she said, "crying and desperate. I told her, 'They won't let him back in school without a prescription. I give up, just get it.'"

The therapist arranged for Julio to see a prescriber who gave him Focalin, a stimulant used in the treatment of ADHD. Sophia gave him the medicine, and noticed an immediate difference. "He completely changed," she said, "into a zombie." His teachers also noted changes and continued to voice concerns.

"They complained if he was too active," Sophia said, "and if he was too still. I was scared. I thought, 'What the fuck? What do you want from me?' Every time I fed my son that medication, I felt like I was hurting him. On weekends, I didn't give him any because I wanted to see my son."

On the medicine, Julio participated less in activities and schoolwork. However, he sat for longer and did not run around the room. He appeared particularly calm in the morning, in the few hours after Sophia gave him the Focalin. School staff wondered whether a second dose, given at noontime, would help his afternoons. They asked Sophia to talk to his prescriber. Wary of the principal's previous threats, and DCF's lurking shadow, Sophia complied.

Julio's therapist at the Child Guidance Clinic left the agency when he was in second grade, and a new clinician was assigned. Sophia filled her in on the school disputes, and they discussed the possibility of the therapist working with him at school. To make the arrangements, the therapist called his guidance counselor. After leaving a few messages and receiving no answer, she asked Sophia to intervene. Sophia left a voicemail. When two more weeks passed without a response, Sophia wrote a formal letter to the principal, requesting that therapy and other services occur on site. After walking Julio to his class one morning, she dropped off the letter to the office. A few hours later, she heard from the guidance counselor.

"Hey, what are those letters you are writing to the school?' she asked.

"I was asking for assistance," Sophia explained, "I really need you to connect with Julio's therapist and set up services."

"I've called her," answered the guidance counselor. "She has not called back."

"Can you try again?" asked Sophia.

"Yes. By the way, I have your son with me."

"Why?"

"Because he was being bad."

"What do you mean?"

"Oh, you know, the sort of stuff he does. So, we gave him extra medication."

"You did what? How much?"

"Just a little."

The exchange spun through Sophia's mind, twining her in a web of panic. Was Julio alright? Would the medicine harm him? What should she do? Already finding his normal dose excessive, she worried about the extra pills. Fingers shaking, she dialed 911 and then ran to the school, three blocks away. She arrived breathless, her heart pounding, just before the ambulance. Proceeding to the counselor's office, she knocked and tried to enter, only to find the door locked.

"Open the door," she said. "I am here to take Julio. An ambulance is waiting and the police are coming." As the door squeaked open, and Julio emerged, Sophia checked on him, scanning his face and body for signs of harm. He explained that the counselor had taken him from class and shown him shiny pens. Then she gave him medicine.

"I was fighting," he said. "I know I am only supposed to get pills at lunch time. But she put them in my mouth." Sophia looked for the guidance counselor, wanting an explanation, and discovered that she had slipped away.

When Sophia and Julio walked into the school's main office, they found three Emergency Medical Technicians (EMTs), three police officers, and a teacher holding a banana. In a single, un-choreographed moment, the teacher attempted to feed Julio the banana, the EMTs examined him, the police asked for the principal and nurse, and Sophia searched for the guidance counselor. "It was a circus," she said.

The guidance counselor entered soon after, registering surprise at the frenetic scene. As she scanned the assembled crew and their activities, she and Sophia locked eyes. "She looked at me," remembered Sophia, "and I looked at her, and she started smiling." The smile resembled a smirk.

Beset with anxiety and anger, with months and years of accumulated frustrations and aggravations, Sophia's outrage unfurled. She lunged, aiming a punch at the counselor, and tackling her to the ground. "I kind of messed up everything when I did that," she said. "But I didn't want anyone messing with my son. What if she had killed him?"

As the police and EMT's hurtled toward them, Sophia released the shaken, but otherwise unharmed, counselor. Later, one of the EMTs told Sophia, "I would have done the same if I were you."

Sophia pressed charges against the counselor, accusing her of assault by means of medication. The counselor also charged Sophia with assault. As a low-income defendant, Sophia was assigned a court-appointed attorney who helped with the accusations against her. As the plaintiff bringing a complaint against the counselor, Sophia received limited legal advice.

The task of dispensing justice falls to the legal system, an institution rife with racial disparities. Imbalances have been documented in arrests, prosecutions, plea negotiations, sentencing, quality of representation, types of charges brought, and sentencing.[20] Data collected in 2011 by the U.S. Department of Justice on police behavior found that black and Latino drivers were ticketed and searched during traffic stops more often than whites, and blacks were more likely to be pulled over in the first place.[21] Almost three times as many black Americans than whites are killed by the police and five times as many when unarmed.[22] Massachusetts's courts show similar lopsidedness, with racial disparities in imprisonment rates that exceed national averages.[23] Juvenile offenders also face differential diagnosis and treatment. Black males, more often than whites, are diagnosed with conduct disorders, rather than ADHD, and one study found them 60 percent less likely to receive psychiatric treatments.[24] Although racial discrepancies are not universal—they vary from judge to judge and jurisdiction to jurisdiction—their prevalence has led many blacks and Latinos to distrust the courts.[25]

Disparities do not just occur in criminal matters, but also when child welfare cases reach the legal system, a circumstance Sophia would later face. Juvenile court attorneys prosecute and defend, and judges review, every case in which DCF removes a child from parental custody. Courts rule on all removals, thus playing a role in the nationwide overrepresentation of black and Native American families, and, in Massachusetts, Latino families, in DCF caseloads and foster care.[26] Reasons for that overrepresentation are not clear. Some of the difference, but not all, may be due to families of color having higher rates of poverty, a risk factor for maltreatment.[27] Other explanations include systemic biases, families' limited access to culturally competent services and resources, and not enough experienced, well-trained DCF workers, judges, and attorneys to make fine-tuned distinctions about maltreatment risks and parenting styles.[28]

When low-income families like Sophia's face charges in criminal or juvenile court, they are assigned a court-appointed lawyer. In Massachusetts, the Committee for Public Counsel Services (CPCS), a state funded agency, provides the legal representation, either through staff or private attorneys. CPCS attorneys receive low rates for their services. Staff attorneys start at $40,000 a year, and private attorneys receive fifty-five dollars an hour (a recent raise from fifty dollars an hour) and must follow stringent guidelines that limit what and how much they can bill. Poor pay discourages many attorneys from pursuing the work and leads to large workloads, high turnover, and staff shortages. As CPCS lawyers are assigned to cases, not chosen, the luck of the draw determines whether a parent or defendant obtains an attorney with sufficient expertise and time to fight effectively for them.

The stresses of court do not just involve worries over fair treatment, but the delays and demands of an overwhelmed system. In 2016, only 62 percent of juvenile court cases in Massachusetts were disposed of within the time limits, down from 73 percent in 2013.[29] By 2017, the dearth of attorneys in Massachusetts available for Care and Protection Cases (in which the court determines if a parent will lose or retain custody of a child) became so severe that the Chief Justice of the state Supreme Judicial Court declared a 'constitutional emergency.' By law, parents are entitled to a timely hearing when their children are removed. But from 2013 to 2016, following the spike in opioid addictions and the death of Jeremiah Oliver in Fitchburg, child removal cases increased by 45 percent, inundating the system.[30] Half of all hearings in the Springfield court were delayed.[31]

"All of this limits access to justice," said Kally Walsh, a private and CPCS criminal and family law attorney in Springfield who has represented children and parents for over twenty years. "While the courts threw money at the delays and cleared out all the temporary hearings, that remedy created a backlog of trials and motions, which means children end up staying in the system longer than they should." Court cases drag on and on. Parents wait to regain custody of children as months or years slide by.

The delays and continuances also mean that litigants need to return to court numerous times, and each time can necessitate long waits. Unless they are there for a trial, the court never knows how long a hearing or motion will take. Sometimes, one side or the other simply wants a continuance. To make sure cases can be heard consecutively, numerous cases are scheduled for the same time and then taken one by one.

"It is more efficient for the court," said Walsh, "not for the clients or for justice. They can end up sitting all day without being called, and then they have to come back and sit all day again. There is a presumption that they have nothing to do but sit in that courthouse. If you have a job, you lose it."

Not everyone needs to sit and wait for days on end. "If you have money," said Walsh, "you are treated substantially differently. If you've hired a private lawyer, the judges and court staff try to get the lawyer in and out before anyone else. You are ushered through."

Judges can also hold views that influence decisions. "Judges have different reputations for leaning in favor of or against parents," said Walsh. "Most are fair. But the law is malleable and interpretable enough, the standard of proof so low, that they can lean in different directions."

Initial Care and Protections hearings in Massachusetts, which are supposed to occur within seventy-two hours of a child's removal, rely on a standard of proof known as "preponderance of the evidence," which means that the facts presented as evidence must be shown to be more probably true than not (more than 50 percent true). When the case goes to trial, the burden of proof is slightly higher. Preponderance of the evidence is the lowest burden of proof, and it is less than what is required to convict in criminal court.[32]

"If someone is going to take your kid," said Walsh, "why isn't it a higher standard? We are talking about the government destroying a family. Poof. Gone. There is a dark, empty place in your life, in your heart, where there once was a kid. There are cases where everyone agrees the child needs to be removed. But for the rest, it is ridiculously easy to meet the fair preponderance standard and find a parent lacking. For instance, I have to prove my client didn't use drugs, if someone said they did."

The low standard weights proceedings against parents, increasing the risk that the court errs on the side of family-breakup, rather than misses harm to a child, and allows more room for bias. Concerned with implicit biases that affect defendants of different races, gender, and income, the Chief Justice in Massachusetts has instituted trainings for court personnel and is working on criminal justice reform.[33] Until those efforts militate change, prejudicial beliefs and practices that asymmetrically affect litigants like Sophia, who are low income and of color, will wind their way into courtrooms.

Sophia understood what she was up against. "It's hard being a Puerto Rican over here," she said. "Police, schools, DCF, and the courts profile us, black people, Mexicans, and other nonwhites as dangerous. Monsters and rapists. Women who just want to have babies and don't want to work. If you live in a low-income neighborhood, you are really at the bottom of the pyramid. You try to better yourself, but it is not respected." As she fought her assault charge, and later, for custody of her children, justice would hang in the balance of a judge's gavel, and the ability of an overwhelmed court system to give her a fair hearing.

Over the next year, the assault charge against Sophia and the complaint against the counselor took much of Sophia's time. There were hearings and proceedings. Postponements. Hours waiting in crowded rooms and hallways for the cases to be heard. Sometimes Sophia would stay at the courthouse all day, only to be told the case had been continued to the next day, or the next week. Then she would sit or stand for a few minutes in front of the black-robed judge while the lawyers asked for more time, or set future dates, or argued about applicable law. With all the delays, continuances, and court dates, Sophia had to stop working.

When Sophia's charges against the guidance counselor were finally argued before a judge, the hearing was short. The school nurse testified that the guidance counselor gave Julio the medication. The guidance counselor said the nurse did it, even though the counselor had been fired for the offense. Without firm proof, the court dismissed the charges. "She had money and she got a lawyer," Sophia said, "a really good attorney. I didn't have money, and I didn't have a lawyer. I was young and did not know what I was doing."

The case against Sophia resulted in a different outcome. As it meandered through the court system, her attorney convinced Sophia to accept a Continuance Without a Finding. In lieu of a trial and possible conviction, she accepted a one-year probation and a postponed decision about her guilt. After one year, if she did not violate probation, the case would be dismissed. If not, a guilty finding and penalties could be imposed.

"I got an assault charge," she said, "and the guidance counselor got off. I wasn't educated, I didn't have any position socially, I was just the Puerto Rican. If this had happened to a white American, society would have been outraged at how my kid was treated."

Julio did not return to the same school after the medication incident. The day after, by coincidence, Sophia was scheduled to move her family to a bigger home, in a different, although still poor, neighborhood. The change in residence necessitated a switch in schools. But the move did not afford a fresh start. The story of what happened, and Sophia's actions, followed them. "We had a reputation," she said. "A guidance counselor was fired because of 'this mom.' As a consequence, no one liked him and no one liked me. I wasn't allowed on the school grounds."

Julio's overstimulation and behaviors continued at the new school. Novel settings and routines unnerved him, and the transition into a building full of wary staff proved difficult. He showed his discomfort with heightened activity and distraction. He could not sit still and learn. The school started to restrain him, removing him from class and holding him down when he failed to comply. With the restraints came bruises and scratches.[34] And more suspensions. And even more questions about medication and Sophia's parenting. She had assaulted a guidance counselor and had a child with behavioral difficulties. Who knew what really happened in the home? In the crime- and drug-ridden neighborhoods in which she lived, abuse and neglect ran rampant.

Because she had hit the guidance counselor in front of her son, DCF opened a case. Sophia was required to meet monthly with a worker, something that proved difficult to arrange. She had obtained a new job, and worked each weekday from 9 a.m. – 5 p.m., as did her worker, who was also not available on weekends. Sophia offered to meet during her lunch break, but the worker needed to come to the house, to check on her apartment and children. Sophia did not mind someone from DCF visiting her home. She had furnished the apartment with curtains and new furniture, kept the refrigerator stocked with food, and cleaned regularly. Her children dressed appropriately. Julio attended therapy, and both children were up to date on medical appointments. DCF also required Sophia to follow a service plan that mandated psychotherapy, an anger management group, and parenting classes. "Some of it was helpful," she said, "you always learn. But some of it was a bit much." She liked going to therapy and made sure to attend her sessions.

More problematic was the narrative that had taken hold and began to follow her. Sophia's parenting and aggression were considered the missing pieces that explained Julio's school behavior. "Basically, according to the DCF reports," she said, "everything was my fault. It was my fault he had so many absences. It was my fault he had trouble learning. It was my fault he wasn't getting the right services at school. 'The mother does not understand the needs of her child,' they said. But I did. No one could understand him the way I could."

An altercation with a neighbor a few months later cemented Sophia's reputation as violent. After an exchange of words and threats, and a loud fracas that attracted the attention of other residents, the police were called. Since the incident violated the terms of Sophia's probation, she was arrested, and DCF called. Sophia spent the night in jail, and DCF took custody of her son and daughter.

When Sophia later went to court for custody hearings, which were delayed months due to staff shortages, she heard DCF's case against her. Workers testified that she kept a dirty house and had no food, but offered no pictures as proof. They claimed she did not attend therapy, as required by her service plan, but provided no documentation. They brought up her record of assaults and her son's difficulties. Sophia's lawyer, whom she had barely met, and who discussed the case with her only minutes before entering the court, asked DCF for substantiation. None was provided. But Sophia also could not prove the claims false. Neither she nor her lawyer had anticipated the testimony or prepared their own evidence prior to the hearing. She brought no letter from her therapist or photographs of her house. Her word dueled against the worker's. With the low standard of proof, a judge could accept DCF's version.

"I had no voice," said Sophia, remembering the experience. "The most powerless feeling is people saying things that aren't true, but when you contest them, nobody is on your side or believes you. They degrade you, dissect you, until you are no more. I ended up feeling ashamed for things that I did not do and should not have felt ashamed for."

When a court investigator later reported that her house was well-kept, a DCF worker wondered how she could afford the furniture and asked her to prove a legal source of income. "They insinuated I must be doing something illegal," Sophia said. "as if someone like me can't have nice things." The judge refused to return custody to Sophia.

Sophia's brother, aged twenty-two, who lived with his girlfriend in a city bordering Springfield, offered to care for the children. DCF approved him as a caregiver on two conditions. He needed to move to a bigger apartment, and he could not let Sophia visit. He agreed. Sophia let him come to the apartment to collect her children's belongings. She gave him their clothes, toys, and bedroom sets. She handed him a debit card to help pay for food and additional necessities.

Julio and his sister, now nine and five years old, moved to a nearby city with their uncle. In the new school and district, teachers noticed Julio's struggles and had him reevaluated. At an IEP meeting, the special education staff proposed placing him in a small, self-contained classroom with a bundle of services: speech therapy, testing accommodations, walks, breaks, extra time on assignments, tutoring, and someone available to read and repeat instructions to him. After receiving the full slate of services, Julio's school behavior changed. His activity level decreased and his learning accelerated. "Look how well he is doing without his mother," the DCF worker noted.

Meanwhile, Sophia lived alone in her apartment, emptied of furniture and the vibrancy of children. One day, awakening to the rumbles of the school bus that used to pick up her son and daughter, she sat on the couch and listened to the squeaking brakes and swooshing doors that opened and shut at each stop. When the bus returned that afternoon, she realized she had not moved. "I was depressed," she said. "There was nobody to cook for. Nobody to get up and move for."

A bevy of DCF workers rotated through. Some she liked and found helpful. One worker let her throw a birthday party for her children, but got removed from the case soon after. Others treated her as dangerous, refusing her unsupervised visitation and referencing case notes as back up. She learned that her file contained a warning about her potential for violence.

Desperate to shed that reputation, and watching the years tick by, Sophia asked for a transfer to a different DCF office. At first, the worker in the new office also felt leery. But as he spent time getting to know her and her children, and how they interacted, he changed his mind. He interviewed her friends, relatives, co-workers, and the family's psychotherapists. Each of them vouched for her. She was allowed to visit with Julio and have him to the house. When the worker noticed their solid relationship, he advocated for Julio's return. "You are nothing like what I read about you," he told her.

Sophia's daughter, however, was not slated to return home. Soon after DCF removed the children and placed them with Sophia's brother, her father agreed to take custody. He lived with his girlfriend in a town about an hour's drive from Springfield and had a criminal history. Sophia also knew him to be a drug addict and a sexual offender. Her DCF worker at the time did not believe her.

As long as DCF had custody of her children, the case fell under the jurisdiction of juvenile court, as a Care and Protection matter. Once DCF returned custody of the children to the parents, the case became a custody dispute between the parents and transferred to probate and family court. One of the juvenile court judges, who had followed Sophia's efforts to win back Julio, seemed partial to her, willing to view her as a competent parent. The probate judge took a harsher view, noting that DCF had awarded the father custody for a reason, and chastising Sophia for the allegations she made against him and his girlfriend. The judge expressed displeasure with Sophia when she reported that the girlfriend had hit her daughter and dragged her by the hair. When she requested the father submit to drug testing. Or when she filed for contempt because the father had not allowed her a court ordered visit. Tired of lacking a voice, and having learned the necessity of a good lawyer, Sophia hired one. He charged $290 an hour. Four years later, after numerous court delays and the accumulation of considerable debt, she won custody of her daughter.

In the meantime, Julio, aged twelve, returned to his mothers' care, and the Springfield schools placed him in a special program for children with behavioral and emotional problems. Class sizes were small, but the students' bodies and difficulties were large. Trying to fit in, Julio started copying the other pupils' behaviors.

"Some of the kids thought it was cool to be disrespectful," Sophia said, "or cut school. They wanted to fight or do drugs because of the neighborhoods they grew up in. They thought, 'It's cool to be a gangster,' or that you have to be a gangster because you have to protect yourself. My son was getting disrespectful. He would tell me, 'I don't have to.' Or, 'Fuck you.' He would do it to get approval from friends." He also leveled his disrespect at the school's staff, earning him a new round of classroom removals and restraints. Bruises appeared on his arms and back. Tears welled in his eyes. On one occasion, when taken to a padded time-out room, a paraprofessional grabbed Julio's head and slammed it against the wall, bursting open his lip. He put Julio in a headlock and pinned him to the floor. The principal, walking by, witnessed the incident and told the paraprofessional to stop. Then she fired him.

Once again, Sophia pressed charges. And once again, a counter complaint was filed, this time against Julio. Now aged thirteen, Julio's assault charge would be heard in juvenile court, where a court-appointed lawyer would represent him. The prospect scared Sophia. She worried that societal and judicial bias would condemn her son, as they had so many other young males of color.

Sophia also worried about the impact of the court process on Julio. Proceedings could entail hours spent sitting in hallways and courtrooms, which meant missed days of school. A trial would necessitate Julio testifying, which posed difficulties for a boy with autism and a stutter. When the paraprofessional offered to drop his charges against Julio, in exchange for Sophia dismissing the ones she had filed against him, Julio's lawyer recommended they accept. She told Sophia, "We can win this, but we never know for sure what the court will do." Sophia concurred. "I wanted what was best for my son," she said. "I didn't want him to have a record."

After years of headaches and heartaches, of brawls with neighbors, disputes with schools, clashes with DCF, and quarrels in the courts, Sophia had to concede that, as a poor, uneducated Puerto Rican, she faced battles she could not win. She wielded little clout with public agencies and waged negligible control over her son's exposure to problematic neighborhoods, schools, and peers. "I thought, 'I can't compete with this,'" she said, "I have to go.' I knew there had to be another way."

Adopting a new tactic, Sophia manufactured her own version of Moving for Opportunity for Fair Housing, the federal housing initiative that raised children's prospects by moving families into better neighborhoods (see Chapter Three for a fuller description of the program). She put her name on the affordable housing waitlists for almost every town in Massachusetts. After a year and a half, when Julio was fourteen, she received an email from a small town outside of Northampton, a quiet, rural community approximately thirty miles north of Springfield with a population of a few thousand residents. An apartment was available, if she wanted it. "Where is that?" she thought, upon hearing the name of the town. "Wherever it is, I'll take it."

Driving that far north for the first time, she noticed how different was the scenery. "It's in the country," she said. "There's a river right next to my home and bike trails. Like a little Puerto Rico. Now my kids could have the experience of throwing rocks in the water, like I did. We could jump off low bridges and swim. One of the neighbors has a horse that she rides around the neighborhood. There are even bears that go through our trash. It's cute. Plus, I fell in love with the washer-dryer hookup."

Not just the scenery, but the town's populace was of a different hue. "The neighbors actually knocked on my door when I moved in," she said, "and offered me cookies and furniture. They check in, make sure we are all right. They can get a little nosy, but they are generally good people, always watching out."

In her new community, the mean income falls close to the state average. The schools perform just above state means. Over 90 percent of the children in the district are white with a low percentage of economically disadvantaged and high-needs students.

Sophia brought Julio's IEP to the new school. She produced the documentation showing his autism and ADHD diagnoses and handed over the school reports that listed his behaviors, restraints, and suspensions. "He came with a long record," she said. "The school staff were scared at first. They asked me about his challenges. I said, 'Did you read his record?' They said, 'Yes.' I told them, 'He's a really good kid, he just needs a chance.' And they took my word for it. It makes me cry."

The school followed the recommendations in the IEP. As the teachers grew familiar with Julio, they added services, such as after-school tutoring. His teachers never pulled him from class or restrained him, and not once did he arrive home shedding tears or complaining of bruises. He tested the school's limits only once, by talking rudely to the principal, which earned him a suspension. Sophia told him, "That's not going to work over here. This is not Springfield. You can't talk back. They respect you, and you need to respect them."

Julio started to excel. The school adjusted his IEP and mainstreamed him into some classes. He brought home improved report cards and test scores. "My son had never passed an MCAS," said Sophia, referring to the Massachusetts Comprehensive Assessment System, the standardized, statewide test that public school students must pass to receive a high school diploma. "In eighth grade, in Springfield, he scribbled hearts and Pokémon all over the answer sheet. The school asked me to get a letter from his therapist saying that he couldn't test. I said I couldn't do that. But in tenth grade, in this school, with extra services and tutoring, he passed every MCAS exam. He is on his way to graduating."

Julio's path to social acceptance took longer. Initially, he felt like an outsider. Or a novelty. "He would come home," said Sophia, "saying kids would approach him, and touch him, and his hair, and pet him, and say, 'Wow, are you really Puerto Rican?'" Julio's first friends were with other nonwhite children—a South American boy and a girl adopted from China, but his popularity slowly rose. "Now everyone knows him," said Sophia, "he has integrated. He goes out with friends and to sleepovers, or they invite him over to dinner. He even has a girlfriend."

Sophia also appreciated how school personnel interacted with her. "They met with me," she said, "and encouraged me. Told me I'm a great mom. They knew my story, yet they accepted me. I feel comfortable here. And safe. Safety is priceless."

Although she feels secure in her current community, Sophia knows that dangers loom. "I worry about Julio every day as a Puerto Rican male," she said. "Even though he looks somewhat white, I always remind him that he's not white, and his last name is Latin. What happens to him depends on who he encounters. I tell him to always try to de-escalate any situation. If a police officer asks your name, just comply. Don't be disrespectful. Don't try to intimidate. Don't get shot. I don't want to see my son in a casket."

Chandice, a middle class black mother, also talks with her teenage son about what it means to be a young man of color. "I am very truthful with him about what is going on in this society," she said. "It started with Trayvon Martin." Trayvon, a seventeen-year-old black high school student was shot in August, 2012 as he walked down the street in Sanders, Florida after purchasing skittles and a soft drink. His killer, George Zimmerman, a self-styled neighborhood vigilante, was tried for murder and acquitted. "My son was eleven, and the incident really upset him. I had to tell him how to conduct himself, what to do. Make him aware that if you are out with your white friends and they are being mischievous, understand that what they do, you can't. Remove yourself, as quickly as you can. Society sees you as a hulking black man. That's the world we occupy. It's not the same world as other mothers experience with their children."

Sophia also worries that her son's autism and ADHD put him at a dangerous disadvantage. "He doesn't catch the big picture," she said, noting his impulsivity and trouble reading cues that signal others' intentions. "Despite all he's been through, he's less aware of the dangers out there. Sometimes I think he has grown comfortable, and children of color can never be too comfortable. He trusts. He has hope. Some people may take advantage of it."

Chandice's son, more than Sophia's, appears aware of the many injustices surrounding him. He is reflective, thinking about life and death, the environment, even the definition of goodness. As a child who once felt forgotten and mocked, he knows how it feels to be left out. He makes efforts to befriend ostracized and bullied peers, including a boy with autism.

"He is coming into his own," said Chandice, "and becoming a man. He believes in equality and social justice, and he thinks there needs to be some standing up for what you believe. But standing up could be the last thing he does. It is impossible to stand up as a black man and not attract negative attention. I am proud of him, but also scared. As a parent, especially as a mother, you feel a tremendous sense of responsibility for your children. If you could, you would take away their pain and discomfort and struggle. But you know, in this world, they will have to develop the muscle to deal."

For Sophia, learning when she could and could not muscle through has resulted in both pain and struggle. When the "rules of the game" apply unevenly to parents of different racial and economic backgrounds, playing by the rules does not guarantee desired outcomes. At first, Sophia tried to level the playing field by force, only to find herself on the losing end of each conflict. But despite the defeats, she has refused to resign herself to the status quo. Aware that justice can best be won through social position, she has returned to college and is considering a career in law.

"I am working with my circumstances," she said, "doing the best I can. I am a woman, a Latina, who has been involved with DCF and the court system. A mom, who loves. I think about how I can do better all the time. I have done some self-reflection, and there are things I wish I had not done. Sometimes you make the wrong choices. Sometimes you don't know. At first, I thought all my troubles were because I was dumb, uneducated, naïve. Maybe in the beginning it was like that, but then I realized it is a systemic problem. If you have no supports, no one backing you up, if you don't have money to pay for a lawyer, then you are messed up. No one is afraid to take advantage of you. But I will never give up or stop fighting."

7. Kim: Alloparents

KIM HAPPENED UPON PARENTHOOD in her early thirties, delighted by the opportunity when it, or rather Hannah, chose her. As a branch manager for a regional bank, and married to a recovering alcoholic eleven years her senior, Kim had not seriously contemplated motherhood. She had enough on her plate: a demanding job and a husband, Dave, who, though maintaining sobriety, required care. They both worked long hours, she forty-five to fifty hours per week at the bank and he at two separate jobs, one as a shipping and receiving supervisor. Their combined salaries allowed them to buy a nice, two-bedroom condominium in the Springfield area, vacation together, and save for the future. Then, a few years into the marriage, Dave fell off a ladder, causing back trouble, disability, and depression. The incident propelled Kim into the role of caretaker and principal supporter of the family, a position she assumed with relative ease.

"I have a tendency to rescue people and animals," she said, as one of her three dogs, a golden retriever adopted from the Dakin Humane Society, nudged her, vying for attention. "My parents always helped other people, and I grew up thinking that's how it was supposed to be. We didn't have a rich life, but we had a good one. My mom used to say, 'You should always give back, and appreciate the good things in life.'"

Kim gave back as much as she could. She served on the board of the AIDS Foundation of Western Massachusetts, dedicating numerous hours to the cause. When friends fell on hard times, they could count on her for a place to stay. When her sister, raising autistic sons, or her mother, a foster parent, needed assistance, she was quick to volunteer.

She spoke from the living room of her modest two-story, four-bedroom house in Springfield, which sits on a short cul-de-sac in a working-class neighborhood of smaller, older homes. Springfield is a city of distinct neighborhoods, some catering to low-income residents, others to professionals or those with modest incomes. Kim lives in one of the more prosperous and safer areas of the city, which she estimates lies about twenty minutes by car from the high crime neighborhoods. She moved there after becoming a mother.

Kim would have considered bearing children, if it were not for Dave and his difficulties. But his disabilities meant she could not depend on him, and given how much care he needed, she worried about how a child would affect their relationship. Then they stumbled on Hannah, a three-year-old foster child, who slowly, surely, and deliberately stole their hearts.

Hannah, along with her three older brothers, lived in the foster home run by Kim's mother and stepfather. Kim and Dave grew to know her and her brothers little by little, relishing their obligations as extended family. They attended school events, teacher conferences, and other activities. By the time Hannah was preparing for kindergarten, they had formed a strong relationship. They enjoyed spending time with her, and received a solid taste of parenting without assuming full-time responsibilities.

However, in a spate of misfortune, Kim's stepfather died abruptly from a heart attack. He fell to the floor, stiff and cold, as five-year-old Hannah stood gaping. Kim's mother, bequeathed the care of four traumatized children while grieving her own loss, felt a heavy shroud had been draped around her shoulders. The responsibility felt unmanageable, but she did not want to separate the siblings. Hannah, wise and wary beyond her years, responding to the uncertainties in her home, asked Kim and Dave to be her mom and dad.

"I said, 'Oh no you don't.'" said Kim. "I had no kids, we had no plans for having kids. But I didn't want her to go back into the foster care system. I thought, 'It's kind of scary to become a parent.' It wasn't in my plans. But my husband was in love with this kid, too."

What frightened Kim most was the thought of raising someone else's child. "If you let them," she said, "they'll take the best of you and then not stick around. That was my worry. Will she wonder about her biological family? Will I raise her for her whole life and then she will want to go with them?" Apprehension pushed at her, but motherhood's draw pulled harder. "It was an epiphany one day," she said. "I thought, I can do this. I could mother her. I wanted to see how Dave would be, but he stepped up."

Dave surprised her by how much he loved Hannah and what he took on. He drove her to dance classes, let her dress him up as a princess, played softball. Dave's mother came every day after school and sat with her, allowing Kim to continue working. They found ways to keep Hannah close to her older brothers by letting them spend the night and sending Hannah with them on family vacations. The arrangement worked.

Despite knowing Hannah fairly well before she moved in, the initial months brought challenges. Hannah's life had not been easy. Her birth mother suffered from epilepsy and schizophrenia, and had grown up in Belchertown State School and Northampton State Hospital, two facilities later closed by lawsuits alleging poor and abusive care.[1] She then terribly abused and neglected her own children. Hannah's mother pushed her oldest daughter down a flight of stairs, breaking both her legs; she fed Drano to her eldest son, who was hospitalized with blue nails and rectal bleeding; she sold the Christmas toys donated to the family to buy other necessities; and once she locked Hannah in the car all night, her only comfort an older brother who came out to touch hands by pressing on the window pane. "She was institutionalized as a child and then became a mother," said Kim. "What chance did she have to learn to parent?"

For the most part, Hannah adjusted well. But numerous times over the first few months, her traumatic reminders and fears emerged and tested Kim's mettle and commitment. One day, Kim left six-year-old Hannah in the bathtub and Hannah drained the water, only to cry hysterically.

"She was a mess," remembered Kim. "I said, 'It's okay, let's put more water in.'"

"You're not mad?" Hannah asked.

"No," replied Kim, trying to understand how emptying the tub might make her angry. Hannah explained that her parents reused water and beat the kids if they let it run out.

A similar incident occurred with food. Right before lunch, Hannah asked what Kim would do if she refused to eat.

"If you don't the eat the meal, you won't get dessert," she replied.

"You won't put anything in my hair?"

"What would be put in your hair?"

"Mustard, ketchup. Maple syrup is the worst," said Hannah.

"No, we don't put things in people's hair," said Kim.

Hannah experienced frequent nightmares, the fears and sadness of her early life creeping into the comforts of her bed under cover of darkness. Sometimes Hannah would awaken and venture into Kim's bed for solace. Other times, Kim would enter Hannah's room to check on her, discern her closed eyes and calm breathing, and note, with bewilderment, the quiet tears running down her daughter's sleeping face.

"At first, I didn't realize how much she had gone through and what she had missed," said Kim. "All I wanted to do was give her what I had as a kid that she didn't. Because I had a mom who loved me. I had a mom who was always there. I had a mom who made sure we always had meals and clean clothes and love. She was an advocate for me, and I wanted Hannah to have that. I would sit on the floor and show her how to do things with Barbies, how to hold and take care of a child or baby. She was fascinated. We sang. We even sang in the bathtub to get her over her fears. That's the kind of childhood I wanted her to have. We went to Florida. We went to Disney World. She went to Maine, and we went to the beach. We did things with the family. We played sports. She did dance. In just a few months, she went from a kid who was terrified to a kid who was singing while we washed her hair. She would laugh and sing and she started to come into her own."

Six months after Hannah arrived in their home, Dave suffered his first relapse. Police arrested him for driving under the influence of alcohol (DUI) and charged him in criminal court. Kim found the incident upsetting, but she worried most about Hannah. She wanted to shield her from the turbulence of Dave's drinking, which included DCF's response.

As a foster child who was not yet adopted, DCF retained ultimate discretion over her placement. Kim called the DCF worker immediate-

ly, tearfully asking what she should do. The worker sounded supportive and told her they would work it out. Kim and Dave had already
disclosed his past alcohol use, and the agency had waived concerns.
"Everyone has problems," their worker had said. "Being honest about
them is what's important."

Still, Kim decided not to take any chances. "I told him to stay out
of the house," she said, "because I was afraid of what would happen, where Hannah would go. I was very protective. He was profusely
apologetic, but I said, 'I can't take a chance, not with her well-being.'"

Dave left the family home on April 24 and returned on November
2 of the same year. DCF visited once during that time to check on
Hannah and the family. For a child who had already suffered numerous parental losses, the household changes and undetermined resolu-
tion engendered a strong reaction.

"Her dream was to have two parents," said Kim, "and that was
not going to happen if he was out of the house. So, she would leave
me drawings, always the same drawing. It was a boat, and she was in
the middle and I was on one side, and Dave was on the other. I used
to find that same picture on my pillow, on the bathroom toilet, on the
kitchen sink. She would also come in to my room at night and touch
my shoulder to make sure I was there. She was clingy. If I was on the
couch, she was on the couch. If I was in the chair, she was in the chair.
When I went to work, I sometimes had to take her with me. She had
a toileting accident at school for the first time ever. She told me she
was worried about going to school because someone from DCF might
come and take her. I told her that would not happen. I could have endured anything, but that was the hardest thing to see. She went from
this happy kid to a kid who was worried about losing her parents.
And I didn't care what I had to do to keep her. If he needed to be out
of my life, I would have done it. He was apologetic, but I was so angry. He put her well-being at risk."

Dave did his best to regain sobriety, while Kim shouldered the
household demands. He went to Alcoholics Anonymous and a day
treatment program. Kim received help from her mother and sister, but
primarily functioned as a single parent, working full-time while carrying the weight of Hannah's misery and anxiety. She had no time for

friends, no time for leisure, no time for anything beyond work, taking care of her child, and managing the fallout of Dave's relapse.

Dave's absence continued to leave Hannah upset and insecure. Thus, in August, Kim called Hannah's DCF worker and asked if Dave could come home. Their worker supported the plan. However, in November, soon after he returned, they received a letter stating that Hannah would be moved because they could not provide a safe and loving placement.

"My stress level was at an all-time high," said Kim. "They had never talked to me about it. Not a word. I had always been honest. So, instead of just having an issue with my husband, they started to have an issue with me. All of a sudden, I went from being this great foster parent who had made a perfect home to a person who 'isn't capable of showing love and affection to any child.' That's what they said about me, what they wrote in a report."

When Kim attended the quarterly foster care reviews for Hannah and her siblings, in which DCF workers, parents, and others working with the child and family meet to discuss progress and goals, she felt the chill of DCF's accusatory verdict. "They would go around the room and skip me," she said, "and I would say, 'Excuse me, let me tell you how Hannah is doing.' And I would show her report card and her medical records. I would tell them how she had grown and thrived. They did not ask me questions like they did the other foster parents. When it was over, I would get out of there and go in the elevator and completely lose it. I felt physically sick. I thought, how does somebody make me out to be this monster because I have a husband that I care about and love? They really did make me feel like I was not competent. They made me question my self-worth. I wondered how I was going to get through it? We are human. We were trying to be honest, we were trying to be upfront. He wasn't driving anymore, he wasn't even driving a vehicle. We did everything we could. And she was never in danger. She was with me."

Kim knew someone who worked as a supervisor at a DCF office. She asked him for advice. He told her DCF was acting "arbitrary and capricious," which gave her legal grounds to fight. He advised her to retain an attorney. Kim used her resources and connections to find one, ending up with one of the best family law attorneys in the area. She asked her attorney what she should do. Whether she should divorce Dave. Her attorney laughed and told her they could work things out. She and Dave did not have to fit into DCF's mold of what a parent should be.

Their appeal was heard at a fair hearing where Dave again offered to leave home. He pleaded with DCF not to make Hannah pay for his mistakes. Their attorney asked DCF a simple question: "If you were so worried about this child, why did you hardly visit her between April and November?" She presented a bonding assessment, prepared by an expert, that highlighted Hannah's connection to the family. The combination of an effective lawyer, an expert's assessment, and Dave's gut-wrenching plea won them the hearing and a path to adoption. But at a price. The bonding assessment and lawyer's fees cost over $10,000. Kim arranged to pay the bills in installments.

Kim found the episode stressful and expensive, and the memory continued to upset her. However, as a professional with contacts and sufficient income, Kim could fight and prevail.

When Hannah was ten years old and adopted, she asked to meet her biological family. The request wrenched Kim. She wondered, would Hannah prefer her birth family? Would meeting them fulfill or disappoint her? Would it diminish Kim's role and identity as a mother? Dialing the phone with trembling fingers, Kim called Hannah's cousins to arrange a get-together. She organized a visit that included Kim's mother and Hannah's brothers. They would meet aunts, uncles, and cousins, but not Hannah's parents.

They discovered a large, tightknit family, well-off and comfortable, living in a beautiful, historical Springfield home that was once used to aid slaves on the underground railroad. After an initial, awkward greeting, the children roamed the landscaped yard and explored the property's nooks, crannies, and hidden passageways. Then, the visit ending, Hannah asked the question on her mind. Why had the family not taken them in? The answer: Hannah's parents were too much for them to handle. They could not cope with her mother's volatility and the contact she would have tried to initiate.

On the way home, Hannah stared thoughtfully out the car window. "If I were an aunt or uncle," she finally said, "I would have done what I needed, and taken care of my family." She announced the next day that she had seen enough. She wanted no further contact with her relatives.

Kim understood Hannah's feelings. She could not understand why the family had not sent birthday cards, Christmas presents, or asked for visits. The house that once sheltered escaping slaves would not extend the same hospitality to its family's youngest members. Protecting itself from the discomfiting hassles and behaviors that accompany parental mental illness, Hannah's family had quashed any impulse towards generosity.

When Hannah and her brothers were first removed from their home, DCF would have sought out Hannah's kin to see if they would assume guardianship. If they passed a criminal background check and a few other hurdles, they would have been approved as caretakers. In this particular case, it seems that lack of willingness, not approval, sent the children to foster care. So, why do some families, like Kim, agree to help while others decline? While hard to know for sure, statistics identify an interesting trend.

Researchers consistently report that those who foster and adopt from the child welfare system do not inhabit the wealthiest segments of society. According to an Annie E. Casey Foundation 2008 report that analyzed Census Bureau data, the mean income of foster families falls about one-third below the mean income of all households with children.[2] The discrepancy derives from higher rates of fostering amongst parents earning $20,000 to $49,000 and much lower incidences amongst those garnering $100,000 and above. The U.S. Department of Health and Human Services, in its 2007 survey of adoptive families, found the same trend.[3] Children adopted out of foster care tend to live in families with average incomes lower than children adopted privately or internationally.

The study also found that most families who foster or adopt do not do it for the money. Government stipends for foster children are low, and contribute only slightly to overall household income.[4] Instead, parents overwhelmingly endorse the wish to provide a child with a permanent home. Altruism, the impulse to help, drives the desire.

The capacity for altruism is built into human biology.[5] The same neurological circuits that entice parents to protect and soothe their children's distress become activated in response to the needs of others. But altruism, like foster parenting, also does not seem to be evenly distributed. Studies suggest that those with fewer resources often give more generously, a finding that even applies to four-year-old children. Socialization begins young.[6]

According to anthropologist and primatologist Sarah Hrdy, a Professor Emerita at University of California, Davis, altruistic systems likely evolved early in evolutionary history to support parenting.[7] Casting her net on millions of years of human adaptation, Hrdy argues that in the Pleistocene age, about 1.8 million years ago, mothers could not have foraged adequate resources for themselves and their children without the help of others. Children's high caloric needs, extended period of dependency, and early weaning, which allows a mother to birth and care for multiple offspring simultaneously, rendered cooperative childrearing a necessity. Babies are thus equipped with inborn interactive abilities, which include looking, smiling, and vocalizing, to attract care and attention from both parental and nonparental figures, or alloparents.

Alloparents, who can be fathers, grandmothers, aunts, siblings, or nonrelative caregivers, provide supervision and nurturance. Their commonness is confirmed by cross-cultural parenting studies.[8] In the stability of small hunter-gatherer clans, with resources best distributed by sharing, cooperation reigned. The idea of an independent nuclear family, scrambling on its own to provide for children, emerged only recently. As populations increased in the Western world, families divided into smaller units, and resources became allocated unevenly, parental efforts focused more and more on helping one's own offspring gain advantage, especially in those segments of society well-resourced enough to sit atop and succeed in the economic food chain.

As Patricia Greenfield notes in her theory of social change (see Chapter Five), less affluent cultures maximize survival by pooling assets and relying on each other.[9] Wealthier cultures boost their offspring's chances of success by breeding autonomy and individualism, traits currently favored in neoliberal societies with higher income job markets.[10] On a daily basis, those with more capital need less help from others and expect others to depend less on them.

The outlook may best be summed up by Stephen Moore, a conservative economic policy analyst and CNN commentator who, in September 2017, criticized The Affordable Care Act by stating, "many people who are healthy are basically saying... 'I don't want to pay for somebody who has got high health care costs.' People want insurance for their own families, not for other people's families."[11] When translated into policy, the result is disregard for the less fortunate. Self-interest takes precedence over community, having over helping.

As policies that limit funding for the social safety net trickle down, they have eroded community institutions and social networks in poorer communities even more rapidly than in wealthier ones.[12] In modern America, extended families and friends still provide crucial supports to parents, and different types of paid childcare exist for those who can afford it. But many families struggle alone. Thus, while alloparents like Kim extend themselves to others, they often find few who are willing or able to provide the same help in return.

As Hannah grew and flourished, Kim prospered alongside her. Kim loved being a mother. She looked forward to coming home after a day at work to cook dinner. She adored throwing Christmas and birthday parties. When Hannah faced difficulties, Kim relished advocating for her. She especially prized talking with Hannah, helping her work out problems when life's bumps sent her tumbling.

Kim came from a big family, with four children and considerable numbers of extended family nearby. During her childhood, her family vacationed yearly at the beach. They packed twenty people into a cottage meant for ten, enjoying every raucous moment. With Hannah, Kim rediscovered the delightful pleasures and energy of family. She wanted a bigger house, filled with more children. Dave, however, felt differently. He grew up with only one brother and preferred peace and quiet. He adored Hannah, but yearned for nothing further.

When Hannah was sixteen, Kim decided to move from their condominium and build her dream house, the dwelling in which she and Dave still live. She built it for Hannah, to give her a larger home, but also with other children in mind—destitute, abandoned children needing a steady place and upbringing. She imagined filling the house with love and laughter.

"Right about the time Hannah was graduating from high school," said Kim, "I was getting a bit of empty nest syndrome. I was forty-five. And I said to my family, 'I would really like to look into adopting another child.'

The family had mixed reactions. "Hannah felt that I was her mother, and there was no sharing. My husband felt he was too old. On my own, I had looked at the Massachusetts Adoption Resource Exchange website and I kept seeing the same little faces of lonely children waiting for families. It broke my heart. And here we were living in this four-bedroom house with plenty of room. Yes, we've had our struggles both financially and family-wise, but I thought, when you've had a good life, and you can do things for others, why not try again?" Her husband reluctantly agreed.

They went to an adoption party where social workers paraded children past prospective parents, hoping their cute smiles and groomed appearances might land them a match. The party upset Hannah. She hated seeing adults gawk at kids as if they were shopping for puppies. Finding it intolerable, she retreated to the car. Kim let her go, remaining inside.

"I kept seeing the same little nine-year-old girl," she said, "who had no expression on her face. You couldn't tell what she was thinking, what she was feeling. She had short pigtails and she was so stoic, and as she was leaving, she said to her social worker, 'I told you no one was going to want me'. Right there, I knew that was our girl."

Like many children removed from their families, the girl, Jenna, had a difficult past. She lived until age four or five in a severely neglectful home with drug-addicted parents. She had rotated through a number of foster homes and faced separation from her siblings. Her behavior included lying, stealing, and fighting. Kim's heart reached out, eager to offer strong enough doses of warmth, attention, and stability to melt the girl's entrenched indifference.

The week of Hannah's high school graduation, Jenna moved in with her inscrutable face and a row of bangs cut ridiculously short across the top of her forehead. Unpacking her bags, she put her clothes and possessions in drawers and on shelves. She placed a snowman doll on her bed, its plush matted and darkened by years of use. Around the room, she judiciously distributed pictures of herself and her biological family. Throughout it all, she did not smile, she did not cry, she did not ask questions or show interest in her new family. The bright, happy, curious child that Kim so easily coaxed into Hannah's being, lay deeply buried inside Jenna's core.

With Kim's thoughts and energies shifting, Hannah started showing difficulties. She would suddenly break down and cry and then run through the house laughing, her moods changing rapidly. She became angry and distant, and talked about moving out. At first, Kim thought it a passing phase. Hannah had a warm and generous nature, and Kim felt confident she would eventually accept Jenna. She talked with Hannah about the importance of helping others. She shared her own conviction that Jenna was the right fit for the family. Jenna resembled them physically. She felt sure that, in time, Jenna would blend in.

"I didn't see what it was doing to Hannah," said Kim, "that she had an identity issue and I had caused it. Because all I meant was, help someone else and you will understand eventually; you are being selfish because you are not understanding. But all she saw was that I had someone who was about to take her place. I think Hannah thought that when she turned eighteen, I would shut her out, because she's adopted. I told her, 'I don't think you understand, but you are a part of me. I may not have physically had you, but you are my daughter and you will always be my daughter. Nothing in this world will change it. I am sorry if I made you feel not important, or that you are not my priority.'"

Kim helped Hannah through the crisis, got her a mental health evaluation and treatment. Hannah's mood lifted, but her relationship with Kim remained troubled. Shortly after, Hannah moved out, rented an apartment, got a job, and started living with her boyfriend, whom the family thought decent enough. She abandoned the dream house that ached to be filled with children. Kim allowed her the space she sought, but not without sensing the contours of its emptiness.

"In the meantime," said Kim, "I have this other kid who has so many issues that weren't diagnosed. Now, I am in this world of crap where I am thinking, 'What have I got myself into?' I wanted this so badly. I wanted a relationship with her, but she was in no way bonded to me. It was very uncomfortable trying to warm up to her. She did not show facial expressions. It was hard to know what she was thinking or feeling or even needing."

Parenting Jenna demanded all of Kim's intuition and knowledge, imparted, or rather, absorbed, through experience and a modicum of foster parent training. She knew enough not to wash the snowman doll, to which the residues of Jenna's previous homes and experiences clung. It had been given to her by her biological mother, along with a gold-colored ring fished out of somebody's couch, and Jenna zealously prized both. Kim also knew to listen when Jenna tentatively, or sometimes provocatively, thrust memories at her. But knowing how to react or what to say when Jenna's anecdotes and actions grew dark and menacing was another matter.

One summer night, a few days after Jenna moved in, they sat together, awkwardly trying to make conversation, when a fruit fly buzzed around them. Kim, trying to lighten the mood, joked about keeping bugs away, but Jenna neither laughed nor smiled. Panicking, she began stammering about bugs, how she had once had them, in her hair, head lice, but no longer.

Kim realized then, how careful she and others would need to be when speaking and interacting with Jenna. She was not a child who could relax, chuckle, or be easily hugged or comforted. She was a youngster who felt perpetually under threat, on guard, sure that disaster or rejection lay right around the corner. A child focused on surviving, at whatever, and whoever's, expense.

Jenna was thus also a child who could not be trusted. Money would disappear out of Kim's purse. An iPod also vanished. Shopping together one day, Jenna volunteered that she was expert at stealing. When she went to stores with her biological mother, her mother would tell her to grab whatever she wanted. "I told her we don't take things," said Kim. "If there's something you want, we can talk about you earning it, but you don't just take it. You can get in trouble. The police can get called. We don't do that."

"Okay," Jenna responded. "I know that it's wrong." But Kim's possessions continued to disappear. Amulets went missing, as well as more money.

Jenna expressed constant irritation at Kim's remarks and efforts, but she also showed hesitant signs of growing interest. At first, when she and Kim talked, she kept her distance, sitting across the room. But as time went on, she moved closer and closer until finally, one day, she sat right next to her. Simultaneously, she expressed full confidence that Kim would one day give up on her. Kim rebuffed the idea, but Jenna insisted.

Kim knew better than to argue. "Okay, suit yourself," she replied.

Jenna exhibited sexual interests, starting when she was just over ten years old. She wanted to wear tight fitting clothes. Obsessed about her looks and what she wore, she dressed, redressed, and stared at her image in the mirror. She tried to leave the house in a bikini, hoping her body would attract attention. When Kim cleaned Jenna's room, she discovered notes describing how she wanted to be touched and caressed. Kim worried what Jenna might do if given the chance. She monitored her closely. She only allowed her to play with other children if they came to the house and Kim could supervise, or if Jenna went to a home where Kim knew and trusted the parents.

One day, when Jenna was a little shy of thirteen years old, Kim peered out her living room window to see the police arrive in the driveway. She had just returned home after a brief foray to her office to complete the payroll, leaving Jenna in Dave's care. The police entered, explaining that they had received a complaint about Jenna. She had been seen with a boy in the backyard of a nearby house. He pulled her pants down, and they had sex.

Jenna denied the incident, claiming she had spent the afternoon next door at a friend's house, but the story gnawed at Kim. Again, and again, she asked Jenna what happened, and again and again, Jenna nonchalantly stuck to her account. Kim felt angry, upset at herself for trusting Dave to supervise. Needing to know what happened, she went the next day to the house that lodged the complaint.

"The guy opens the door," said Kim, "and said, 'What took you so long to get here? I know whose mother you are.' And I said, 'Can you tell me what happened?' He said, 'Yeah. I came down with my four children—we are about to have Sunday breakfast. I open the window. My children are about to come and look out, and you can tell that there are people in the back having sex. There were two boys, and your daughter.'"

Although she was prepared for such an account, Kim was surprised at her own reaction. "I don't even know what I was feeling at that moment," said Kim. "It was just complete shame. We always liked it here, but I almost thought I had to move. It was so embarrassing, enough that it was hard for me to walk out my front door and get in my car. And then I see our whole neighborhood start to treat us like pariahs. They didn't want their kids playing with her. She'd sit in the living room and watch these kids go to camp, and they didn't want her. They went to cheer practice; they didn't want her. They'd play outside; they didn't want her. If she came out, they all went in. So, I am watching this and I know I need to find some sort of help."

After Kim's previous experiences with DCF, she had decided she would adopt her second child through Berkshire Children and Families. Berkshire is an agency that contracts with DCF, but places children in homes that it independently recruits, educates, and supports. At the time, Linda Dugas was an adoption worker with Berkshire, and the social worker for Kim and Dave.

Dugas said that she and Berkshire did their best to support families and to refer them to resources, but their involvement stopped when children were adopted, at which point other services took over. Even with sustained effort, finding and enlisting the right help could be a struggle. [13] Dugas tried to find therapists for the children, but the best therapists were often full and not taking new cases. She also gave families reading material, talked to them, and tried to have them attend support groups, but parents would tell her they did not have time. "It's enough for me to get my kids to therapy," they would say, "let alone me."

Training for foster or adoptive parents cannot prepare them for all they will encounter. "MAPP class is woefully inadequate," Dugas said, referring to the thirty-hour "Massachusetts Approach to Partnership in Parenting" class all families fostering or adopting through DCF must take.[14] "All it does is skim the surface and terrify you, if you can take it all in."

Dugas thinks that part of the problem comes from a misunderstanding of what children who have been abused, and their parents, need. "We have this belief," she said, "that as long as a child makes it to a loving family, all will be well. But kids like Jenna can suck all the air out of a family, so it can be hard to hang in. Especially since most families are struggling in isolation, doing it on their own. They run up against judgment, anger, and misunderstanding in schools and family members.[15] They hear, 'The child should be able to do that!' Or, 'You don't need to do this, send that kid back, it's not your kid.' Families need an incredible support system. It's the hardest job they will ever have, and they can't leave their kid with just anyone. But the people they know and count on run away. They are not signing up to help."

Even workers can find the demands strenuous, causing some to flee. "One of the first cases I was given," remembered Dugas, "I had to do a child assessment, and I was reviewing the file. It was nine volumes. I read every bit of it, and it absolutely pained me to the core. The history of physical and sexual abuse and neglect was so intense. The number of times this little girl was in and out of care. I thought, What chance does she have?' I remember going home that day, and curling up on the couch, and just sobbing."

Early in her career, Dugas also felt triggered by meeting and working with birth parents. "When I first started, I had a negative take on these families. All these families neglecting and abusing their kids. But one of my first cases was this dad who was horribly abusive to his kids. He literally tied them to the bed when he sexually abused them. I had to go to the prison to interview him. I remember thinking that this was going to be the hardest thing I have ever done in my life. And I would say that, within two minutes, it was clear to me that I was sitting across from a two-year-old boy. He was so immature, undeveloped. Something in me shifted. I realized that was what most of these parents were. Of course they couldn't parent. They were just reproducing what came down the pike for them. That was a pivotal moment. I started to see everybody in a more humane way."

At first, Dugas wondered if she could, or should, stay in the job. It affected her so strongly. But she decided she could do it. Even do it well. "I thought, 'Okay, I am crying,'" she said, remembering the experiences. "It's touched me in some way. That does not mean I should run away."

Dugas hung in for three very difficult years before she reached the other side of the pain and exposure. Part of what helped was her agency's structure, and the way it made a difference to the work. "For me," she said, "the appeal was the team. Berkshire created a little family. There were seven or eight people working together. We met every Thursday for three, four, sometimes five hours. We discussed every case, every crisis. No one ever felt they were making decisions in isolation. To not feel solely responsible was huge. And thank goodness for my supervisor, who was a seasoned worker. She was such a grounding force. It was very sustaining."

Years and many cases later, when Dugas started supervising, she saw how the work affected others, sometimes interfering with their ability to provide support and guidance. "One worker wasn't sleeping, wasn't eating," she said. "The stress of the work, what she was exposed to, the responsibility of finding a home for a child, and wondering if it was going to be the right home, really felled her. So, with her, we decided she needed to move on."

The supportive work environment propelled Dugas to remain in the same agency for twenty years, despite low pay. She could have earned more working for DCF, but does not think she would have enjoyed that culture or the less supportive environment. "Many of the DCF workers come in without a lot of training or experience," she said. "They can be very punitive with their families. I think they get frustrated and disappointed when something goes wrong. When a family experiences trouble or a placement does not work, people have a tendency to feel angry because of their sense of responsibility and guilt. And some take it out on and blame the family. The consultation group at Berkshire would stop us from acting on those feelings."

At one point, DCF asked Berkshire for training on how to replicate their higher success rates with families. Dugas and a colleague conducted a workshop, in which they outlined their protocols and structure. "DCF felt that economically they couldn't do that," said Dugas. "Take four hours out of a worker's schedule each week to sit around and talk? But a lot of crucial education and support happened in that four hours."

Researchers have unequivocally found that children do better, parents feel less stress, and maltreatment and neglect decreases when parents are supported.[16] The same appears to be true for workers.[17] But assistance can backfire, if not sensitively fine-tuned and delivered in the right manner.[18] As seen with Kim, and in the previous stories of Diana, Angelina, Jacob, and Sophia, families can feel humiliated, coerced, blamed, and inadequate when decisions and unwanted services are hoisted upon them. Employees can react similarly, at which point they may shift the burdens, responsibility, and blame back to the families.[19] Berkshire circumvented that cycle by providing alloparenting to its staff, who then improved outcomes by nurturing and supporting clients in similar ways.

Unfortunately, however, by the time Jenna's difficulties became extreme, she was legally adopted and Dugas's agency was no longer working with the family. Although post-adoption services were available through Adoption Journeys, a state-wide program established with funding from the state legislature in 1997 at the behest of parent advocates and DCF, Kim did not know of its existence.[20] With nowhere else to turn, she needed to scour for help in the only other forum available, the fragmented and equally over-burdened mental health system.

When Jenna first came to the family, she saw a psychotherapist near her old foster home in Greenfield. Driving from Springfield to the therapist's office took an hour each way, and Jenna showed no real connection to that person. Nor did she seem to benefit from the services. Kim discontinued the therapy and looked for help nearby. She had to understand Jenna better, get a diagnosis. Find someone who could help resolve the issues driving her behaviors. "If I can't help her," she thought, "what will her future be? If I can't get through to her, learn to deal with this, what will become of her?" She called a local outpatient clinic that accepted Jenna's state insurance and made an appointment.

The clinic assigned her a young therapist, eager and energetic, newly minted from graduate school. The therapist wanted to help, but could not provide Kim with guidance or explanations for Jenna's behavior. She also could not get Jenna to open up or talk, so the two of them played cards and board games together, in silence. The therapist told Kim maybe they could build trust, little by little, that way.

"I thought that wouldn't work well for Jenna," said Kim. "This is a kid who at age four was changing her younger sibling's diapers, who got herself off the school bus by age three. You don't have to play games with a kid like that. Why didn't she see that? She needed to get to know her. Talk about friends, school, her thoughts. Show she can understand and handle stuff. Then maybe Jenna would trust her and give her a little peek into what she is living."

After half a year, Kim gave up on therapist number two and switched Jenna to a therapist in private practice, whose name she got from her pediatrician. The third therapist, an older woman, sweet and well-meaning, had just recovered from cancer. She talked to Jenna as if speaking to a younger child, in a high-pitched, sing-song voice. The tone bothered Jenna. The therapist also started appointments late, sometimes by a full hour; and she fell asleep more than once during their sessions. She told Kim to knock on the door and interrupt when they were waiting too long.

"I thought she should be on time for clients," said Kim, "and I shouldn't have to tell her that. I had a little girl who was nervous and antsy sitting out there. Didn't she get that?" Nonetheless, Kim gave the therapist a chance for one and a half years. She was recovering from cancer, and Kim felt sorry for her. But it was a year and a half of wasted time.

Therapist number four came as a referral from Jenna's high school guidance counselor. She was young, full of energy, with a style that Kim thought might work. Kim told the therapist about Jenna's sexual behaviors, stealing, and lack of affection and reciprocity. The therapist said she likely exhibited Reactive Attachment Disorder (RAD), a condition that begins in early childhood with the absence of a strong bond to a caretaker.[21] She told Kim that children who do not get critical care in their first few years end up neurologically wired differently. They exhibit difficulties with relationships and self-control. Problems often persist. Kim appreciated the diagnosis and explanation.

The therapist met with Jenna and tried to form a relationship with her. She spoke with Kim on the side, but also respected Jenna's confidentiality. Jenna did not seem eager to attend, but she went, claiming that she told her therapist little. When she returned home from sessions, she would sit and talk with Kim. Like an onion slowly peeling its skin and revealing its inner layers, she began telling Kim more and more about her past. She described a night when the electricity was shut off and she was thirsty. In the living room, when she fumbled in the dark to find a drink, she saw a bottle lying on the floor and picked it up. "Have you ever drunk anything with cigarettes in it?" she asked. "It's gross."

She explained how she would wake up to find strangers strewn about. Different people came and went, none of whom she knew. She told Kim about a guy in a jacket, white t-shirt, and jeans, with dark hair, who always wanted her to sit on his lap and how uncomfortable that felt. She had nightmares about him. Then she would fall silent, refusing to say anything more.

"I told her that she didn't have to tell me," said Kim, "but I wanted her to know that it wasn't okay that anyone made her uncomfortable. If I was there, I would have beat the crap out of him. That was a little girl and it's not that little girl's fault that somebody she trusted left her in the care of that person.

"What I heard should never have happened in any kid's life. Then I understood. So, I read everything I could on RAD. I had to help her. Why was she not feeling remorse? She was wired different. How do I get through to her? She had different issues than my other kid."

Jenna reported the story and the nightmares to Kim numerous times, but refused to tell her therapist. The stories disturbed Kim. She prized and prioritized helping. Yet she kept unearthing abundant examples of other people inflicting harm.

History and nature are filled not only with noble accounts of generosity, but also with episodes of harsh reality. In times of scarcity, when prospects look dire, humans and mammals abandon, neglect, or kill their young.[22] The battle for resources is ruthless, causing the less fortunate to die. Cross culturally and throughout history, child abuse and infanticide have been common when parents are overwhelmed and do not have the means to ensure survival. Sarah Hrdy notes that prior to 15,000 years ago, children born into conditions like Hannah and Jenna would not have survived. They endure today because of interventions from police, DCF, and the courts, but services aimed at helping them remain rudimentary.

The primary intervention for children like Jenna is to place them in foster or pre-adoptive families, to give them emotional bonds that provide nurturing, protection, and security. While stable caregiving promotes attachment and decreases a child's symptoms, rewiring brains that have been severely dysregulated by early trauma is a gargantuan task. Children require intensive efforts targeting emotional regulation, attention, cognitive understanding, relationships, and self-concept.[23] Psychotherapy can help, but it is rarely delivered in strong enough doses, or by practitioners with sufficient knowledge, to relieve a parent from the bulk of the work. Thus, as Kim discovered, Jenna's rehabilitation would depend largely on the relationship they formed and the efforts Kim made. As Linda Blum found in her studies on mothers raising children with invisible social-emotional-behavioral disorders (see Chapter Two), Kim would be required to gain expertise in navigating services and delivering interventions.

One of the reasons that the responsibility for saving children falls so strongly on parents like Kim has to do with psychology's understanding of attachment. John Bowlby, a British psychiatrist, noted the deep distress of children separated from their mothers and the importance of the mother-child relationship for social, emotional, and cognitive development.[24] Bowlby generated his theory in the 1950s, right at the height of cultural attitudes idealizing stay-at-home motherhood. He understood that "just as children are absolutely dependent on their parents for sustenance, so...are parents, especially their mothers, dependent on a greater society for economic provision."[25] The bulk of his research (and subsequent studies by others in the decades following) left out the society part, focusing instead on the mother-infant relationship. Alloparenting, and its possibilities, was never wholeheartedly embraced or evaluated. What followed has been reams of research on the importance of sensitive, responsive, mother-child relationships, generously distributed to the general public through parenting manuals and psychotherapeutic advice, that lends scientific reinforcement to the primacy of the parent-child bond.[26]

The theories and research are not wrong, just stretched beyond their reasonable conclusions. It should not be surprising that in America and other child-centered cultures, children who form secure attachments to their parents achieve the best developmental outcomes. Parental effort exerts an outsized influence in societies in which parents provide the bulk of care. For caretakers with the resources to meet their children's needs, the arrangement works well. But that is hardly the best model for those facing economic, health, or mental health constraints or who live in communities offering few supports or opportunities.

Remaining sensitive, intensely child-centered, and fostering autonomy, while in the midst of a tumultuous life, is extremely hard and sometimes counterproductive.[27] As seen in the various stories in this book, the pressure to meet the needs of a child struggling with ill health or the effects of trauma can necessitate inattention to competing relationships or to a parent's own health. A parent's difficulties can interfere with sustained attention to a child's needs. Kim's efforts to help Jenna came at the expense of her husband, older daughter, and herself.

Linda Dugas has embraced a different approach in her private and professional life. "My partner and I," she said, "live in a rural community of small farmers and gardeners that showcases community at its best. We are part of a neighborhood of at least twenty families who are unbelievably connected. If someone is sick, someone is bringing them a meal, and someone else is taking them to a doctor's appointment. We are aware of how rare this is. But we are all committed to it. We may die in our house because of the supports we have."

She has also helped nurture a similar sense of solidarity as a clinical supervisor at the Treehouse Community, the intergenerational village for foster and adoptive families in which Victoria and Nathaniel, whose twins were born premature and with disabilities, wanted to live.[28]

A sixty-home complex in Easthampton, Massachusetts, that opened in 2006, Treehouse was built in an idyllic pasture with exquisite views of nearby Mount Tom. It contains twelve family homes interspersed with forty-eight smaller units for seniors. Dwellings are built around a circle, with a Community Center in the middle. The layout and landscaping are purposefully designed to foster a sense of beauty, value, and community, which contrasts with the impoverished, desolate neighborhoods from which most of the children originate.

Treehouse boasts a staff of six who strive to provide whatever families require. Social workers are available onsite to talk over problems and find resources. An educational advocate helps parents understand children's academic needs and represent them to schools. A scholastic coordinator spends afternoons in the Community Center, helping youth with homework and training them in social, behavioral, and emotional skills. Afterschool recreational activities are provided; and one-to-one mentoring exists for older adolescents and emerging adults.

A sense of community is instilled; natural supports grow and blossom. Parents aid other parents. Seniors volunteer to provide childcare, drive children to activities or appointments, and lend out their cars. Parents do not need to become expert in every aspect of their child's care; and children do not need to bring every question or anxiety home to their parents. Thus far, outcomes for children at Treehouse have exceeded the norm for those fostered or adopted from the child welfare system.[29]

Kerry Homstead, the program's onsite leader, holds the title of "Community Facilitator" to stress the program's nonhierarchical structure. "It's about partnership and connection," she said. "We don't consider residents 'clients.' They are partners. We are a community. Everyone's backgrounds are very different and not everyone likes each other and gets along, but we build understanding and tolerance. We have deep conversations about racism, cultural discrimination, and the barriers and experiences people bring with them. It gets to the heart of how we support people."

Their understanding extends to the different ways a parent may choose to raise a child. "Every parent has a different parenting style," said Homstead. "The field got rigid in terms of expectations from parents. Parent curriculums. What's going on with that? They are preset values. Kind of like MAPP course. Take that and you will be all set. Not at all."

As Kim discovered, and Treehouse knows, parenting children with difficulties can be full of surprises that no curriculum can completely foretell or forestall. The strenuousness compels some parents to give up, causing foster children to move from place to place, which damages them even more. "How do people hang in there through it all?" asked Homstead. "That's what Treehouse is about. We hang in. We surround you with support and an invested community. As a staff, we pursue ongoing education, conversation, problem-solving, and not giving up. If something doesn't work, we go back, rethink, and try something else. Next year will look different from last year because the kids are different. We need to be very adaptable. It's an attitude. It tends to stymie larger agencies like DCF, who can't be as flexible."

Part of that attitude consists of fostering a nonjudgmental stance. "Treehouse doesn't blame parents when something does not work," Dugas said. "The staff has a deep sense that these families have taken on something enormous. It's not our job to be judgmental, but to hold them. Families don't have to be perfect."

Heather, a grandmother raising two grandsons, finds the environment sustaining. She first moved into the elder housing at Treehouse after working as an outreach worker to senior centers. "I saw firsthand what happened to seniors and other people when they get isolated," she said. "People die faster; they are lonelier; they become bitter. It's not what I wanted." Retired, and on a limited income, she had few housing options. Treehouse was affordable and offered the promise of connections.

"They weren't instant," she said. "I don't think anything in a community is instant. You have to find your niche. Mine happens to be cooking. I wanted to figure out something I could do with the kids and adults. So, I started a Saturday morning café and made breakfast for everybody. That was the beginning. I was also active with the kids in the theater groups that came in. All the kids know me and I know all the kids. It is a big, extended family. We are very loving. Even my own family has been welcomed into the throng of this community."

A couple years after arriving, one of her adult children underwent a crisis and her grandsons, aged eight and fourteen, moved into the one bedroom apartment Heather shared with three cats and a dog. When it became clear that her daughter's difficulties were not diminishing, and the boys would be hers to raise, they moved into a family home at Treehouse.

Heather's youngest grandson suffered from depression, anxiety, and agoraphobia, which interfered with his ability to attend school. Since school is mandatory, and he refused to go, the family got referred to DCF and the court system. Heather did all she could to help him and avoid court intervention, but found her knowledge and power limited. "To try to wade through the system is impossible," she said, "when you have absolutely no idea what's available, what the next step is, or what they are talking about. It's like everyone talking a separate language. Nobody tries to help you understand."

Treehouse, however, helped. Two mothers in the community, who have been through similar difficulties, provided support and understanding. A female staff member accompanied her to court. "I got to the hearings," said Heather, "and I couldn't remember what I was going to say because I was on an emotional roller coaster ride. She was my voice, which was wonderful."

Treehouse also provided an educational advocate, who represented her grandson and helped formulate a school plan. "She does a wonderful job," said Heather. "If I wasn't here, I wouldn't know that such a person even existed. Because it's not written down anywhere. There is no set of rules for people trying to raise a child in the system. I didn't have any trouble with my kids when they were young, so I did not know any of this stuff."

Mariana, another Treehouse resident, also found the supports crucial, and very different from what she experienced elsewhere. Mariana had adopted two children before she and her partner came to Treehouse from a crime-ridden neighborhood in Holyoke. After her seven-year-old witnessed a stabbing outside their apartment, she knew she had to leave. Within a month, she moved to Treehouse, her application expedited when the program learned about her circumstances.

"The first day that we brought a few things over," she remembered, "all the neighbors came out and welcomed us. We thought it was weird at first. Where we came from, people didn't speak to their neighbors. You didn't know who was safe."

She quickly grew to appreciate the friendliness of the community. "The staff found therapists and specialists," said Mariana. "Helped with educational stuff. Provided activities that I would never have thought of doing because they weren't in my experience. Or my budget. The first year we were here, they gave the kids ski lessons at Berkshire East. Somehow, with neighbors' help, my kids now have full gear, and friends take them along when they are going to the ski area. Treehouse also got them scholarships to Farm Camp, which they love, and found a place for my daughter to take care of horses in exchange for riding lessons. They look at what kids are interested in and try to find it."

Mariana's children also utilize the program's homework help. "One day," she said, "the kids asked for help with their math and we looked at it and said, 'Oh, not sure about that.' So, we sent them to the community center where they got help. Now the staff make sure that the first thing they get done is their math. They partner with us."

She is most impressed by the contrast with her earlier experiences. "It was overwhelming in Holyoke," she said. "We were constantly fighting the school for services I knew my children needed. My husband has dyslexia. When we went to IEP meetings, they started throwing out all of these terms and scores, and he felt like his head would explode. Now we go to IEP meetings and don't feel stressed. A staff member goes with us, and we have an educational advocate. We have a team of people backing us up. I feel I can voice what I need to say. He has people who explain."

Although Kim had supportive family and friends, she knew very few professionals or other adoptive parents who understood her situation, could explain how various systems worked, and were savvy enough to provide helpful information. Besieged by one new challenge after another, she continuously found herself trying to develop expertise and locate adequate resources.

When Kim and Dave adopted Jenna, they signed an open adoption agreement with her parents that included contact and visits. They sat together at a large table in the Greenfield DCF office, along with lawyers and social workers, to negotiate the agreement. Jenna's parents thanked Kim for taking care of their child and announced they wanted what was best for her. Kim agreed they could visit—three times a year for her biological mother and four for her father. The parents needed to contact Kim during certain months to arrange the visits. If they missed more than two, future contacts would be cancelled. Kim made only one request: they keep their commitments and not let Jenna down. She had already seen Jenna's disappointment when her mother failed to make earlier visits arranged by DCF.

The biological parents called late to arrange the first visit. Kim let it go, but warned them about future meetings. They met up at Yankee Candle, a popular Christmas store with interior exhibits of a Bavarian Village, Santa's Workshop, electric trains, and other activities.

Jenna appeared uncomfortable, alternately trudging next to her biological mother and running to Kim's side. Her father and brother walked by themselves, paying little attention to anyone, despite not having seen Jenna in a year and a half. On the next visit, Jenna's mother showed up late and clearly drunk. She left after a short time. Jenna looked devastated, but bravely stated, "It's okay, I have my own mom now."

Another time, Jenna's mother, brother, aunts, and uncles came to watch her play soccer. When she talked, her mother's mouth sported a row of black, decaying teeth and eye pupils reduced to tiny dots. A friend told Kim that the tooth decay signified "meth mouth," indicating long-term drug use, and her constricted pupils meant she was high.

After that, Kim and Jenna did not see Jenna's biological family again. Jenna refused further opportunities to visit, although she continued to treasure the ring and snowman doll. Her mother called a few years later, asking if she could send a Christmas present, which never arrived. She also told Kim that Jenna had probably suffered sexual abuse. Kim told her she should have filed a child abuse report against the perpetrator.

"I didn't know about all of this," said Kim, "so, I was getting agitated. RAD. Drug use. It's all this stuff that I've never encountered. It was an eye opener. But I was committed. So, simultaneously I got my own therapist who gave me support for years. I told her, 'I'm not equipped for this. I can't take this kid who shows no feelings, no remorse when she does something wrong. Who just sits and looks at me.' Once, she put mac and cheese in the microwave. It smoked up the house, the fire department came, and she wouldn't tell them a word."

High school brought more challenges. Smart and wily, Jenna could whizz through the work when she applied herself, although she rarely did. The school, seeing her potential, refused to give her a special education plan, so she muddled through. Kim made sure that she did. After a couple of incidents when Jenna skipped school, went to a nearby park, smoked pot, and had sex, Kim told her she would escort her to and from the door of her classroom if necessary. From then on, Kim drove her back and forth from school and called at random times to make sure she stayed in class.

Jenna's behavior kept Kim on high alert. When Jenna took pictures of her rear end and cleavage and posted them on social media, Kim took them down. When Jenna stole another student's shoes, Kim made her give them back. After Jenna ran off in the middle of the night with older men and hung out with gang members, Kim installed GPS tracking on her phone. Kim used it to find her and bring her home. One day, Kim received a letter stating that Jenna had been caught shoplifting at Sears.

"She was doing more than I knew," said Kim. "I didn't want to believe all that she was doing. She was putting her life in danger, again and again. She might as well have been walking on a tightrope between twenty-story buildings. I thought, 'I'm going to get a phone call, and this kid is going to be dead.'"

Kim slept poorly, wondering what Jenna was doing, and with whom. She lost weight, a lot of weight. "I would think of her wandering the streets and taking off," said Kim, "and I was bombing in the toilet because I was so upset. My heart was racing. I can't tell you how many nights were like that. I felt I wasn't equipped to deal with it, and yet I knew no one else was going to help her unless I got through this. I never thought of giving up. My husband did. He was just done."

Her husband's feelings and behaviors compounded the problems. He told Kim that he loved Hannah, but not Jenna. He told Jenna that she was not his daughter. While Kim struggled to understand, and help Jenna, Dave began a slide of his own. Besieged by continued back problems and faltering cognition, both possibly connected to his earlier fall, he worked sparingly, taking on a few jobs here and there. He slept many hours, even during the day, and suffered a handful of relapses, single events of drinking that upset Kim, although Jenna seemed unconcerned.

Dave, sinking into sullenness, could not understand why Jenna differed so much from Hannah. Why she did not warm up to them. Now that she lived in their safe and loving home, he thought she should snap out of her old ways and settle in. He called her a loser, hoping he could yank or shame her into behaving and, in the process, protect Kim from further stress and torment. Failing in his efforts, he distanced himself from Kim and the two began to argue. His drinking and abrasive moods and comments, aimed mostly at Jenna, ruined two Christmas celebrations.

Kim once again found herself functioning as a single parent, working full-time, and managing the finances and the household. Her family's conflicts also trapped her between competing needs, and she found herself shielding her fractious daughter from her disabled, agitated husband.

"I was defending her to him, of all people," she said. "I was really irritated, and losing respect and getting angry. I was ready to be out of the marriage. There was one night that I got in the car and just drove. I thought, 'I just want to leave them all.' She's not changing. She's not doing anything to change. I'm trying to help her, and she's fighting me every step of the way. And he's making stupid comments, and sleeping all day, and sleeping all night, and leaving all the housework to me. All the responsibility. I told him not to parent her. Let me take care of the issues and the problems. I put myself last."

With home life more and more difficult, Kim took refuge in work. "At work, I got recognition and raises and promotions," said Kim. "Now, instead of one bank branch I had two, so I was managing two staffs while I was trying to deal with this issue. But I had great people around me. And that made the difference. When I needed help at work, they stepped up. Probably what sustained me. Being at work was my sanctuary."

Her sister and mother also chipped in. Sometimes her sister took Jenna for a week to give Kim and Dave breathing space.

Kim slimmed life down to motherhood and work. She could manage nothing else. Whenever the bank sent her on business trips, she felt nervous, so she went on as few as possible. She limited her social life and resigned her board seat at the AIDS Foundation. Her time was spent monitoring and managing Jenna. Staying vigilant. She even relinquished the dream of a home filled with children. Her hands felt indescribably full, yet she wondered, always and incessantly, if she was doing enough.

Kim spoke with Jenna's therapist, who suggested medication. Jenna's doctor referred them to a psychiatrist, but an agonizing few months passed before Jenna got an appointment and started on antidepressants. After a series of arguments that resulted in Jenna smashing a mirror and the police again arriving in their driveway, they received a referral to a family stabilization team from a nearby community mental health clinic.

Despite the service's aim to help families in crisis, they waited more months before a team of two therapists met with them. The therapists assessed Jenna, thought she was not at risk for self-harm, and referred them to an in-home team of two more therapists. The in-home workers tried to bring the family closer together. They took Jenna out and spoke with her about her life and behavior. They worked with the parents to adjust their tone and demeanor. One of the therapists also gave Jenna a pocketknife. The interventions helped a little, but Kim had trouble fathoming the choice of gift.

All in all, beginning with the clinician in Greenfield, Jenna worked with eight different psychotherapists, a psychiatrist, and various school counselors. None of the therapies substantially curbed her behaviors.

The school counselor suggested Kim look into what the courts could offer. She advised that, because Jenna was seventeen and almost aged out of the juvenile system, Kim might need to push and insist. Pushing and insisting was something Kim knew how to do.

She talked with a probation officer and pleaded for help. The officer convened a meeting, at which she told Jenna that her shoplifting and delinquency could put her in jail. She could avoid incarceration only by attending school, performing community service, and remaining under her mother's authority until she graduated, even if that fell past her eighteenth birthday. Jenna complied, completing all the program requirements.

One night, right before she graduated high school, Jenna came home, put her book bag down, and casually looked at Kim. "Hey mom," she said, "I love you." It was the first time she had uttered those words.

"You love me?" Kim asked in surprise.

"Yeah," Jenna said, retreating upstairs to her room, "Can't a girl tell her mom she loves her? What's wrong with you?"

For a while, on medication and following court ordered constraints, Jenna appeared less snippy and snappy. She talked more readily and showed an interest in her future. When she finished high school, she began working twelve to twenty hours a week and enrolled in college. Kim hoped she had turned the corner. Jenna talked as though she had. She said she wished she could go back in time and change what she did—the stealing, fighting, and hanging with gang members. However, in a matter of months, Jenna stopped taking her medication, moved out to live with a boyfriend, and failed college. She smoked a lot of marijuana.

Hannah, however, slowly returned to the fold. She married, got pregnant, and let Kim hold her hand during labor. Kim wonders at what a good mother she has become and how much Dave adores their grandchild. Hannah chats with Kim almost every day.

As Jenna neared her twenty-first birthday, she began to settle down, reflect, and reengage. She worked more hours, smoked less, and agreed to save money in a retirement account. For the first time in years, she gave her mother a birthday card. "I never knew how badly I made people feel by not thinking about them," she said, as she delivered it. "I did not know how good I had it. But I always knew you loved me."

"My love for Jenna is probably one of the biggest factors that got me through," said Kim. "My love for both my kids. Love means a lot. I wasn't ever going to be a mother, but when I became one, it was like a whole different realm, and there's some sort of badge of honor that comes with it. I have no regrets. I think that if you are going to adopt a kid from the system, you have to understand that they come with a lot. They may have experienced more abuse in a week than others do in a lifetime. Whatever problems Jenna may still have, I feel like she is a part of me and I am a part of her, and that is not going to change. It would have been easy to give up. So many times, I felt I couldn't do this, and others told me no one would hold it against me if I bailed. But I can't give up. I tell my girls, 'Always know you were wanted and loved. No matter what happens, I will be there to help.'"

8. Conclusion:
Getting From Here To There

The Current Landscape

ALL THE PARENTS IN THIS BOOK, who range from poor to middle class, found it difficult to locate and engage help across a span of different needs and human services systems. Their exertions stretched their families thin, triggering widespread repercussions.

Nathaniel and Victoria, in Chapter Two, felt debilitated by the effort to juggle the care of their twins while striving to obtain knowledgeable school, medical, and disability services.

Diana, in Chapter Three, exhausted herself with futile attempts to engage programs that would save her daughter from drug addiction.

Robin, in Chapter Four, sampled numerous therapies, books, and self-help programs before finding a mix that could direct her parenting.

Angelina and Jacob, in Chapter Five, found the hurdles and judgments DCF placed upon them almost impossible to surmount.

Sophia, in Chapter Six, fought to be heard in schools and the courts.

Kim, in Chapter Seven, struggled to find expert mental health services and supports for her adopted daughter.

The pressures degraded families' health, mental health, and income. Nathaniel and Sophia left work to care for their children, putting them in precarious financial situations. Angelina dropped out of college and felt too debilitated to leave the house. Diana's inability to obtain services led to the loss of her daughter and exacerbated her depression and anxiety. Victoria and Nathaniel, as well as Kim, found the strains precluded giving sufficient attention to their healthier daughters. Tensions also threatened Nathaniel, Victoria, and Kim's spousal relationships. For parents already overwhelmed by the acute needs of their children, grappling with systemic demands created hardship. As one of the participants in Professor Linda Blum's study of mothers raising children with mild-to-moderate invisible disabilities told her, the strains, struggles, and judgments added scars and scar tissue on top of the original problems.

When familial adversity builds, the fallout reverberates through society. The worsening conditions of parents and children increases the demand for services and taxes already overburdened schools, mental health services, courts, child welfare, and other institutions, none of which are positioned to meet the need. Agencies react by deflecting requests, restricting access, or shifting burdens back on parents. In this way, difficulties perpetuate, creating impossible dilemmas for families and the overworked, under-resourced workers and institutions trying to support them.

Families face relentless pressure to do more and more for their children. They feel blamed and criticized when schools, courts, family members, or DCF insinuate they are not doing enough. But none of the parents in this book abdicated responsibility or rigorous effort. Instead, each of them toiled hard, trying to lift themselves and their children with bootstraps that were stretched and fraying from the pull of their circumstances. What they needed most was recognition of their needs, combined with communities and services better positioned to address them.

Establishing more effective policies and practices will take imagination and will. They require systemic changes. But powerful precedents exist. Alongside larger, more static institutions, many local, small, and innovative programs, some of which have been profiled in this book, are making a difference. Replicating their successes requires increased focus on the following elements:

- Revising the narrative.
- Strengthening communities.
- Developing a better-equipped workforce.
- Encouraging innovation.

Revising the Narrative

"WHAT WOULD IT LOOK LIKE if we didn't have all these additional experiences compounding problems?" asked Professor Blum. "What if we started from a place of more acceptance?"

One of the hallmarks of the Treehouse Community (see Chapter Seven), that serves foster and adoptive families, and The Care Center (see Chapter Five), that educates teenage mothers, is dedication to providing comprehensive supports without judgment. Both programs accept parental limitations as normative, and provide help as a right, thus allaying the debilitating blame and extraneous strains families experience. Assistance is offered through a wide range of options that respect different parenting styles and goals. Barriers to seeking help, in the form of stigma, criticism, or inaccessibility of services, are lessened. Parents do not find one problem addressed at the expense or exacerbation of others. They do not encounter expectations that are out of line with reality. Restructuring the social services system to function in a similar way is a necessary, but difficult, undertaking.

Stymieing efforts at reform, and obscuring the necessity, is America's mantra of individualism, the belief that withstanding the slings and arrows of outrageous fortune occurs through strengthening the self, regardless of the sea of troubles in which people find themselves. Seminal ideas about resiliency, personal responsibility, and self-sufficiency have become wedged into the recesses of society, where they hide unnoticed, influencing policies and the systems built around them. Governments, agencies, schools, television shows, and professionals then create programs and interventions that reinforce those ideas. The end result is that parents are expected to do more and more with less and less.

Success stories about parents and children who thrive, despite poverty, illness, or disability, shame those who cannot. But vast differences exist in parents' abilities and circumstances, which in part determines their clout. Families with sufficient supports, money, status, and/or education learn to work the system, advocating for themselves or hiring professionals who can lobby on their behalf. They also find organizations more responsive to their needs. In contrast, parents with less power and means get lost in the shuffle. America's schools, courts, and helping systems do not grant everyone an equally working chance.

Inequity in America, rather than diminishing ideals of individualism and self-sufficiency, has increased them. A culture that offers scant help, and rewards standing out over fitting in, becoming over being, and self over community, elevates the need for autonomy and resilience. Without those traits, it is hard to survive.

The emphasis on self-efficacy and resilience intensifies demands on parents to train children with those skills. Parenting manuals, psychotherapeutic interventions, and public media campaigns promote middle class parenting styles, geared towards autonomy, as the ticket to privilege and high-paying jobs. Parent training is routinely suggested as the salve to help families struggling in poverty or accused of maltreatment, with variable outcomes.[1] As parents raise children to survive their particular circumstances, advising a switch in strategies without a concomitant change of circumstances is tantamount to asking families to swim against the tide of the communities in which they live and interdepend.

When it comes to raising a child with severe disabilities or mental health issues, most parents lack the complex mix of skills needed to advocate for their children or help them develop to their full potential, especially when navigating the stresses of low-income jobs and neighborhoods or their own physical or mental health difficulties. Current policies and recommendations again emphasize parent training as a prime remedy for that deficit. However, while parents appreciate learning to care better for their children, overwhelming them with parent training, when they barely have time to shower, is not an adequate solution. Even with enhanced parent training, most parents will not be able to master and implement intricate, time-consuming treatment plans that require moment by moment adjustments. When they try, they may find the effort diminishes their families' physical, fiscal, and mental health. More acknowledgment of parents' legitimate hardships comprises the first step towards establishing and funding service systems that are broad and deep enough to relieve, rather than add to, parental burdens.

The culture's increased emphasis on mental health, and psychotherapy as a way to sustain it, also reinforces the notion of personal responsibility for well-being.[2] While psychotherapy can treat and improve many conditions, it rarely delivers outcomes equal to those attained by people who have suffered little. Despite the recognition that adversity and ACEs (Adverse Childhood Experiences, see Chapter Four) underlie a host of difficulties, current efforts to change, fix, or strengthen individuals moves the focus away from preventative interventions.[3]

As Professor Blum noted, "Many causes of ill health and health inequality in the United States are because of large, political, institutional causes, not personal ones. Our lack of enforcing the Clean Water Act, or the Clean Air Act. Racism. Poverty. Where people have to live because they can't afford housing. Parents having to work, be in school. Or with health issues of their own. Kids or family members with needs. The emphasis on personal responsibility and health maximization ignores the entire social environment. No matter how many kale smoothies people devour, it's not going to make a huge difference."

Strengthening Communities

FAMILIES FARE BEST when they live in environments that promote wellbeing. They need neighborhoods that are safe and cohesive.[4] Communities with parks, green spaces, healthy food, and affordable housing. Jobs paying wages that confer a viable quality of life. Places where neighbors help neighbors and schools and social service agencies meet students and families' needs. Just as adversity spreads like a contagion, quality programs and atmospheres immunize.[5] A child happy and thriving in school, or in the community, puts less stress on parents, allowing those parents, in return, to provide better support. Strengthening communities and community services should be a national priority.

Alloparenting, the voluntary care given by nonparental figures (see Chapter Seven), has diminished alongside urbanization and the primacy of the nuclear family, although in some communities, such as where adoption worker Linda Dugas lives, residents still provide substantial help to one other. While wealthy, industrialized societies, structured around individualism, are unlikely to return to communal caregiving, with its tendency to favor stricter norms and conformity, alloparenting's lessons should not be lost. Researchers find that social support is the most important protective factor for sustaining people and improving mental health.[6]

Social supports can come from family, neighbors, or other community members, such as Dugas, Robin, and Sophia found, or through loosely knit groups. Agencies can also serve that function. Most of the programs favored by families in this book were small and community-based. Robin found Alcoholics Anonymous and Al-Anon effective because they offered social connection as well as practical tips on managing daily challenges. The Care Center established comprehensive supports and mentoring for the teenage parents it served, integrating numerous different services on site. At the Treehouse Community, residents aided each other and staff flexibly responded to their needs. Religious organizations and community centers can also fulfill those functions, and often do. But those and other programs must be able to extend to families such as Victoria and Nathaniel who are isolated due to overwhelming responsibilities and multiple needs. More deliberatively designed, well-resourced, flexible, accessible programs, embedded within communities, are needed.

Local programs are best positioned to provide sustaining supports because they can monitor and adapt to communities' needs and constraints, although they require infrastructure and funding to do so. Large public administrations, such as DCF or state and federal governments, often lack the nimbleness and local knowledge required to tailor service delivery to individual needs. As Bette Jenks, coordinator of the Athol PATCH program, noted, "You can't come in and dictate. You have to work with the community. Find out what is needed. What a family resource center looks like in Athol should not look anything like one in Boston." When decision-making occurs in remote legislatures or bigger bureaucracies, it rarely satisfies local needs.

America's skewed playing field will only even out through a balance of individualism and community. The benefits would be felt not just by challenged families, such as profiled in this book, but households of every socioeconomic and racial background. In a recent survey, Switzerland, the Scandinavian countries, and the Netherlands, more equal societies that offer substantial social supports, were rated as the happiest and healthiest countries in which to live.[7] Their residents pay for the privilege through higher taxes. If parity is to take root in America, it will need to be enacted through leadership, policies aimed at supporting families and communities, incentives and funding provided by state and federal governments, and a change of narrative. Europeans feel a personal responsibility not just for themselves, but for the wellbeing of others, including their workers.[8]

Developing A Better Equipped Workforce

KEN EPSTEIN, the Children, Youth and Family System of Care Director for San Francisco County Community Behavioral Health Services, likes to tell the following story: When a new Chief Executive Officer (CEO) took command of a faltering program, the outgoing CEO gave her advice. "I am going to give you three letters," he said. "When you run into trouble, just open the letters and follow their instructions." For a while the job went well, and the new CEO had no need for guidance. However, a year later, difficulties began to assail her. Opening the first letter, she read, "Blame your predecessor." She denounced the policies of the old CEO and her reputation rebounded. Another two years passed before discord hit again. Needing direction, she opened the second letter, which told her, "Restructure." A reorganization plan carried her through another year or two. The agency's intrinsic difficulties then became apparent, and she found herself faulted for not correcting them. She consulted the third note, which advised, "Write three letters."

According to Epstein, that formula for reform—blame, restructure, retire—tends to repeat, limiting deep change. "Bureaucracies are built to protect and maintain themselves," he said over lunch, his voice fighting to be heard above the din of a popular Thai restaurant, whose atmosphere accentuated the barriers he described. He explained that while accountability is necessary, regulations hinder innovation because they aim to limit risk or increase efficiency and productivity. However, those priorities ignore the complexity of peoples' lives. Social service jobs, which aim to help people in precarious and inconstant circumstances, cannot be made certain or efficient. The work is messy, meandering, and sometimes expensive. When programs ignore that reality, they produce services and work environments that are user-unfriendly.[9]

"The problem," he continued, "is that we put people in paradigms that are wrongly conceived. When we change the system, we still keep the paradigm. Put new workers in the same equation and you will get the same results." He believes that transforming bureaucracies requires revamping the workplace: "Those of us who work and manage large organizations need to try every day to make them more humane."

Overwhelmed systems looking to contain costs often cut exactly what most sustained Linda Dugas in her job as an adoption worker: training, substantial supervision and support, and workable caseloads. Skimping on salaries is another common tactic. But when workers are not given the basic tools needed to manage their lives and work, they cannot perform well. Turnover in the human service field is considerable, limiting the acquisition of expertise. For agencies, high levels of attrition are also expensive, costing funds that could go to other purposes.[10]

ServiceNet tries hard to limit turnover in its agency through a number of initiatives. "I think people who work here appreciate certain things," said Karen Franklin, the director of outpatient services. "People like the training, quality of care, and collegial atmosphere we offer. They feel their work is valued. People come from other agencies and feel less micromanaged." ServiceNet allows staff input on what types of treatments to train in and offer and tries to accommodate therapists' interests and passions. Low pay still leads workers to leave, but less often than in other offices.

A similar recipe has been used by Finland to transform its educational system into one of the best in the world.[11] In the past four decades, Finland invested in its elementary and secondary school teachers. The country created rigorous, competitive academic programs, as well as offered teachers pleasant, supportive working environments, opportunities for creativity and growth, and moderate teaching loads. Teachers receive good compensation and a high degree of respect. As a consequence, teaching has become a sought after profession, and training programs can select those most likely to succeed (they have a 10 percent acceptance rate). Only 9 percent of teachers leave, and careers frequently span forty years. Through its reforms, Finland has built a contented, motivated, highly trained, experienced, and stable workforce that produces results for the students it serves.

The United States of America has not bestowed the same care in the training and retaining of human service employees. Those professions do not pay well, command respect, or uniformly provide pleasant, feasible working conditions. Ongoing, quality training is not guaranteed. In addition, no mechanism exists to make sure the workforce is large enough or sufficiently trained to serve the complex needs of the populations it serves. As a consequence, service delivery is haphazard, ranging from deficient to excellent. Unfortunately, when institutions and services flounder, communities and governments lose trust in them, which also erodes willingness to fund and reform them. When that happens, quick, inadequate fixes get applied, and innovation slackens.

Encouraging Innovation

ALTHOUGH THE SOCIAL SERVICE SYSTEM contains many deficits, its record also includes innovation and progress. Over the last century, the government has passed laws requiring schools to educate all children, closed abusive residential facilities, and forced insurance plans to provide equitable coverage for mental health and substance abuse treatment.[12] Mistreatment of individuals with disabilities and mental illness has lessened. Stigma over seeking help has diminished. Access to mental health treatment has improved. Many smaller, private organizations that aim to fill community needs have cropped up, like the Treehouse Community, The Care Center, ServiceNet, and Adoption Journeys. Across the country, numerous resourceful programs tackle public problems.

Massachusetts has also enacted statewide initiatives to provide comprehensive and integrated services. In 2008, in response to a class action lawsuit, the State instituted the MassHealth Children's Behavioral Health Initiative (CBHI), which provides a menu of in-home treatments for children and families on Medicaid.[13] In 2018, it created Accountable Care Organizations (ACOs) meant to coordinate and integrate services through primary care doctors.[14] Despite these efforts and improvements, problems remain. According to a review conducted in 2017, the quality of CBHI services is inconsistent, especially as the programs tend to be staffed by inexperienced workers.[15] While it is too soon to gauge the impact of the ACO model, it, too, is unlikely to dent shortages in services and providers, impact the low pay and varied quality of services, or integrate services across non-ACO entities. However, despite the limitations, the State's willingness to reform is laudable and can encourage other novel ideas.

Innovation requires moving away from rigid organizational structures toward ideas that combine and mobilize community resources in new ways. Anne Teschner and Ana Rodriguez transformed The Care Center into an educational success after considering programs and models not usually provided to teen parents. "We saw that students who attend prep schools may not be the smartest in the world," said Teschner, "but they generally succeed. It is a question of who gets resources, and who doesn't, and what are those resources. Prep schools have arts, humanities, athletics, small class sizes, and the expectation of success. So, we took the GED (General Education Development) model and dumped on top of it the prep school model in the hope that it would ignite learning."

The plan has succeeded, but not without creative efforts to overcome cultural, political, and fiscal barriers, another important element of innovation. Teschner spends a lot of time fundraising, grant writing, and countering others' presumptions. "It was a risk," she said, "there were lots of naysayers who said the young women have enough on their plate. They don't need to be rowing. They don't need to be studying philosophy. They don't need any of this. Just give them a job, and maybe a little bit of parent education, but not too much, because they are going to be bad parents, anyway. But it worked. We just sort of stopped the whole wheel."

Successful programs also consider the needs of consumers and involve them in the creation and administration of services. At Treehouse, residents partner with staff to both receive and deliver help. "We respond to emerging needs," said Kerry Homstead, the community facilitator, "it's an attitude. We are always looking for what families need and how to find solutions. We bring in volunteers and programs from inside and outside the community. Parents use them as they want. Everything is very individualized." Innovative services are those attuned to time and place and able to accommodate to an ever-changing social and political landscape.

One of the forces working against innovation is over-concern about efficiency and cost-cutting. Productivity and economizing are important goals, especially when the money comes from taxes, but both tend to result from innovation, rather than engender it. The development of new techniques and ideas are undermined when stringent budgets cut time and resources for thought, supervision, research, and experimentation. In human services, like other complex fields, the work proceeds in fits and starts, with tinkering and tweaking. Yet unlike other disciplines, human services are rarely provided sufficient money for those endeavors. In contrast, fields such as medicine and business enjoy strong reputations for inventiveness and receive funding and opportunities to test out promising avenues, even when they result in high failure rates.[16] Human services can only innovate and meet community needs if given the resources. Efficiency and effectiveness will follow.

OVER ONE HUNDRED YEARS AGO, an Italian immigrant to Ellis Island purportedly made the following statement: "I came to America because I heard the streets were paved with gold. When I got here, I found out three things: First, the streets weren't paved with gold; second, they weren't paved at all; and third, I was expected to pave them." Despite falling short, the American Dream, that promises equal opportunity and a better future, does not need to be abandoned. The country's unfinished support networks can still be built up, if everyone pitches in. In addition to government funding and workplace reform, citizens can help. They can reach out to neighbors, befriend an isolated or struggling family, volunteer in local social service organizations, mentor a youth, lend high quality, pro bono professional services to those who cannot afford them, advocate for reform—the list and possibilities are endless. By revising the numerous narratives that inhibit change combined with a concerted community effort, significant progress can be made in the circumstances of families and the supports they receive.

Acknowledgements

IF THIS BOOK LAUDS THE POWER of communities to uplift and sustain, it also reflects that notion. The book has never been an individual effort. Numerous parents, professionals, and academics contributed both directly and indirectly to the ideas and stories gracing these pages. Their voices, reflected in quotes and insights, shape the book's narrative and argument. Without their generous and astute input, and the time they cleared from their busy schedules, this project would not have been completed.

I am indebted first and foremost to the many families I interviewed, both whose stories I recount and those I left out, who opened up their lives and hearts to me. We spent many hours together as I poked and prodded their memories, coaxing them to reveal difficult feelings and experiences that brought them, and me, to tears. I remain in awe of the honesty and bravery they showed, as well as their good will. Each of the parents participated with the hope that, by sharing their stories, others would benefit.

This book leaned heavily on the support of my own community, which responded with enthusiasm to my requests for help. Besides the professionals and researchers named in the manuscript, many more friends and colleagues backed my efforts by recruiting parents, giving advice, listening to my endless chatter, reading sections of the manuscript, or simply believing in the project's worth and my ability to complete it. I thank Sarah Abel, Jean Beard, Jaime Bersch, Ashlee Bianchine, David B., Teri Cain, Susan Crane, Hilary Cronin, Claudia Donald, Seth Dunn, Kathy Harrison, Rose Evans, Patricia Everett, Shelly Bathe Lenn, Cathy Luna, Marie Mintz, Eileen Messer, Melissa Mateus, Pat Ononibaku, Sally Popper, Betty Sharpe, Bev Swetcky, and Allison Weissman. I am also grateful for the patience, understanding, and support of my family, which includes my parents, siblings and their spouses, nieces and nephews, husband, and children, who allowed me the space and time to write, even when it meant I had less time and energy for them.

Then there is Diana Gordon, who started out as my editor and ended up a friend. Without her encouragement and sage advice, I may never have persevered through what she calls "the long, lonely cowgirl hours in the saddle," those days when I sat alone, staring at my computer, while words and ideas fled and progress seemed elusive. She also taught me the true meaning of "less is more" by gently snipping some of the outlandish sentences that I had mistaken for gems. I struggled against a few of the cuts, but in the end, had to concede that she was right. Both I, and the readers, owe her wholehearted thanks.

I have been privileged to work with Steve Strimer of Levellers Press whose commitment to untold stories compelled him to make time for this book in his already overworked schedule. Sharon Bially of Book-Savvy PR offered optimisim, advice, and expertise in pushing for the book's recognition when the demands of promotion flummoxed me.

Last and certainly not least, I owe a debt of gratitude to all of the families I have worked with throughout the years, who have let me into their lives and struggles, and taught me so much. I wrote this book with them in mind.

National, State, and Local Resources

DISABILITY:

The Arc of the United States
National office (with chapters throughout the country):
1825 K Street NW, Suite 1200
Washington, DC 20006
Phone: 202-534-3700 / 800-433-5255
https://www.thearc.org

Provides supports and services for people with intellectual and developmental disabilities, information and referral, advocacy, family and residential support, employment, leisure, and recreational programs.

Autism Speaks
National office:
888-288-4762
En Español 888-772-9050
familyservices@autismspeaks.org
https://www.autismspeaks.org

Funds research and connects families to information, resources, and opportunities.

Center for Parent Information and Resources (CPR)
National office:
c/o Statewide Parent Advocacy Network
35 Halsey Street, Fourth Floor
Newark, NJ 07102
973-642-8100
malizo@spannj.org

A central resource of information and products to the community of Parent Training Information (PTI) Centers and the Community Parent Resource Centers (CPRCs), to help them better serve families of children with disabilities.

Department of Developmental Services
State headquarters (other states have similar agencies):
500 Harrison Avenue
Boston, MA 02118
617-727-5608
TTY: 617-624-7783
https://www.mass.gov/service-details/department-of-developmental-
services-dds

Provides service coordination, family support services, residential supports, respite care, and transportation services. DDS provides some of
these services directly, and others are available from providers in the
community.

Federation for Children with Special Needs
State offices:
The Shrafft Center
529 Main Street, Suite 1M3
Boston, MA 02129
Phone/TTY: 617-236-7210
Toll Free: 800-331-0688 (Massachusetts only)
Satellite office Western Massachusetts: 413-323-0681 or
866-323-0681
info@fcsn.org

Provides information, referral, advocacy, and support to parents and
others working with children with disabilities, (ages birth to twenty-two) particularly in obtaining appropriate educational services.

Sunshine Foundation
1041 Mill Creek Drive
Feasterville, PA 19053
215-396 4770
info@sunshinefoundation.org
https://www.sunshinefoundation.org

Provides funds to answer the dreams of chronically or seriously
ill, physically challenged, or abused children, whose families suffer
financial strain.

GENERAL PARENT SUPPORT:

It Takes a Village:
Physical address:
2 Main Street
Cummington, MA 01026

Mailing address:
PO Box 146
Cummington, MA 01026
413-650-3640
info@hilltownvillage.org
http://www.hilltownvillage.org

Free postpartum support: home visits, support groups, donation site for free baby items.

Parents Anonymous
National office:
250 West First Street, Suite 250
Claremont, CA 91711
909-621-6184
National Parent Helpline 855-4AParent (1-855-427-2736)
http://parentsanonymous.org

Provides support groups for parents, children, and youth, referrals, emergency support through helpline, functions as both an intervention and prevention program.

Parents Helping Parents
State resource, but similar organizations exist in other states:
Parental Stress Line: 800-632-8188
info@parentshelpingparents.org
https://www.parentshelpingparents.org

Provides support, support groups, and a guide for those whose children are in DCF custody.

Parents without Partners
National office, with chapters throughout the country:
1100-H Brandywine Boulevard.
Zanesville, OH 43701-7303
Phone: 800-637-7974
parentswithoutpartners.org

For single parents: educational, family, and adult social and recreational activities.

LEGAL:

Disability Law Center
Massachusetts headquarters, national services offered through National Disability Rights Network:
617-723-8455
Toll Free: 800-872-9992
Northampton, MA: 413 584-6337, 800-222-5619
mail@dlc-ma.org

Provides free legal services and advocacy to low-income people with disabilities in the areas of special education, accessibility to community service, health care, disability benefits and rights, and conditions in facilities.

Massachusetts Legal Assistance Corporation
State headquarters, similar programs exist in other states:
18 Tremont Street, Suite 1010
Boston, MA 02108
info@mlac.org
Phone: 617-367-8544
http://mlac.org/help

Provides advice, information, and referrals to free legal services across the state.

National Disability Rights Network
National office:
820 1st Street NE, Suite 740
Washington, DC 20002
202-408-9514
TTY: 220-408-9521
info@ndrn.org.
http://www.ndrn.org

Provides legally based advocacy services to people with disabilities in the United States. There is an agency in every state, which can be located through the website.

USA.gov
844-USA-GOV1
https://www.usa.gov/legal-aid

Provides links to free and low-cost legal resources across the United States.

MENTAL HEALTH:

Referrals to local services or private practice clinicians can be obtained from physicians, insurance plans, schools, or others who know the resources in the area. Community mental health clinics can be located through the SAMSHA website (see below).

American Academy of Child and Adolescent Psychiatry (AACAP)
National office:
3615 Wisconsin Avenue, NW
Washington, DC 20016-3007
Phone: 202-966-7300
https://www.aacap.org/

Information on child and adolescent psychiatry, fact sheets for parents and caregivers, current research, practice guidelines.

Children and Adults with Attention-Deficit/Hyperactivity Disorder (CHADD)
National office:
4601 Presidents Drive, Suite 300
Lanham, MD 20706
301-306-7070
Helpline: 800-233-4050
http://www.chadd.org/default.aspx

Support groups, evidence-based information, advocacy.

Department of Mental Health
Massachusetts headquarters (other states have similar agencies):
25 Staniford Street
Boston, MA 02114
617-626-8000
TTY: 617-727-9842
dmhinfo@dmh.state.ma.us
https://www.mass.gov/orgs/massachusetts-department-of-mental-health

Provides services, supports, and case management to children and adults with qualifying mental health problems, funds residential services and specialized activities for children.

National Alliance on Mental Illness (NAMI)
National office:
3803 N. Fairfax Drive, Suite 100
Arlington, VA 22203
Helpline: 800-950-NAMI
Main line: 703-524-7600
https://www.nami.org

Massachusetts Chapter of NAMI
The Schrafft Center
529 Main Street, Suite 1M17
Boston, MA 02129
617-580-8541

Helpline: 800-370-9085
https://namimass.org

Provides family-to-family education, support groups, and information and referral to people with mental illness and their families.

National Suicide Prevention Lifeline
800-273-8255
https://suicidepreventionlifeline.org/

Provides 24/7, free and confidential support for people in distress and their families, prevention and crisis resources, and best practices information for professionals.

Substance Abuse and Mental Health Services Administration (SAMHSA)
National office:
5600 Fishers Lane
Rockville, MD 20857
National helpline: 800-662-4357
TTY: 1-800-487-4889
https://findtreatment.samhsa.gov

The national helpline provides referrals in English and Spanish to local treatment facilities, support groups, and community-based organizations. Callers can also order free publications and other information. A database of mental health services, that is searchable by address, is available on the website, as well as online resources and information.

SCHOOL ADVOCACY

Federation for Children with Special Needs
Massachusetts offices (similar services exist in other states):
The Shrafft Center
529 Main Street, Suite 1M3
Boston, MA 02129
Phone/TTY: 617-236-7210

Toll Free: 800-331-0688 (Massachusetts only)
Satellite office Western Mass: 413-323-0681 or 866-323-0681
fcsninfo@fcsn.org

Provides educational advocates and training to become educational advocates for children with special needs.

Massachusetts Advocacy for Children
State offices:
25 Kingston Street, 2nd Floor
Boston, MA 02111
Helpline: 617-357-8431ext. 3224
https://massadvocates.org

Prioritizes help to children with disabilities, homeless children, children who have been expelled or suspended, and children traumatized by adverse experiences.

Stand for Children
National offices:
2121 SW Broadway #111
Portland, OR 97201
800-663-4032
http://stand.org

Works across ten states to close the achievement gap by passing policies that insure access to quality public education.

SUBSTANCE ABUSE

Al-Anon/Alateen
National offices:
1600 Corporate Landing Parkway
Virginia Beach, VA 23454-5617
wso@al-anon.org
Toll-free Meeting Line: 888-425-2666
https://al-anon.org

Support groups for teens and family members who are worried about someone's drinking. Programs are offered free of charge.

Alcoholics Anonymous
National offices:
475 Riverside Drive at West 120th Street – 11th Floor
New York, NY 10115
212-870-3400
http://www.aa.org/pages/en_US

Support group for individuals with a drinking problem. Programs are offered free of charge.

Narcotics Anonymous
National offices:
PO Box 9999
Van Nuys, California USA 91409
818-773-9999
https://www.na.org

Support groups for those in recovery from substance addiction. Programs are offered free of charge.

Substance Abuse and Mental Health Services Administration (SAMHSA)
National office:
5600 Fishers Lane
Rockville, MD 20857
National helpline: 800-662-4357
TTY: 1-800-487-4889
https://findtreatment.samhsa.gov

The national helpline provides referrals in English and Spanish to local treatment facilities, support groups, and community-based organizations. Callers can also order free publications and other information. A database of substance abuse services, that is searchable by address, is available on the website, as well as online resources and information.

TRAUMA, FOSTER CARE, and ADOPTION:

Adoption Journeys
Child & Family Services
P.O. Box 60006
140 Pine Street Suite 12
Florence, MA 01062
413-320-4680, (800) 972-2734

Offices throughout the state provide information and referrals,
assessment, and support for families experiencing stress, support
groups, child care respite, social and recreational activities, trainings
to parents, schools, and professionals. Some other states provide
similar services.

A Home Within
95 3rd Street, Suite 224
San Francisco CA 94103
888-898-2249
admin@ahomewithin.org
https://www.ahomewithin.org

Provides pro bono psychotherapy to current and former foster youth
and alumni through networks of private practice clinicians in various
parts of the country.

Court-Appointed Special Advocates: (CASA)
National offices:
100 West Harrison Street North Tower, Suite 500
Seattle, WA 98119
OR
1625 Massachusetts Avenue, NW, Suite 520
Washington, DC 20036
800-628-3233
http://www.casaforchildren.org/

CASA/GAL volunteers are appointed by judges to watch over and
advocate for abused and neglected children, to make sure they don't
get lost in the system.

FOCUS: Foster Futures
Friends of Children
245 Russell St #22,
Hadley MA 01035
413-586-0011
focus@friendsofchildreninc.org
https://joinfocus.org/

A community-based program that connects youth who age out of foster care with teams of volunteer mentors.

KidsNet
Massachusetts offices:
Boston: 617-983-5800
Metro: 508-753-2967 or 888-754-4535
Northeast: 978-682-9222
Central: 508-753-2967
West: 413-734-4978 or 413-747-0040
Southeast: 508-586-2660
http://www.mspcc.org

Offers training, information and referral, family respite, and campership opportunities for DCF foster, pre-adoptive, and kinship parents.

National Child Traumatic Stress Network (NCTSN)
National office:
Center for Mental Health Services
Substance Abuse and Mental Health Services Administration
Department of Health and Human Services
5600 Fishers Lane
Parklawn Building, Room 17C-26
Rockville, MD 20857
https://www.nctsn.org

Website includes many resources for parents, educators, and professionals that includes research, information, and trainings, including handouts and toolkits.

National Foster Care Association
National office:
1102 Prairie Ridge Trail
Pflugerville, TX 78660
800-557-5238
Info@NFPAonline.org
https://nfpaonline.org

Supports foster parents in achieving safety, permanence, and well-being for the children and youth in their care.

North American Council on Adoptable Children (NACAC)
National offices:
970 Raymond Avenue, Suite 106
Saint Paul, MN 55114
651-644-3036
info@nacac.org
nacac.org

Offers education, parent support, research, and advocacy for parents and professionals, including information on adoption subsidies.

Treehouse Communities
1 Treehouse Circle
Easthampton, MA 01027
413-527-7966
admin@refca.net
https://refca.net/what-we-do/treehouse-community/

Intergenerational, residential community that supports families who foster or adopt through the public foster care system. The program began in Easthampton and is expanding to California and MetroWest Boston. Other intergenerational communities for vulnerable populations exist in other parts of the country through Generations of Hope: http://ghdc.generationsofhope.org.

About the Author

KAREN ZILBERSTEIN is a psychotherapist and passionate advocate for children and families, especially those touched by trauma and the foster care system. A sought after speaker on this and other parenting and child development topics, Karen also serves as Clinical Director of the Northampton, Massachusetts chapter of A Home Within, a national nonprofit that provides pro bono psychotherapy for individuals who have experienced foster care. Prior to this, Karen taught at Smith College School for Social Work and coordinated its child development team. Co-author of a children's book, *Calming Stormy Feelings: A Child's Introduction to Psychotherapy*, she has published numerous journal articles in her field.

Notes

Chapter One

1 Previous estimates by the National Center for Children in Poverty and census data put the poverty rate at 1 in 5 children, but there are indications of a recent reduction in the rate. Shapiro, I., & Trisi, D, (October 5, 2017). *Child poverty falls to record low, comprehensive measure shows stronger government policies account for long-term improvement.* Center on Budget and Policy Priorities. Retrieved from https://www.cbpp.org/research/poverty-and-inequality/child-poverty-falls-to-record-low-comprehensive-measure-shows.

2 Boyle C., Boulet S., Schieve L., Cohen R., Blumberg S., Yeargin-Allsopp M., Visser, S., & Kogan, M. (2011). Trends in the prevalence of developmental disabilities in US children, 1997–2008. *Pediatrics,* 27, 1034-1042. Brault, M. (2011). *School-aged children with disabilities in U.S. metropolitan statistical areas:* 2010. U.S. Census Bureau, American Community Survey Briefs.

3 Merikangas, K., He, J., Burstein, M., Swanson, S., Avenevoli S., Cui, L., Benjet, C., Georgiades, K., & Swendsen, J. (2010). Lifetime prevalence of mental disorders in U.S. adolescents: Results from the National Comorbidity Study-Adolescent Supplement (NCS-A). *Journal of the American Academy of Children & Adolescent Psychiatry,* 49(10), 980–989.

4 A majority of people experience at least one traumatic event in their lifetime, but only a small subset develop PTSD. Lifetime prevalence of PTSD is thought to be higher in women than in men. Interpersonal violence leads to more PTSD symptoms than do accidents or disasters. In the general population, lifetime prevalence of PTSD stands at approximately 8%. Breslau, N., Davis, G., Andreski, P., et al. (1991). Traumatic events and posttraumatic stress disorder in an urban population of young adults. *Archives of General Psychiatry,* 48, 216–22. Kessler, R.C., Sonnega A., Bromet E., et al. (1995). Posttraumatic stress disorder in the National Comorbidity Survey. *Archives of General Psychiatry,* 52,1048–1060. Javdi, H., & Yadollahie, M. (2012). Post-traumatic Stress Disorder. *International Journal of Occupational and Environmental Medicine,* 3(1), 2–9.

5 Anderson, K. (2013). Diagnosing discrimination: Stress from perceived racism and the mental and physical health effects. *Sociological Inquiry,* 83(1), 55–81. U.S. Census Bureau, *Quick Facts.* Retrieved from https://www.census.gov/quickfacts/fact/table/US/PST045216.

6 Wang, Q. (2005). *Disability and American families*: 2000 U.S. Census Bureau.

7 The Annie E. Casey Foundation. (2017). *Kids count data book: Trends in child well-being.* Baltimore, MD: Author. Retrieved from www.aecf.org.

8 Isenberg, N. (2016). *White Trash.* New York: Viking.

9 The history in this chapter is drawn from the following sources: Abel, E. (2000). *Hearts of wisdom: American women caring for kin, 1850-1940.* Cambridge, MA: Harvard University Press. Alwin, D. (1988). From Obedience to autonomy: Changes in traits desired in children, 1924-1978. *The Public Opinion Quarterly,* 52(1), 33-52. Apple. R. (2006). *Perfect motherhood: Science and childrearing in America.* New Brunswick, NJ: Rutgers University Press. Courtwright, D. (1985). New England families in historical perspective. In P. Benes (Ed.). *Families and children.* Boston University: The Dublin seminar for New England folklife annual proceedings. Descartes, L., & Kottak, C. (2009). *Media and middle class moms: Images and realities of work and family.* New York: Routledge. Fass, P. (2016). *The end of American childhood: A history of parenting from life on the frontier to the managed child.* New Jersey: Princeton University Press. Hulbert, A. (2003). *Raising America: Experts, parents, and a century of advice about children.* New York, NY: Alfred K. Knopf. McMahon, M. (1995). *Engendering motherhood: Identity and self-transformation in women's lives.* New York: The Guilford Press. Mintz, S. (2004). *Huck's raft: A history of American childhood.* Cambridge, MA: Belknap Press of Harvard University.

10 The characterization is attributed to the Connecticut minister, Horace Bushnell (1802–1876), in Fass, *The end of American childhood,* 36.

11 Ibid, 40.

12 Kanner L. (1949). Problems of nosology and psychodynamics in early childhood autism. *American Journal of Orthopsychiatry,* 19(3), 416–26.

13 Hulbert, *Raising America,* 116.

14 U.S. Department of Labor (2016). Working mothers issue brief. Available from https://www.dol.gov/wb/resources/WB_WorkingMothers_508_FinalJune13.pdf.

In March 2015, 69.9% of mothers worked compared to 47.4% in 1975. Black mothers have the highest rates of working, with 76.3% in the labor force in 2015. Three-quarters of mothers work full-time, the rest part-time. Single parent families have also doubled since 1975.

15 This has been dubbed "intensive parenting" by Hays, S. (1996). *The*

cultural contradictions of motherhood. New Haven: The Yale University Press.

16 Flouri, E., Midouhas, E., & Hoshi, H. (2014). The role of urban neighbourhood green space in children's emotional and behavioural resilience. *Journal of Environmental Psychology*, 40, 179–18. Roubinov, D., Hagan, M., Boyce, W., Adler, N., & Bush, N. (2018) Family socioeconomic status, cortisol, and physical health in early childhood: The role of advantageous neighborhood characteristics. *Psychosomatic Medicine*. Shonkoff, J., & Deborah, P. (Eds.) (2000). *From neurons to neighborhoods: The science of early childhood development*. Washington, D.C.: National Academy Press. Younan, D. et al., (2016). Environmental determinants of aggression in adolescents: Role of urban neighborhood greenspace. *Journal of the American Academy of Child & Adolescent Psychiatry*, 55(7), 591-601.

17 For examples and discussions about how neoliberal policies and philosophies affect families: Blum, L. (2015). *Raising generation Rx: Mothering kids with invisible disabilities in an age of inequality*. New York: New York University Press. Cooper, M. (2014). *Cut adrift: Families in insecure times*. Oakland, CA: University of California Press. Garrett, R., Jensen, T., & Voela, A. (Eds.). (2016). We need to talk about family: essays on neoliberalism, the family and popular culture. United Kingdom: Cambridge Scholars Publishing. Putnam, R. (2015). *Our kids: The American dream in crisis*. New York: Simon & Schuster.

18 Allard, S. (2009). *Out of reach: Place, poverty, and the new American welfare state*. New Haven, CT: Yale University Press. Edin, K., & Shaefer, H. (2015). *$2.00 a day: Living on almost nothing in America*. New York: Houghton Mifflin Harcourt.

19 Dionne, E. J. (2012). *Our divided political heart: The battle for the American idea in an age of discontent*. New York: Bloomsbury. Petev, I. (2013). The association of social class and lifestyles: Persistence in American sociability, 1974 and 2010. *American Sociological Review*, 78, 633–61. Putnam, R. (2000). *Bowling alone: The collapse and revival of American community*. New York: Simon & Schuster.

20 Edin & Shaefer, *$2.00 a day*. Lindhert, P., & Williamson, J. (2016). *Unequal gains: American growth and inequality since 1700*. Princeton, NJ: Princeton University Press. Schulte, B. (June 23, 2014). The U.S. ranks last in every measure when it comes to family policy, in ten charts. *The Washington Post*. Smeeding, T., Erikson, R., & Janti, M. (2011). *Persistence, privilege, and parenting: The comparative study of intergenerational*

mobility. Russell Sage Foundation. Pew Research Center (November, 2015). *Global support for principle of free expression, but opposition to some forms of speech.* Retrieved from http://assets.pewresearch.org/wp-content/uploads/sites/2/2015/11/Pew-Research-Center-Democracy-Report-FINAL-November-18-2015.pdf. U.S. Department of Labor (2016). Working mothers issue brief. Available from https://www.dol.gov/wb/resources/WB_WorkingMothers_508_FinalJune13.pdf.

21   Deming, D. (2015). *The growing importance of social skills in the labor market.* (Working Paper Series No. 21473). Cambridge, MA: National Bureau of Economic Research. Heckman, J., Stixrud, J., & Urzua, S. (2006). *The effects of cognitive and noncognitive abilities on labor market outcomes and social behavior* (Working Paper Series No. 12006). Cambridge, MA: National Bureau of Economic Research.

22   Pew Research Center: Social and Demographic Trends. (2015). *Parenting in America: Outlook, worries, aspirations are strongly linked to financial situation.* Retrieved from http://www.pewsocialtrends. org/2015/12/17/parenting-in-america/.

Chapter Two

1   Guyer, R. (2006). *Baby at risk: The uncertain legacies of medical miracles for babies, families, and society.* Herndon, Virginia: Capital Books, Inc.

2   Blum, *Raising Generation Rx.* Bopti, A., Brown, T., & Lentin, P. (2016). Family quality of life: A key outcome in early childhood intervention services—A scoping review. *Journal of Early Intervention,* 38(4), 191–211. Inta, I., Alda, J., Chamorro, M., Espadas, M., & Huguet, A. (2018). Difference in psychic distress lived by parents with ADHD children and parents with healthy children: Focus on gender differences. *Journal of Attention Disorders,* published online August 2, 2018. Karp, D. (2002). *Burden of sympathy: How families cope with mental illness.* Cary, North Carolina: Oxford University Press. McConell, D., Savage, A., & Breitkreuz, R. (2014). Resilience in families raising children with disabilities and behavior problems. *Research in Developmental Disabilities,* 35, 833–848. Tint, A., & Weiss, J. (2016). Family wellbeing of individuals with autism spectrum disorder: A scoping review. *Autism,* 20(3), 262–275. U.S. Department of Health and Human Services, Health Resources and Services Administration, Maternal and Child Health Bureau. (2103). *The National Survey of Children with Special Health Care Needs Chartbook* 2009–2010. Rockville, Maryland: U.S. Department of Health and Human Services. Retrieved from https://mchb.hrsa.gov/cshcn0910/more/pdf/nscshcn0910. pdf.

3 Habitat for Humanity: https://www.habitat.org/housing-help/apply.

4 Treehouse Communities: https://refca.net/what-we-do/treehouse-community/treehouse-easthampton.html.

5 A list of grants is available at https://www.homeadvisor.com/r/grants-for-home-modification/.

6 Information on SSI COLAs are available at https://www.ssa.gov/oact/cola/colaseries.html. For food stamps, the information is available at https://www.fns.usda.gov/snap/cost-living-adjustment-cola-information.

7 DDS services are outlined in the Annual Family Support plan, available at http://www.mass.gov/eohhs/docs/dmr/reports/family-support/annual-plan-family-support-fy16.pdf.

8 Blum, *Raising Generation Rx.*

9 For a fairly comprehensive history see the article, "Historical background and development of Social Security" on the Social Security website: https://www.ssa.gov/history/briefhistory3.html.

10 https://www.servicenet.org

11 For fiscal year 2018, Health and Human Services, which includes mental health and disability programs, takes up a 56% share of the Massachusetts state budget. Massachusetts is more generous than other states, but services remain underfunded, and there are always legislative debates over which programs to prioritize and how to allocate funds. See http: http://budget.digital.mass.gov/bb/h1/fy18h1/brec_18/ga_18/hdefault.html. Hodgkin, D., & Karpman, H. (2010). Economic crises and public spending on mental health care. *International Journal of Mental Health,* 39(2), 91–106.

12 Psychiatric and other service shortages are prevalent throughout the country, and worse in rural areas. The demands on parents to advocate and find services is also high. Anderson, J. et al. (2017). A scoping literature review of service-level barriers for access and engagement with mental health services for children and young people. *Children and Youth Services Review,* 77, 164–176. Hazen, E., & Prager, L. (2017). A quiet crisis: Pediatric patients waiting for inpatient psychiatric care. *Journal of the American Academy of Child & Adolescent Psychiatry,* 56(8), 631-633. Levin, A. (2017). Report details national shortage of psychiatrists and possible solutions. *Psychiatric News,* American Psychiatric Association. Retrieved from http://psychnews.psychiatryonline.org/doi/full/10.1176/appi.pn.2017.4b24. Marshall, J., Adelman, A., Kesten, S., Natale, R., & Elbaum, B. (2017). Parents' experiences navigating intervention systems for young children with mild language delays. *Journal of Early Intervention,* 39(3), 180–198.

13 Orzechowski, E. (2016). *"You'll Like It Here" — The Story of Donald Vitkus, Belchertown Patient #3394*. Amherst, MA: Levellers Press. Olmstead v. L.C. Retrieved from https://en.wikipedia.org/wiki/Olmstead_v._L.C. Page. Ricci v. Okin Retrieved from Civil Rights Litigation Clearinghouse, Retrieved from https://www.clearinghouse.net/detail.php?id=454.

14 Pan, D. (April 29, 2013). TIMELINE: Deinstitutionalization and its Consequences. *Mother Jones*. Pollack, H. (June 12, 2013). What happened to U.S. mental health care after deinstitutionalization? *The Washington Post*. Torrey, E. (1997). *Out of the shadows: Confronting America's mental illness crisis*. New York: John Wiley & Sons.

Chapter Three

1 Athol statistics: Athol, MA government statistics retrieved form http://www.athol-ma.gov/sites/atholma/files/quick_facts_athol.pdf. For census data on income levels: https://www.census.gov. School data from the Massachusetts Department of Elementary and Secondary Education is available at http://profiles.doe.mass.edu/general/general.aspx?topNavID=1&leftNavId=100&orgcode=06150000&orgtypecode=5. Information on teen births retrieved from Office of Data Management and Outcomes Assessment, Massachusetts Department of Public Health, December 2014: http://www.mass.gov/eohhs/docs/dph/research-epi/teen-births-2013.pdf.

2 Lord, W. (1953). *History of Athol, Massachusetts*. Madison, Wisconsin: The University of Wisconsin–Madison. Montachusett Regional Planning Commission and the Franklin Regional Council of Governments. (2002). *Economic development chapter-Athol master plan*. Retrieved from http://www.athol-ma.gov/sites/atholma/files/file/file/600031227723406.pdf.

3 Conuel, T. (1990). *Quabbin: The Accidental Wilderness*. Amherst, Massachusetts: University of Massachusetts Press. Green, J. (2001). *The creation of Quabbin Reservoir: The death of the Swift River Valley*. Athol, MA: The Transcript Press.

4 Athol, MA government statistics retrieved from http://www.athol-ma.gov/sites/atholma/files/quick_facts_athol.pdf.

5 Article 14, otherwise known as Chapter 14, according to military statutes, is a discharge given to a soldier due to a pattern of minor misconduct, conduct lacking good order and discipline, or a single act of serious misconduct.

6 Massachusetts Department of Children and Families: https://www.mass.gov/orgs/massachusetts-department-of-children-families.

7 North Quabbin Patch Program: http://valuingourchildren.org/patch.html.

8 CDC-Kaiser ACE Study: https://www.cdc.gov/violenceprevention/acestudy/about.html.

9 The National Survey of Children's Health: http://www.childhealthdata.org/learn/NSCH.

10 Child Trends Data Bank. (2013). *Adverse experiences: Indicators of child and youth well-being*. Retrieved from https://www.childtrends.org/wp-content/uploads/2013/07/124_Adverse_Experiences-1.pdf.

11 Conger, R., Conger, K., & Martin, M. (2010). Socioeconomic status, family processes, and individual development. *Journal of Marriage and Family, 72*, 685–704. Gillies, V. (2007). *Marginalized mothers: Exploring working-class experiences in parenting*. New York, NY: Routledge. Hanson, T., McLanahan, S., & Thomson, E. (1999). Economic resources, parental practices and children's well-being. In G. Duncan & J. Brooks-Gunn (Eds.), *Consequences of growing up poor* (pp. 190–258). New York: Russell Sage Foundation. Jones, T., Nurius, P., Song, S., & Fleming, C. (2018). Modeling life course pathways from adverse childhood experiences to adult mental health. *Child Abuse & Neglect, 80*, 32–40. Lareau, A. (2011). *Unequal childhoods: Class, race and family life*. Berkeley: University of California Press. Lynch, J. W., Kaplan, G. A., & Shema, S. J. (1997). Cumulative impact of sustained economic hardship on physical, cognitive, psychological, and social functioning. *The New England Journal of Medicine, 337*(26), 1889-1895. Maguire-Jack, K., & Wang, X. (2016). Pathways from neighborhood to neglect: The mediating effects of social support and parenting stress. *Children and Youth Services Review 66*, 28–34. Pelton, L. (2015). The continuing role of material factors in child maltreatment and placement. *Child Abuse & Neglect, 41*, 30–39. Russell. M., Harris, B., & Gockel, A. (2008). Parenting in poverty: Perspectives of high-risk parents. *Journal of Children and Poverty, 14*, 83–98. Schneider, W., Waldfogel, J., & Brooks-Gunn, J. (2015). The great recession and behavior problems in 9-year old children. *Developmental Psychology, 51*, 1615–1629. Sharkey, P., & Elwert, F. (2011). The legacy of disadvantage: Multigenerational neighborhood effects on cognitive ability. *American Journal of Sociology, 116* (6), 1934–1981. Shonkoff, J., Garner, A, et al. (2012). The lifelong effects of early childhood adversity and toxic stress. *Pediatrics, 129*, e232–e246. Smeeding, T. Erikson, R., & Janti, M. (2011). *Persistence, privilege, and parenting*: The comparative study of intergenerational mobility. Russell Sage Foundation.

12   Pew Research Center: Social and Demographic Trends (2015) "Parenting in America: Outlook, worries, aspirations are strongly linked to financial situation." Retrieved from http://www.pewsocialtrends.org/2015/12/17/
parenting-in-america/.

13   Furstenberg, F. (2007). *Destinies of the disadvantaged: The politics of
teen childbearing.* Russel Sage Foundation, 164.

14   Gunnar, M., & Quevedo, K. (2007). The neurobiology of stress and
development. *Annual Review of Psychology,* 58, 145–173. Kochanska, G.,
Philibert, R., & Barry, R. (2009). Interplay of genes and early mother–child
relationship in the development of self-regulation from toddler to preschool
age. *Journal of Child Psychology and Psychiatry,* 50(11), 1331–1338.
Luthar, S. S. (Ed.) (2003). *Resilience and vulnerability: Adaptation in the
context of childhood adversities.* New York: Cambridge University Press.
Schore, A. (2001). Effects of a secure attachment relationship on right brain
development, affect regulation, and infant mental health. *Infant Mental
Health Journal,* 22 (1/2), 7–66. Smeekens, S., Riksen-Walraven, J., & van
Bakel, H. (2007). Multiple determinants of externalizing behavior in 5-year-
olds: A longitudinal model. *Journal of Abnormal Psychology,* 35, 347–361.
Sroufe, L. A., Egeland, B., Carlson, E. A., & Collins, W. A. (2005). *The
development of the person: The Minnesota study of risk and adaptation
from birth to adulthood.* New York: Guilford Press.

15   Brody, G., Yu, T., Chen, E., Miller, G., Kogan, S., & Beach, S. (2013). Is
resilience only skin deep? Rural African Americans' socio- economic status-
related risk and competence in preadolescence and psychological adjustment
and allostatic load at age 19. *Psychological Science,* 24(7), 1285–1293.
Miller, G., Yu, T., Chen, E., & Brody, G. (2015). Self-control forecasts
better psychosocial outcomes but faster epigenetic aging in low-SES youth
*Proceedings of the National Academy of Sciences of the United States of
America,* 112(33), 10325–10330.

16   Bristow, G. (2016). *The sociology of generations: New directions and
challenges.* United Kingdom: Palgrave Macmillan. Cancian, M., Yang, M. &
Slack, K. (2013). The effect of additional child support income on the risk
of child maltreatment. *Social Service Review,* 87(3), 417-437. Desmond, M.
(2016). *Evicted: Poverty and profit in the American City.* New York: Crown
Publishers. Janczewski, C. (2015). The influence of differential response
on decision-making in child protective service agencies. *Child Abuse &
Neglect,* 39, 50–60. Putnam, *Our kids.* Paruch, D. (2006). The orphaning
of underprivileged children: America's failed child welfare law and policy.
Journal of Law and Family Studies, 8, 119–165. Wright, T. (2013) 'Making
It' versus satisfaction: How women raising young children in poverty assess

how well they are doing. *Journal of Social Service Research*, 39(2), 269-280.

17 Cooke, K. Rohde, D., & McNeil, R. (December 20, 2012). Special Report: The Unequal State of America–Lean times for the "undeserving poor." Retrieved from https://www.reuters.com/article/us-equality-indiana/special-report-the-unequal-state-of-america-lean-times-for-the-undeserving-poor-idUSBRE8BJ0IO20121220. "ambivalence about helping the poor is widespread. A Reuters/Ipsos poll of Americans in October and November found that 52 percent of respondents said the government isn't doing enough to help the poor. Yet 40 percent said that most people who receive aid don't deserve it, a follow-up survey found."

This attitude has also been expressed by a number of conservatives as a reason to limit benefits and entitlements. Starting with Reagan's claims of "welfare queens" who were cheating the system, and earning benefits without trying to better themselves, this argument has been put forward. In fact, the US spends a lot of money on anti-poverty programs, and they have been shown to help, although they remain insufficient. Ideology and poorly run programs helped turn the tide against providing more generous benefits. For a larger discussion see: Edin & Shaefer, *$2.00 a day*. Irwin, N. (April 15, 2017). Supply-side economics, but for liberals. *New York Times*.

18 Edin & Shaefer, *$2.00 a day*.

19 Center for Poverty Research, University of California, Davis. Retrieved from https://poverty.ucdavis.edu/faq/what-current-poverty-rate-united-states.

20 Blaustein, M., & Kinniburgh, K. (2010). *Treating traumatic stress in children and adolescents: How to foster resilience through attachment, self-regulation, and competency*. New York, NY: Guilford Press. Holmes, J. (2017). Roots and routes to resilience and its role in psychotherapy: Lieberman, A., & Van Horn, P. (2008). *Psychotherapy with infants and young children: Repairing the effects of stress and trauma on early attachments*. New York, NY: Guilford Press. Padesky, C., & Mooney, K. (2012). Strengths-based cognitive–behavioural therapy: A four-step model to build resilience. *Clinical Psychology & Psychotherapy*, 19(4), 283–290.

21 Moving to Opportunity for Fair Housing: https://www.hud.gov/programdescription/mto.

22 Chetty, R., Hendren, N., & Katz, L. (2016). The effects of exposure to better neighborhoods on children: New evidence from the moving to opportunity project. *American Economic Review* 106(4), 855–902. Another study with similar conclusions: Schwarz, H. (2010). *Housing policy is school policy: Economically integrative housing promotes academic success*

in Montgomery county, Maryland. The Century Foundation. Retrieved from https://tcf.org/assets/downloads/tcf-Schwartz.pdf.

23   Chetty, R., & Hendren, N. (2016). *The impacts of neighborhoods on intergenerational mobility: Childhood exposure effects and county-level estimates.* Working paper retrieved from https://scholar.harvard.edu/files/hendren/files/nbhds_paper.pdf.

24   Brooks-Gunn, J., & Duncan, G. (1997). The effects of poverty on children. *The Future of Children, 7*(2), 55–71. Cancian, M., Yang, M. & Slack, K. (2013). The effect of additional child support income on the risk of child maltreatment. *Social Service Review, 87*(3), 417–437. Conger, R., Conger, K., & Martin, M. (2010). Socioeconomic status, family processes, and individual development. *Journal of Marriage and Family, 72*, 685–704. Pelton, L. (2015). The continuing role of material factors in child maltreatment and placement. *Child Abuse & Neglect, 41*, 30–39. Raffington, L., Prindle, J., & Shing, Y. (2018). Income gains predict cognitive functioning longitudinally throughout later childhood in poor children. *Developmental Psychology, 54*(7), 1232-1243.

25   There are a number of constraints that also limit welfare's usefulness besides the low amount of income it provides: Time limits, the need to work or volunteer to receive benefits (without provisions to ensure people get jobs), and the transferring of benefits to non-cash allowances for food and other resources so that families do not have flexibility in spending the money and may not be able to pay other bills. Edin & Shaefer, $2.00 *a day.*

26   Desmond, *Evicted.* Schaak, G., Sloane, L., Arienti, F., & Zolvistoski, A. (2017). *Priced out: The housing crisis for people with disabilities.* Boston, MA: Technical Assistance Collaborative, Inc. In Massachusetts, as in other areas of the country, waiting lists for subsidized housing are long and it can take years before receiving housing. The cost of renting has also gone up in many communities. The cost of housing has far outpaced SSI benefits, making housing difficult to attain.

27   As noted in the earlier chapter, a shortage of mental health providers exists and waiting lists can be long. Communities must also decide what services to offer and so some may not be available in a certain locale.

28   Substance Abuse and Mental Health Services Administration (2015). *Behavioral Health Barometer: Massachusetts,* 2015. HHS Publication No. SMA–16–Baro–2015–MA. Rockville, MD: Substance Abuse and Mental Health Services Administration.

29   Commonwealth of Massachusetts (November 14, 2017). *Governor's*

working group on opioids update: *Action Items*. Available from https://www.mass.gov/files/documents/2017/11/15/2017-annual-update-action-items-gov-working-group.pdf.

Chapter Four

1 Wilder, L. I. (1953). *Little house in the Big Woods*. New York: Harper Collins Publishers, Inc., 44.

2 Information about Northampton is available at the city's website: http://www.northamptonma.gov/150/Demographics-Statistics or through census data: https://factfinder.census.gov/faces/nav/jsf/pages/community_facts.xhtml?src=bkmk.

The city is also listed on a number of websites as being friendly to lesbians:

https://www.autostraddle.com/the-21-most-lesbianish-cities-in-the-us-128377/. https://www.liveabout.com/top-itemcount-top-lesbian-cities-in-the-united-states-2171190.

3 Sears, B., & Sears, M. (2001). *The attachment parenting book: A commonsense guide to understanding and nurturing your baby*. New York, Boston: Little, Brown and Company.

4 Davis, L. (1997). *Becoming the parent you want to be: A sourcebook of strategies for the first five years*. New York: Broadway Books. Leach, P. (1978). *Your baby and child: From birth to five*. New York: Knopf Doubleday Publishing Group.

5 United States Department of Labor Children's Bureau. (1914). *Infant Care*. Washington D.C.: United States Government Printing office. Revised edition, published in 1929 is available online: https://archive.org/details/infantcareoounit.

6 Hulbert, *Raising America*.

7 Ibid. Fass, *The end of American childhood*.

8 Spock, B. (1946). *The common sense book of baby and child care*. New York: Duel, Sloan and Pearce. According to Wikipedia (https://en.wikipedia.org/wiki/The_Common_Sense_Book_of_Baby_and_Child_Care), the book is one of the biggest selling books of the twentieth century. It sold fifty million copies by the time of Spock's death and has been translated into thirty-nine languages.

9 Fass, *The end of American childhood*.

10 Ibid. Hays, *Intensive parenting*. Hulbert, *Raising America*.

11 Dominant childrearing methods include books such as written by Leach and Davis, as well as Brazelton, T., & Sparrow, J. (2002). *Touchpoints 3 to 6*. USA: DeCapo Lifelong Books. The ideas also show up in parent training curriculum offered to parents. Three of the most prominent include the following programs: Eyberg, S. M., & Bussing, R. (2010). Parent-child interaction therapy. In M. Murrihy, A. Kidman, & T. Ollendick (Eds.), *A clinician's handbook for the assessment and treatment of conduct problems in youth*, (pp. 139–162). New York, NY: Springer. Sanders, M. (2008). Triple P-Positive Parenting Program as a public health approach to strengthening parenting. *Journal of Family Psychology, 22*, 506–517. Webster-Stratton, C. (2005). *The Incredible Years: A trouble-shooting guide for parents of children aged 2–8 years*. The Incredible Years. For a review, see Zilberstein, K. (2016). Class matters in parenting interventions. *Clinical Child Psychology and Psychiatry, 21*(3), 359–367.

12 Sunderland, M. (2006). *The science of parenting*. New York: DK Publishing.

13 Christopher, K. (2012). Extensive mothering: Employed mothers' constructions of the good mother. *Gender & Society, 26*(1), 73–96. Cooper, *Cut adrift*. Edin, K., & Kefalas, M. (2005). *Promises I can keep: Why poor women put motherhood before marriage*. Berkeley, CA: University of California Press. Gillies, *Marginalized mothers*. McMahon, M. (1995). *Engendering motherhood: Identity and self-transformation in women's lives*. New York: The Guilford Press. Lareau, *Unequal childhoods*.

14 Lancy, D. (2008). *The anthropology of childhood: Cherubs, chattel, changelings*. Cambridge, U.K.: Cambridge University Press.

15 Arnett, J. (2004). *Emerging adulthood: The winding road from the late teens through the twenties*. New York: Oxford University Press. Twenge, J., & Campbell, W. (2018). Cultural individualism is linked to later onset of adult-role responsibilities across time and regions. *Journal of Cross-Cultural Psychology*. Published online ahead of print.

16 Ford, J. (2009). Neurobiological and developmental research: Clinical implications. In C. Courtis & J. Ford (Eds.), *Treating complex traumatic stress disorders: An evidence-based guide* (pp. 31–58). New York, NY: Guilford Press. Gunnar & Quevedo, The neurobiology of stress and development. McCrory, E., DeBrito, S., & Viding, E. (2010). Research review: The neurobiology and genetics of maltreatment and adversity. *Journal of Child Psychology and Psychiatry, 51*(10), 1079–1095.

17 Dworkin, R. (Spring, 2012). Psychotherapy and the pursuit of happiness. *The New Atlantis*, 69–83. Gopaldas, A. (2016). Therapy. *Consumption Markets & Culture, 19*(3), 264–268.

18 Harris Poll. (2015). *A survey about mental health and suicide in the United States.* Retrieved from

http://actionallianceforsuicideprevention.org/sitesactionallianceforsuicidepr
evention.org/files/Mental%20Health%20and%20Suicide%2Executive%20
Summary%208%2027%2015%20(2).pdf.

19 Siegenthaler, E., Munder, T., & Egger, M. (2012). Effect of preventive interventions in mentally ill parents on the mental health of the offspring: Systematic review and meta-analysis. *Journal of the American Academy of Child & Adolescent Psychiatry,* 51(1), 8–17. Slade, A. (2005). Parental reflective functioning: An introduction. *Attachment & Human Development,* 7(3), 269–281.

20 Petev, The association of social class and lifestyles: Persistence in American sociability. Putnam, *Bowling alone.*

21 Abuse and Mental Health Services Administration (2015). *Behavioral Health Barometer: Massachusetts,* 2015. HHS Publication No. SMA–16–Baro–2015–MA. Rockville, MD: Substance Abuse and Mental Health Services Administration.

22 Baglivio, M., Wolff, K., Piquero, A., Greenwald, M., & Epps, N. (2017). Racial/ethnic disproportionality in psychiatric diagnoses and treatment in a sample of serious juvenile offenders. *Journal of Youth and Adolescence, 46,* 1424–1451. Chen, J., & Rizzo, J. (2010). Racial and ethnic disparities in use of psychotherapy: Evidence from U.S. National Survey data. *Psychiatric Services,* 61(4), 364–372. Epping, J., & Geyer, S. (2017). Social inequalities in the utilization of outpatient psychotherapy: Analyses of registry data from German statutory health insurance. *International Journal for Equity in Health,* 16, 147–155. Goodman, L., Pugach, M., Skolnik, A., & Smith, L. (2013). Poverty and mental health practice: Within and beyond the 50-minute hour. *Journal of Clinical Psychology: In Session,* 69(2), 182–190. Fernandez, M. (2011). Treatment outcome for low socioeconomic status African American families in parent child interaction therapy: A pilot study. *Child & Family Behavior Therapy,* 33, 32–48. Pugach, M., & Goodman, L. (2015). Low-income women's experiences in outpatient psychotherapy: A qualitative descriptive analysis. *Counselling Psychology Quarterly,* 28(4), 403–426. Zilberstein, K. (2016). Class matters in parenting interviews. Clinical Child Psychology and Psychiatry, 21(3), 359–367. Zuvekas, S., & Fleishman, J. (2008). Self-rated mental health and racial/ethnic disparities in mental health service use. *Medical Care,* 46(9), 915-923.

23 Fraynt, R., Ross, L., Baker, B., Rystad, I., Lee, J., & Briggs, E. (2014). Predictors of treatment engagement in ethnically diverse, urban children receiving treatment for trauma exposure. *Journal of Traumatic Stress,* 27, 66–

73. Snowden, L. (2003). Bias in mental health assessment and intervention: Theory and evidence. *American Journal of Public Health*, 93(2), 239–243. Whaley A. L. (2011). Clinicians' competence in assessing cultural mistrust among African American psychiatric patients. *Journal of Black Psychology*, 37, 387-406.

24 Anandi, M., Mullainathan, S., Shafir, E., & Zhao, J. (2013). Poverty impedes cognitive function. *Science*, 341, 976–980. Conger, R., Conger, K., & Martin, M. (2010). Socioeconomic status, family processes, and individual development. *Journal of Marriage and Family*, 72, 685–704. Lareau, *Unequal childhoods*. Russell, M., Harris, B., & Gockel, A. (2008). Parenting in poverty: Perspectives of high risk parents. *Journal of Children and Poverty*, 14, 83–98.

25 Chen, X., Bian, Y., Xin, T., Wang, L., & Silbereisen, R. K. (2010). Perceived social change and childrearing attitudes in China. *European Psychologist*, 15, 260–270. Gillies, *Marginalized mothers*. Lareau, *Unequal childhoods*. Winslow, E., Bonds, D., Wolchik, S., Sandler, I., & Braver, S. (2009). Predictors of enrollment and retention in a preventive parenting intervention for divorced families. *The Journal of Primary Prevention*, 30, 151–172.

26 Cushman, P. (1995). *Constructing the self, constructing America: A cultural history of psyhotherapy*. USA: Da Capo Press. Grogan, J. (2013). *Encountering America: Humanistic psychology, sixties culture and the shaping of the modern self*. New York: Harper Perennial. Illouz, E. (2008). *Saving the modern soul: Therapy, emotions and the culture of self-help*. Berkeley, CA: Universtity of California Press. Kirmayer, L. (2007). Psychotherapy and the cultural concept of the person. *Transcultural Psychiatry*, 44(2), 232-257. Rustin, M. (2015). Psychotherapy in a neoliberal world. *European Journal of Psychotherapy & Counselling*, 17(3), 225-239.

27 One recent trend in psychotherapy concerns an emphasis on attachment and close relationships and how psychotherapy can enhance those. Another is the use of cognitive behavioral techniques to build relationship and self-regulation skills, which have now been incorporated into a variety of different therapies, including Dialectical Behavioral Therapy and various therapies for survivors of childhood trauma or those with severe mental illnesses such as bipolar disorder or schizophrenia. For example: Blaustein & Kinniburgh, *Treating traumatic stress*. Holmes, J. (2017). Roots and routes to resilience and its role in psychotherapy: A selective, attachment-informed review. *Attachment & Human Development*, 19(4), 364–381. Linehan, M. (2014). *DBT Skills Training Manual*. (Second Ed.) New York: The Guilford Press. Misch, D. (2000). Basic strategies of dynamic supportive therapy.

Journal of Psychotherapy Practice and Research 9(4), 173–189. Padesky, C., & Mooney, K. (2012). Strengths-based cognitive–behavioural therapy: A four-step model to build resilience. *Clinical Psychology & Psychotherapy,* 19(4), 283–290.

28 The episode aired in fall of 2016.

Chapter Five

1 Job Corps is a federally funded program for low-income youth that provides academic and job skills training on residential campuses throughout the United States. Website: https://www.jobcorps.gov.

2 Centers for Disease Control and Prevention. *About teen pregnancy.* Retrieved from https://www.cdc.gov/teenpregnancy/about/.

3 Furstenberg, *Destinies of the disadvantaged.* Furstenberg, F. (2007). Teenage mothers in later life (and the researchers who study them). *Contexts,* 6(3), 78–79.

4 Flanagan, P. (1998). Teen mothers. Countering the myths of dysfunction and developmental disruption. In C. Garcia Coll, J. L. Surrey, & K. Weingarten (Eds.), *Mothering against the odds: Diverse voices of contemporary mothers.* New York: Guilford Press. Geronimus, A., & Sanders, K. (1992). The socioeconomic consequences of teen childbearing reconsidered. *Quarterly Journal of Economics,* 107(4), 1187–1214. Hoffman, S. (2015). Teen childbearing and economics: A short history of a 25-year research love affair. *Societies,* 5, 646–663. Kearney, M., &. Levine, P. (2010.). Socioeconomic disadvantage and early childbearing. In J Gruber (Ed.). *The problems of disadvantaged youth: An economic perspective.* Chicago: University of Chicago Press.

5 The Care Center: http://www.carecenterholyoke.org.

6 Wistariahurst. *Elizabeth Towne.* Retrieved from https://wistariahurst. org/women-making-change/elizabeth-towne/.

7 Studies confirm that school failure often precedes pregnancy and that supports are critical to how well teen parents perform: Brosh, J., Weigel, D., & Evans, W. (2007). Pregnant and parenting adolescents' perception of sources and supports in relation to educational goals. *Child & Adolescent Social Work Journal,* 24(6), 565–578. Melhado, L. (2007). Teenage parents' educational attainment is affected more by available resources than by parenthood. *Perspectives on Sexual and Reproductive Health,* 39(3), 184–185. SmithBattle, L. (2007). "I wanna have a good future": Teen

mothers' rise in educational aspirations, competing demands, and limited school support. *Youth & Society,* 38(3), 348–371. Zachry, E. M. (2005). Getting my education: Teen mothers' experiences in school before and after motherhood. *Teachers College Record,* 107(12), 2566–2598.

8   Edin & Kefalas, *Promises I can Keep.* Flanagan, *Mothering against the odds.* Furstenberg, *Destinies of the disadvantaged.* Gregson, J. (2009). *The culture of teenage mothers.* Albany, New York: State University of New York Press. Rolfe, A. (2008). 'You've got to grow up when you've got a kid': Marginalized young women's accounts of motherhood. *Journal of Community & Applied Social Psychology,* 18, 299–314.

9   Greenfield, P. (2009). Linking social change and developmental change: Shifting pathways of human development. *Developmental Psychology,* 45, 401–418. Greenfield, P. (2016). Social change, cultural evolution, and human development. *Current Opinion in Psychology,* 8, 84–92.

10   Lareau, *Unequal childhoods.*

11   This trend has been shown to occur cross-culturally. Chen, X., Bian, Y., Xin, T., Wang, L., & Silbereisen, R. K. (2010). Perceived social change and childrearing attitudes in China. *European Psychologist,* 15, 260–270. Keller, H. (2012). Autonomy and relatedness revisited: Cultural manifestations of universal human needs. *Child Development Perspectives,* 6, 12–18. Lancy, *The anthropology of childhood.* Lareau, *Unequal childhood.* Martins, G., Goncalves, T., Marin, A., Piccinini, C., Spern, T., & Tudge, J. (2015). Social class, workplace experience, and child-rearing values of mothers and fathers in southern Brazil. *Journal of Cross-Cultural Psychology,* 46, 996–1009. Park, H., Coello, J., & Lau, A. (2014). Child socialization goals in East Asian versus western nations from 1989 to 2010: Evidence for social change in parenting. *Parenting: Science and Practice,* 14, 69–91.

12   Gillies, *Marginalized mothers,* 83.

13   For information on subsidized housing in Massachusetts: https://www.mass.gov/service-details/a-guide-to-obtaining-housing-assistance:

"How to apply for state public housing: You must put your name on a waiting list that is kept by the local housing authority. Applicants may put their name on more than one waiting list if they qualify for more than one program. Waiting lists for public housing tend to be long. When your name comes to the top of the list, the housing authority will contact you. Be sure to notify a housing authority if you change your address while you are waiting for a public housing unit."

14 Bond, G., Resnock, S., Drake, R., Xie, H., McHugo, G., & Bebout, R. (2001). Does competitive employment improve nonvocational outcomes for people with severe mental illness? *Journal of Consulting and Clinical Psychology*, 69(3), 489–501. Breslau, J., Lane, M., Sampson, N., & Kessler, R. (2008). Mental disorders and subsequent educational attainment in a US national sample. *Journal of Psychiatric Research*, 42(9), 708–716. Lehman, A., Goldberg, R., Dixon, L., McNary, S., Postrado, L., Hackman A., & McDonnell, K. (2002). Improving employment outcomes for persons with severe mental illnesses. *Archives of General Psychiatry*, 59, 165–172. Sherman, M. (2007). Reaching out to children of parents with mental illness. *Social Work Today*, 7(5), 26. U.S. Department of Health & Human Services, Administration for Children and Families, Administration on Children, Youth and Families, Children's Bureau. (2017). *Child Maltreatment 2015*. Available from http://www.acf.hhs.gov/programs/cb/research-data-technology/statistics-research/child-maltreatment.

15 Dong, M., Anda, R., Felitti, V., Dube, S., Williamson, D., Thompson, T., Loo, C., & Giles, W. (2004). The interrelatedness of multiple forms of childhood abuse, neglect, and household dysfunction. *Child Abuse & Neglect* 28, 771–784.

16 American Academy of Child and Adolescent Psychiatry. (2008). Children of parents with mental illness. *Facts for families*, 39. Washington D.C. Duncan, S., & Reder, P. (2000). Children's experience of major psychiatric disorders in their parents: An overview. In P. Reder, M. McClure, & A. Jolley (Eds.), *Family matters*: (pp. 83–96). London: Routledge. Gela, N., & Corrigan, P. (2015). The stigma of families with mental illness. In J. Arditti (Ed.). *Family problems: Stress, risk, and resilience,* (pp. 33–49) United Kingdom: John Wiley & Sons, Inc. (pp. 33–49). Nomura, Y., Wickramaratne, P., Warner, V., Mufson, L., & Weissman, M. (2002). Family discord, parental depression and psychopathology in offspring: Ten-year follow-up. *Journal of American Academy of Child and Adolescent Psychiatry*, 41, 402–409. Sherman, M. (2007). Reaching out to children of parents with mental illness. *Social Work Today*, 7(5), 26. Siegenthaler, E., Munder, T., & Egger, M. (2012). Effect of preventive interventions in mentally ill parents on the mental health of the offspring: Systematic review and meta-analysis. *Journal of the American Academy of Child & Adolescent Psychiatry*, 51(1), 8–17.

17 For a discussion and descriptions of the pressures and competing demands on workers, see Duerr Berrick, J. (2017). *The Impossible imperative: Navigating the competing principles of child protection.* Oxford University Press. Kindle Edition.

18   Statistics show that of the 676,000 child victims served by child welfare in 2016:

- 74.8% were neglected
- 18.2 percent were physically abused
- 8.5 percent were sexually abused
- 1,700 died of abuse and neglect
- 3,472,000 children received an investigation or some other response from the system, an increase of 9.5% from 2012.

U.S. Department of Health & Human Services, Administration for Children and Families, Administration on Children, Youth and Families, Children's Bureau. (2018). *Child maltreatment 2016*. Available from https://www.acf.hhs.gov/cb/research-data-technology/statistics-research/child-maltreatment.

19   For a history and explanations of the child welfare system: *APSAC Advisor*. (2016). Issue 28(2). Fass, *The end of American childhood*. Lepore, J. (February 1, 2016). Baby Doe: A political history of tragedy. *The New Yorker*. Retrieved from https://www.newyorker.com/magazine/2016/02/01/baby-doe. McGowan, B. (2005). Historical evolution of child welfare services. In G. Mellon, & P. Hess (Eds.), *Child welfare for the twenty-first century*. New York: Columbia University Press. Wildeman, C., & Waldfogel, J. (2014). Somebody's children or nobody's children? How the sociological perspective could enliven research on foster care. *Annual Review of Sociology*, 40, 599–618.

20   Lepore, Baby Doe.

21   Hughes, R., & Vandervort, F. (2016). Differential response: A misrepresentation of investigation and case fact finding in child protective services. *APSAC Advisor*, 28(2), 12.

22   Bristow, *The sociology of generations*. Bywaters, P., Brady, G., Sparks, T., & Bos, E. (2016). Child welfare inequalities: New evidence, further questions. *Child & Family Social Work*, 21, 369–380. Paruch, D. (2006). The orphaning of underprivileged children: America's failed child welfare law and policy. *Journal of Law and Family Studies*, 8, 119–165.

23   Dill, K. (2007). Impact of stressors on front-line child welfare supervisors. *Clinical Supervisor*, 26(1/2), 177–193. Figley, C. (1995). *Compassion fatigue: Coping with secondary traumatic stress disorder in those who treat the traumatized*. Bristol, PA: Brunner/Mazel. Grffiths, A., Royce, D., & Walker, R. (2018). Stress among child protective service workers: Self-reported health consequences. *Children and Youth Services Review*, 90, 46–53. Pearlman, L., & Saakvitne, K. (1995). *Trauma and the therapist: Countertransference and vicarious traumatization in psychotherapy with incest survivors*. New York:

Norton. Sprang, G., Craig, C., & Clark, J. (2011). Secondary traumatic stress and burnout in child welfare workers: A comparative analysis of occupational distress across professional groups. *Child Welfare*, 90(6), 149–168.

24 Edwards, F., & Wildeman, C. (2018). Characteristics of the front-line child welfare workforce. *Children and Youth Services Review*, 89, 13–26.

Chapter Six

1 Census bureau statistics for Springfield can be found at https://www.census.gov/quickfacts/fact/table/springfieldcitymassachusetts/PST045217.

2 See Section 300.174 of the Individuals with Disabilities Education Act: Prohibition on mandatory medication. Retrieved from https://sites.ed.gov/idea/regs/b/b/300.174.

3 Lareau, *Unequal Childhoods*. Lareau, A. (2015). Cultural knowledge and social inequality. *American Sociological Review*, 80(1), 1–27.

4 Blum, *Raising Generation Rx*. Gillies, *Marginalized mothers*.

5 US Department of Justice, *Individuals with disabilities act*. Website: https://sites.ed.gov/idea/.

6 Chingos, M. (June 15, 2017). *How progressive is school funding in the United States?* Brookings Institute. Retrieved from https://www.brookings.edu/research/how-progressive-is-school-funding-in-the-united-states/.

7 Dixson, A., Clayton, D., Peoples, L., & Reynolds, R. (2016). The impact of racism on education and the educational experiences of students of color. In A. Alvarez, C. Liang, & H. Neville (Eds.) *The cost of racism for people of color: Contextualizing experiences of discrimination* (pp. 189–201). American Psychological Association. Mary, J., Calhoun, M., Tejada, J., & Jenson, J. (2018). Perceptions of academic achievement and educational opportunities among Black and African American youth. *Child and Adolescent Social Work Journal*. Published online ahead of print. Wiggan, G. (2014). Student achievement for whom? High-performing and still 'playing the game,' the meaning of school achievement among high achieving African American students. *Urban Review*, 46,476–492.

8 *School and district profiles*. Massachusetts Department of Elementary and Secondary Education. Retrieved from http://profiles.doe.mass.edu.

9 Vostanis, P., Taylor, H., Day, C., Edwards, R., Street, C., Weare, K., & Wolpert, M. (2011). Child mental health practitioners' knowledge and experiences of children's educational needs and services. *Clinical Child*

Psychology and Psychiatry, 16, 385–405. Zilberstein, K., & Popper, S. (2016). Clinical competencies for the effective treatment of foster children. *Clinical Child Psychology and Psychiatry*, 21(1), 32–47.

10   More information about the Federation for Children with Special Needs can be found on its website: https://fcsn.org/about-us/.

11   *FY 19 First-view budget*. Presented to the Northampton School Committee, February 27, 2018. Retrieved from https://drive.google.com/file/d/1Qd4yi2YupGfHFOweAf8Hv-zWEMgMeEZA/view. *School and district profiles*. Massachusetts Department of Elementary and Secondary Education. Retrieved from http://profiles.doe.mass.edu.

12   *Current opioid statistics*. Retrieved from https://www.mass.gov/lists/current-opioid-statistics#updated-data---q2-2018---as-of-august-2018-.

13   According to news reports, Springfield took in 590 students displaced by Hurricane Maria, the highest of any school district in Massachusetts. See https://www.masslive.com/news/index.ssf/2018/01/springfield_has_highest_number.html.

14   Dixson, et.al., *The cost of racism*. Nicholson-Crotty, S., Grisson, J., Nicholson-Crotty, J., & Redding, C. (2016). Disentangling the causal mechanism of representative bureaucracy: Evidence from assignment of students to gifted programs. *Journal of Public Administration and Theory*, 26(4), 745–757. Posey-Maddox, L. (2017). Race in place: Black parents, family–school relations, and multispatial microaggressions in a predominantly white suburb. *Teachers College Record* 119(110304), 1–42. U.S. Department of Justice. (2014). 2013–2014 *Civil rights data collection: A first Look: Key data highlights on equity and opportunity gaps in our nation's public schools*. Retrieved from https://www2.ed.gov/about/offices/list/ocr/docs/2013-14-first-look.pdf.

15   *FY 19 First-view budget*. Presented to the Northampton School Committee, February 27, 2018. Retrieved from https://drive.google.com/file/d/1Qd4yi2YupGfHFOweAf8Hv-zWEMgMeEZA/view. *School and district profiles*. Massachusetts Department of Elementary and Secondary Education. Retrieved from http://profiles.doe.mass.edu.

16   Graves, S., & Ye, F. (2017). Are special education labels accurate for black children? Racial differences in academic trajectories of youth diagnosed with specific learning and intellectual disabilities. *Journal of Black Psychology*, 43(2) 192–213. Mandell, D., Davis, J., Bevans, K., & Guevara, J. (2008). Ethnic disparities in special education labeling among children with Attention-Deficit/Hyperactivity Disorder. *Journal of Emotional and Behavioral Disorders*, 16(1), 42-51.

17 Derald Wing Sue, a professor of education and psychology at Columbia University's Teachers College, defines microaggressions as the unconscious snubs, "dismissive looks, gestures, and tones" directed at people of color, "that impair performance... [sap] the psychic and spiritual energy of recipients and [create] inequities." Sue, D., Capodilup, C., Torino, G., Bucceri, A., Holder, B., Nadal, K., & Esquilin, M. (2007). Racial microaggressions in everyday life. *American Psychologist*, 62(4), 271–286, p. 273. Racism and microaggressions count as traumas, or adverse experiences, delivering the same effects as other ACES. As exposures pile up, they impair physical and mental health. Common responses include anxiety, depression, fear, stress, anger, and lowered self-esteem. See: Hollingsworth, D., Cole, A., O'Keefe, V., Tucker, R., Story, C., & Wingate, L. (2017). Experiencing racial microaggressions influences suicide ideation through perceived burdensomeness in African Americans. *Journal of Counseling Psychology*, 64(1), 104–111. Lanier, Y., Sommers, M., Fletcher, J., Sutton, M., & Roberts, D. (2017). Examining racial discrimination frequency, racial discrimination stress, and psychological well- being among black early adolescents. *Journal of Black Psychology*, 3(3), 219–229. Nadal, K. (2018). *Microaggressions and traumatic stress: Theory, research, and clinical treatment.* American Psychological Association. Weng, C., & West, L. (2016). Social connectedness and intolerance of uncertainty as moderators between racial microaggressions and anxiety among black individuals. *Journal of Counseling Psychology*, 63(2), 240–246.

18 Posey-Maddox, L. (2017). Race in place: Black parents, family–school relations, and multispatial microaggressions in a predominantly white suburb. *Teachers College Record* 119(110304), 1–42.

19 McKay, M., Atkins, M., Hawkins, T., Brown, C., & Lynn, C. (2003). Inner-city African American parental involvement in children's schooling: Racial socialization and social support from the parent community. *American Journal of Community Psychology*, 32(1/2), 107–114.

20 American Civil Liberties Union. (October 27, 2014). Racial disparities in sentencing. Written submission to the Hearing on Reports of Racism in the Justice System of the United States. Retrieved from https://www.aclu.org/sites/default/files/assets/141027_iachr_racial_disparities_aclu_submission_0. pdf. Rhodes, W., Kling, R., Luallen, J., & Dyous, C. (2015). *Federal sentencing disparity:* 2005–2012. Bureau of Justice Statistics, United States Department of Justice. Retrieved from https://www.bjs.gov/content/pub/pdf/fsdo512.pdf.

21 Langton, L., & Durose, M. (2013). *Police behavior during traffic and street stops,* 2011. (NCJ 242937). Washington, DC: Bureau of Justice Statistics, U.S. Department of Justice. Retrieved from https://www.bjs.gov/

content/pub/pdf/pbtss11.pdf. Teasley, M., Schiele, J., Adams, C., & Okliwa, N. (2018). Trayvon Martin: Racial profiling, black male stigma, and social work practice. *Social Work, 63*(1), 37–45.

22 Bor, J., Venkataramani, A., Williams. D., & Tsai, A. (June 21, 2018). Police killings and their spillover effects on the mental health of black Americans: A population-based, quasi-experimental study. *The Lancet.* Retrieved from https://www.thelancet.com/pdfs/journals/lancet/PIIS0140-6736(18)31130-9.pdf.

23 *Annual report on the state of the Massachusetts court system FY2017.* Retrieved from https://www.mass.gov/files/documents/2018/05/15/fy17-annual-report.pdf.

24 Baglivio, M., Wolff, K., Piquero, A., Greenwald, M., & Epps, N. (2017). Racial/ethnic disproportionality in psychiatric diagnoses and treatment in a sample of serious juvenile offenders. *Journal of Youth and Adolescence, 46,* 1424–1451.

25 Anderson, M. (August 12, 2014). *Vast majority of blacks view the criminal justice system as unfair.* Pew Research Center. Retrieved from http://www.pewresearch.org/fact-tank/2014/08/12/vast-majority-of-blacks-view-the-criminal-justice-system-as-unfair/.

26 Detlaff, A. (2011). Disproportionality of Latino children in child welfare. In D. Green, K. Belanger, & R. McRoy (Eds.). *Challenging racial disproportionality in child welfare: Research, policy & practice* (p. 119–129). Child Welfare League of America. Detlaff, A. & Rycraft, J. (2010). Factors contributing to disproportionality in the child welfare system: Views from the legal system. *Social Work, 55*(3), 213–224. Fluke, J., Harden, B., Jenkins, M., & Ruehrdanz, A. (2011). *A research synthesis on child welfare disproportionality and disparities.* Retrieved from http://www.cssp.org/publications/childwelfare/alliance/Disparities-and-Disproportionality-in-Child-Welfare_An-Analysis-of- the Research-December-2011.pdf . Font, S., Berger, L. & Slack, K. (2012). Examining racial disproportionality in child protective services case decisions. *Children and Youth Services Review, 34,* 2188–2200. Maguire-Jack, K., Lanier, P., Johnson-Motoyama, M., Welch, H., & Dineen, M. (2015). Geographic variation in racial disparities in child maltreatment: The influence of county poverty and population density. *Child Abuse & Neglect, 47,* 1–13. Putnam-Hornstein, E., Needell, B., King, B., & Johnson- Motoyama, M. (2013). Racial and ethnic disparities: A population-based examination of risk factors for involvement with child protective services. *Child Abuse & Neglect, 37,* 33–46.

27 Outley, A. (2006). Overcoming barriers to permanency: Recommen- dations for juvenile and dependency courts. *Family Court Review, 44*(2),

244-257. Summers, A., Gatowski, S., & Dobbin, S. (2012). Terminating parental rights: The relation of judicial experience and expectancy-related factors to risk perceptions in child protection cases. *Psychology, Crime & Law,* 18(1), 95–112.

28   Azar, S., & Cote, L. (2002). Sociocultural issues in the evaluation of the needs of children in custody decision making: What do our current frameworks for evaluating parenting practices have to offer? *International Journal of Law and Psychiatry,* 25, 193–217. Zilberstein, K. (2016). Parenting in families of low socioeconomic status: A review with implications for child welfare practice. *Family Court Review,* 54(2), 221–231.

29   *Annual report on the state of the Massachusetts court system FY2017.*

30   A fuller description of the Oliver case and its repercussions can be found in Chapter Five.

31   McDonald, D. (October 27, 2017). SJC chief calls attorney shortage for child care and protection cases 'a constitutional emergency.' *The Boston Globe.*

32   Stevenson, L. (1999). Fair play or a stacked deck?: In search of a proper standard of proof in juvenile dependency hearings. *Pepperdine Law Review,* 26(3), 613–630. McWey, L., Henderson, T., & Alexander, J. (2008). Parental rights and the foster care system: A glimpse of decision-making in Virginia. *Journal of Family Issues,* 29(8), 1031–1050.

33   *Annual report on the state of the Massachusetts court system FY2017.*

34   "Kids come home from school with bruises," said educational advocate, Alison Greene, "from behavior that wasn't prevented, self-injury, or restraints. Certain types of restraint are legal as a last result to prevent serious bodily harm. Every district has staff who have been specially trained in restraints. But there are also people, in every district, who do it wrong." For more information, see Bulter, J. (2017). *How safe is the schoolhouse? An analysis of state seclusion and restraint laws and policies.* Retrieved from http://www.autcom.org/pdf/HowSafeSchoolhouse.pdf.

Chapter Seven

1   See discussion in Chapter Three of the history and controversy surrounding those institutions.

2   O'Hare, W. (2008). *Data on children in foster care from the Census Bureau.* Baltimore, MD: The Annie E. Casey Foundation. Retrieved from http://www.lists.mobile.aecf.org/m/pdf/FosterChildren-July-2008.pdf. Other reports show similar findings: Kirby, K. (1997). Foster parent demographics: A research note. *The Journal of Sociology & Social Welfare,* 24(2), 135–141.

3   Vandivere, S., Malm, K., & Radel, L. (2009). *Adoption USA: A chartbook based on the* 2007 *National Survey of Adoptive Parents*. Washington, D.C.: The U.S. Department of Health and Human Services, Office of the Assistant Secretary for Planning and Evaluation.

4   Ahn, H., DePanfilis, D., Frick, K., & Barth, R. (2018). Estimating minimum adequate foster care costs for children in the United States. *Children and Youth Services Review, 84,* 55–67. The study found that rates paid to foster parents in all but four states do not cover adequate costs of raising a child.

5   Kurzban, R., Burton-Chellew, M., & West, S. (2015). The evolution of altruism in humans. *Annual Review of Psychology, 66,* 575–599. Marsh, A. (2016). Neural, cognitive, and evolutionary foundations of human altruism. *WIREs Cognitive Science, 7,* 59–71. Preston, S. (2013). The origins of altruism in offspring care. *Psychological Bulletin,* 139(6), 1305-1341.

6   Miller, J., Kahle, S., & Hastings, P. (2015). Roots and benefits of costly giving: Children who are more altruistic have greater autonomic flexibility and less family wealth. *Psychological Science,* 26(7), 1038–1045. Piff, P., & Robinson, A. (2017). Social class and prosocial behavior: Current evidence, caveats, and questions. *Current Opinion in Psychology,* 18, 6–10. Stellar, J., Manzo, V., Kraus, M., & Keltner, D. (2012). Class and compassion: Socioeconomic factors predict responses to suffering. *Emotion,* 12(3), 449–459.

7   Hrdy, S. (2000). *Mother nature: Maternal instincts and how they shape the human species.* New York: Ballantine Books. Hrdy, S. (2009). *Mothers and others.* Cambridge, MA: Harvard University Press.

8   Barlow, K. (2004). Critiquing the "good enough" mother: A perspective based on the Murik of Papua New Guinea. *Ethos,* 32(4), 514–537. Keller, H. (2012). Autonomy and relatedness revisted: Cultural manifestations of human needs. *Child Development Perspectives,* 6, 12–18. Tronick, E., Morelli, G., & Winn, S. (1987). Multiple caretaking of Efe (Pygmy) infants. *American Anthropologist,* 89(1), 96–106. Quinn, N., & Mageo, J. (2013). *Attachment reconsidered: Cultural perspectives on a western theory.* USA: Palgrave MacMillan.

9   Greenfield, P. (2009). Linking social change and developmental change: Shifting pathways of human development. *Developmental Psychology,* 45, 401–418. Greenfield, P. (2016). Social change, cultural evolution, and human development. *Current Opinion in Psychology,* 8, 84–92.

10 Chen, X., Bian, Y., Xin, T., Wang, L., & Silbereisen, R. K. (2010). Perceived social change and childrearing attitudes in China. *European Psychologist,* 15, 260–270. Deming, *The growing importance of social skills in the labor market.* Heckman et al., *The effects of cognitive and noncognitive abilities on labor market outcomes and social behavior.* Lancy,

The anthropology of childhood. Park, H., Coello, J., & Lau, A. (2014). Child socialization goals in East Asian versus western nations from 1989 to 2010: Evidence for social change in parenting. *Parenting: Science and Practice,* 14, 69–91.

11   See a partial transcript at Media Matters: https://www.mediamatters. org/print/758931.

12   McArthur, M., & Winkworth, G. (2017). What do we know about the social networks of single parents who do not use supportive services? *Child & Family Social Work,* 22(2), 638–64. Maguire-Jack, K., & Wang, X. (2016). Pathways from neighborhood to neglect: The mediating effects of social support and parenting stress. *Children and Youth Services Review,* 66, 28 –34. Putnam, *Bowling alone.* Rajendran, K., Smith, B., & Videka, L. (2015). Association of caregiver social support with the safety, permanency, and well-being of children in child welfare. *Children and Youth Services Review,* 48, 150–158. Thompson, R. (2015). Social support and child protection: Lessons learned and learning. *Child Abuse & Neglect,* 41, 19–29.

13   Numerous studies document the lack of adequate mental health services for children adopted out of the child welfare system: Bellamy, J., Goplan, G., & Traube, D. (2010). A national study of the impact of outpatient mental health services for children in long-term foster care. *Clinical Child Psychology and Psychiatry,* 15, 467–479. Brodzinsky, D. (2013). *A need to know: Enhancing adoption competence among mental health professionals.* New York, NY: The Donaldson Adoption Institute. Kerker, B., & Dore, M. (2006). Mental health needs and treatment of foster youth: Barriers and opportunities. *American Journal of Orthopsychiatry,* 76, 138–147. Tarren-Sweeney, M. (2010). It's time to rethink mental health services for children in care, and those adopted from care. *Clinical Child Psychology and Psychiatry,* 15, 613–626. Zilberstein, K., & Popper, S. (2016). Clinical competencies for the effective treatment of foster children. *Clinical Child Psychology and Psychiatry,* 21(1), 32–47.

14   Information on the MAPP curriculum is available at https://www.mass. gov/how-to/mapp-training.

15   Chronister, J., Chou, C., & Liao, H. (2013). The role of stigma, coping and social support in mediating the effect of societal stigma on internalised stigma, mental health recovery, and quality of life among people with serious mental illness. *Journal of Community Psychology,* 41(5), 582–600. Rushton, A. (2003). Support for adoptive families: A review of current evidence on problems, needs and effectiveness. *Adoption & Fostering,* 27(3), 41–50. Wegar, K. (2000). Adoption, family ideology, and social stigma: Bias in community attitudes, adoption research, and practice. *Family Relations* 49(4), 363–369. Weistra, S., & Luke, N. (2017). Adoptive parents' experiences of social support and attitudes towards adoption. *Adoption & Fostering,* 41(3), 228–241.

16 McArthur, M., & Winkworth, G. (2017). What do we know about the social networks of single parents who do not use supportive services? *Child & Family Social Work,* 22(2), 638–64. Maguire-Jack, K., & Wang, X. (2016). Pathways from neighborhood to neglect: The mediating effects of social support and parenting stress. *Children and Youth Services Review* 66, 28–34. Putnam, *Bowling alone.* Rajendran, K., Smith, B., & Videka, L. (2015). Association of caregiver social support with the safety, permanency, and well-being of children in child welfare. *Children and Youth Services Review,* 48, 150–158.

17 Haight, W., Sugrue, E., & Calhoun, M. (2017). Moral injury among child protection professionals: Implications for the ethical treatment and retention of workers. *Children and Youth Services Review,* 82, 27–41. McElvaney, R., & Tatlow-Golden, M. (2016). A traumatised and traumatising system: Professionals' experiences in meeting the mental health needs of young people in the care and youth justice systems in Ireland. *Children and Youth Services Review,* 65, 62–69. Nissly, J., Mor Barak, M., & Levin, A. (2005). Stress, social support, and workers' intentions to leave their jobs in public child welfare. *Administration in Social Work,* 29(1), 79–100. Smith, B. (2005). Job retention in child welfare: Effects of perceived organizational support, supervisor support, and intrinsic job value. *Children and Youth Services Review,* 27(2), 153–169.

18 Thompson, R. (2015). Social support and child protection: Lessons learned and learning. *Child Abuse & Neglect,* 41, 19–29.

19 Pelton, L. (2011). Concluding commentary: Varied perspectives on child welfare. *Children and Youth Services Review,* 33, 481–485. Pelton, L. (2016). Separating coercion from provision in child welfare. *Child Abuse & Neglect,* 51, 427–434. Smithson, R., & Gibson, M. (2017). Less than human: A qualitative study into the experience of parents involved in the child protection system. *Child & Family Social Work,* 22, 565–574.

20 A robust literature shows the importance of knowledgeable, post-adoptive services for supporting families and stabilizing placements. Brodzinsky, D. (2008). *Adoptive parent preparation project phase I: Meeting the mental health and developmental needs of adopted children.* The Donaldson Adoption Institute. Brodzinsky, D. (2013). *A need to know* Zilberstein, K., & Popper, S. (2016). Clinical competencies for the effective treatment of foster children. *Clinical Child Psychology and Psychiatry,* 21(1), 32–47.

21 American Psychiatric Association. (2013). *Diagnostic and statistical manual of mental disorders,* (5th ed.) *(DSM-5).* Washington, DC: American Psychiatric Association. Jonkman, C., Oosterman, M., Shuengel, C., Bolle, E., Boer, F., & Lindauer, R. (2014). Disturbances in attachment: Inhibited and disinhibited symptoms in foster children. *Child and Adolescent Psychiatry and*

Mental Health, 8, 21–28. Kay, C., & Green, J. (2013). Reactive attachment disorder following early maltreatment: Systematic evidence beyond the institution. *Journal of Abnormal Child Psychology*, 41, 571–581. Zeanah, C., & Gleason, M. (2015). Annual research review: Attachment disorders in early childhood–Clinical presentation, causes, correlates, and treatment. *Journal of Child Psychology and Psychiatry*, 56(3), 207–222. Zilberstein, K. (2016). Reactive attachment disorder. In R. Levesque (Ed.), *Encyclopedia of Adolescence*, (2nd edition). New York: Springer.

22 Hrdy, *Mothers and others*. Hrdy, S. *Mother nature*. Lancy, *The anthropology of childhood*.

23 Beckett, C., Maughan, B., Rutter, M., Castle, J., Colvert, C., Groothues, C.,...Sonuga- Barke, E. (2006). Do the effects of early severe deprivation on cognition persist into early adolescence? Findings from the English and Romanian adoptees study. *Child Development*, 77(3), 696–711. Beers, S., & De Bellis, M. (2002). Neuropsychological function in children with maltreatment-related posttraumatic stress disorder. *American Journal of Psychiatry*, 159, 483–486. Belsky, J., & Pluess, M. (2009). The nature (and nurture?) of plasticity in early human development. *Perspectives on Psychological Science*, 4(4), 345–351.Cicchetti, D. (2013). Research review: Resilient functioning in maltreated children—Past, present and future perspectives. *Journal of Child Psychology and Psychiatry*, 54(4), 402–422. McCrory, E., DeBrito, S., & Viding, E. (2010). Research review: The neurobiology and genetics of maltreatment and adversity. *Journal of Child Psychology and Psychiatry*, 51(10), 1079–1095. Perry, B., & Pollard, R. (1998). Homeostasis, stress and adaptation: A neurodevelopmental view of childhood trauma. *Stress in Children*, 7(1), 33–51. Shonk, S., & Cicchetti, C. (2001). Maltreatment, competency deficits, and risk for academic and behavioral maladjustment. *Developmental Psychology*, 37(1), 3–17. Zeanah, C., Chesher, T., Boris, N., and the American Academy of Child and Adolescent Psychiatry Committee on Quality Issues. (2016). Practice parameter for the assessment and treatment of children and adolescents with reactive attachment disorder and disinhibited social engagement disorder. *Journal of The American Academy Of Child & Adolescent Psychiatry*, 55(11), 991–1003.

24 Bowlby, J. (1982). *Attachment and loss: Attachment* (2nd ed.). New York: Basic Books. Inge, B. (1992). The origins of attachment theory: John Bowlby and Mary Ainsworth. *Developmental Psychology*, 28, 759-775.

25 Bowlby, J. (1951). Maternal care and mental health (p. 84). *World Health Organization Monograph* (Serial No. 2).

26 Hrdy presented this criticism in her book, *Mothers and others*. A large body of research and clinical reports derive from attachment concepts, mostly along dyadic lines, but they are beginning to branch out into wider systems:

Ainsworth, M. D. S., Blehar, M. C., Waters, E., & Wall, S. (1978). *Patterns of attachment: A psychological study of the strange situation*. Hillsdale, NJ: Erlbaum. Brazelton, T., & Cramer, B. (1991). *The earliest relationship: Parents, infants, and the drama of early attachment*. USA: DeCapo Lifelong Books. De Wolff, M. S., & Van IJzendoorn, M. H. (1997). Sensitivity and attachment: A meta-analysis on parental antecedents of infant attachment. *Child Development, 68*, 571–591. Diamond, G., Diamond, G., & Hogue, A. (2007). Attachment-based family therapy: Adherence and differentiation. *Journal of Marital and Family Therapy, 33*, 177–191. Rutter, M. (1997). Clinical implications of attachment concepts: Retrospect and prospect. In L. Atkinson & K. Zucker (Eds.), *Attachment and psychopathology* (pp. 17–46). New York: Guilford Press. Lieberman & Van Horn, *Psychotherapy with infants and young children*. Sears & Sears, *The Attachment Parenting Book*. Schore, A. (2001). Effects of a secure attachment relationship on right brain development, affect regulation, and infant mental health. *Infant Mental Health Journal, 22*, 7–66. Sroufe, L., Carlson, E., Levy, A., & Egeland, B. (1999). Implications of attachment theory for developmental psychopathology. *Development and Psychopathology, 11*, 1–13. Sroufe, L. et al. *The development of the person*. Sunderland, *The science of parenting*. Zeanah, C., Berlin, L., & Boris, N. (2009). Practitioner review: Clinical applications of attachment theory and research for infants and young children. *Journal of Child Psychology and Psychiatry, 52*, 819–833. Zilberstein, K. (2014). The use and limitations of attachment theory in child psychotherapy. *Psychotherapy, 51*, 93–103.

27   Ireland, M., & Pakenham, K. (2010). Youth adjustment to parental illness or disability: The role of illness characteristics, caregiving, and attachment. *Psychological Health & Medicine, 15*(6), 632–645. Kalil, A., Ryan, R., & Chor, E. (2014). Time investments in children across family structures. *The Annals of the American Academy of Political and Social Science, 654*(1), 150–168. Moss, E., Rousseau, D., Parent, S., St.-Laurent, D., & Saintonge, J. (1998). Correlates of attachment at school age: Maternal reported stress, mother-child interaction, and behavior problems. *Child Development 69*(5), 1390-1405. Radke-Yarrow, M., Cummings, E., Kuczynski, L., & Chapman, M. (1985). Patterns of attachment in two- and three-year-olds in normal families and families with parental depression. *Child Development 56*(4), 884–893. Schechter, D., & Willheim, E. (2009). Disturbances of attachment and parental psychopathology in early childhood. *Child and Adolescent Psychiatric Clinics of North America, 18*(3), 665–686.

28   Treehouse website: https://refca.net/what-we-do/treehouse-community/treehouse-easthampton.html.

29   Comparison of Treehouse youth and national averages for foster youth, according to the *Treehouse Foundation's* 2018 *Prospectus and Invitation for Investors*:

Children and Youth at Treehouse Easthampton 2006 - 2018 (N=101)		
(Citations available on request)	National Averages for Foster Youth	Treehouse Youth
High School Graduates	58%	95%
Attending College or Vocational Training	< 10%	100%
High School Drop Outs	(ANNUALLY) 8 -14%	(TOTAL OVER 12 YRS.) 5%
Children Repeating One or More Grades in School	33 - 46%	2%
Arrests	46%	0
Teens/Young Adults Parenting	48%	2%
Failed Placements / Children Returning to DCF	16%	0

Chapter Eight

1   Gross, D., Belcher, H., Ofonedu, M., Breitenstein, S., Frick, K., & Chakra, B. (2014). Study protocol for a comparative effectiveness trial of two parent training programs in a fee-for-service mental health clinic: Can we improve mental health services to low-income families? *Trials*, 15(1). Retrieved from http://www.trialsjournal.com/content/15/1/70. Fernandez, M. (2011). Treatment outcome for low socioeconomic status African American families in parent child interaction therapy: A pilot study. *Child & Family Behavior Therapy*, 33, 32–48. Leijten, P., Raaijmakers, M., de Castro, B., & Matthys, W. (2013). Does socioeconomic status matter? A meta-analysis on parent training effectiveness for disruptive child behavior. *Journal of Clinical Child & Adolescent Psychology*, 42, 384–392. Lundahl, B., Risser, H., & Lovejoy, C. (2006). A meta-analysis of parent training: Moderators and follow-up effects. *Clinical Psychology Review*, 26, 86–104. Pereira, M. Negrão, M. Soares, I. & Mesman, J. (2014). Decreasing harsh discipline in mothers at risk for maltreatment: A randomized control trial. *Infant Mental Health Journal*, 35(6), 604-613.

2   Whitaker, R. (2015). The triumph of American psychiatry: How it created the modern therapeutic state. *European Journal of Psychotherapy & Counselling*, 17(4), 326–341.

3   Arango, C. et al. (2018). Preventive strategies for mental health. *Lancet Psychiatry*. Published online ahead of print.

4   Flouri, E., Midouhas, E., & Hoshi, H. (2014). The role of urban neighbourhood green space in children's emotional and behavioural resilience. *Journal of Environmental Psychology*, 40, 179–18. Greenberg, M. (2006). Promoting resilience in children and youth: Preventative interventions and their interface with neuroscience. *Annals of the New York Academy of*

Science, 1094, 139–150. Maguire-Jack, K., & Wang, X. (2016). Pathways from neighborhood to neglect: The mediating effects of social support and parenting stress. *Children and Youth Services Review*, 66, 28 –34. Putnam, *Bowling alone*. Roubinov, D., Hagan, M., Boyce, W., Adler, N., & Bush, N. (2018) Family socioeconomic status, cortisol, and physical health in early childhood: The role of advantageous neighborhood characteristics. *Psychosomatic Medicine*. Published online ahead of print. Younan, D. et al., (2016). Environmental determinants of aggression in adolescents: Role of urban neighborhood greenspace. *Journal of the American Academy of Child & Adolescent Psychiatry*, 55(7), 591-601

5   Clark, A., Fleche, S., Layard, R., Powdthavee, N., & Ward, G. (2018). *The origins of happiness: The science of well-being over the life course*. New Jersey: Princeton University Press.

6   Chronister, J, Chou, C, & Liao, H. (2013). The role of stigma coping and social support in mediating the effect of societal stigma on internalised stigma, mental health recovery, and quality of life among people with serious mental illness. *Journal of Community Psychology*, 41(5): 582–600. Maguire-Jack, K., & Wang, X. (2016). Pathways from neighborhood to neglect: The mediating effects of social support and parenting stress. *Children and Youth Services Review*, 66, 28–34. Putnam, *Bowling alone*. Racine, N., Madigan, S., Plamondon, A., Hetherington, E., McDonald, S., & Tought, S. (2018). Maternal adverse childhood experiences and antepartum risks: The moderating role of social support. *Archives of Women's Mental Health*, 21(6), 663-370. Rajendran, K., Smith, B., & Videka, L. (2015). Association of caregiver social support with the safety, permanency, and well-being of children in child welfare. *Children and Youth Services Review*, 48, 150–158.

7   Helliwell, J., Layard, R., & Sachs, J. (2018). *World happiness report* 2018. New York: Sustainable Development Solutions Network. Retrieved from http://worldhappiness.report/ed/2018/.

8   Not just policies differ between the USA and Europe, but also popular ideas about the role of government and individuality. American policies may reflect those differences: "Americans tend to prioritize individual liberty, while Europeans tend to value the role of the state to ensure no one in society is in need." For more details see: Pew Research Center. (November, 2015). *Global support for principle of free expression, but opposition to some forms of speech*. Retrieved from http://assets.pewresearch.org/wp-content/uploads/sites/2/2015/11/Pew-Research-Center-Democracy-Report-FINAL-November-18-2015.pdf.

9   Epstein, E. (in press). Relational healing and organizational change in the time of evidence. In M. McGoldrick & K. Hardy (Eds.), *Re-visioning Family Therapy: Race, Culture, and Gender in Clinical Practice* (3rd ed.). New York: Guildford Press.

10   Edwards, F., & Wildeman, C. (2018). Characteristics of the front-line child welfare workforce. *Children and Youth Services Review*, 89, 13–26.

11   Sahlberg, P. (2015). *Finnish lessons 2.0: What can the world learn from educational change in Finland?* (2nd ed.). New York: Teachers College Press.

12   Carey, A. (2014). Parents reflections of professionals, the support system, and the family in the twentieth-century United States. In S. Burch, & M. Rembis (Eds.) *Disability Histories*. Urbana, US: University of Illinois Press. Coy A., (2006). Mental health in colonial America. *The Hospitalist.*, 6(5). Retrieved from http://www.the-hospitalist.org/hopitalist/article/123117/ mental-health-colonial-america. National Alliance on Mental Illness. *What is mental health parity?* Retrieved from https://www.nami.org/find-support/ living-with-a-mental-health-condition/understanding-health-insurance/ what-is-mental-health-parity. Orzechowski, *You'll like it here.*

13   See the CBHI website at https://www.mass.gov/masshealth-childrens-behavioral-health-initiative.

14   See the ACO website at https://www.mass.gov/service-details/primary-care-aco-plans.

15   Masshealth Children's Behavioral Health Initiative and Technical Assistance Collaborative. (2017). *Massachusetts Practice Review Summary Report*. Retrieved from https://www.mass.gov/service-details/cbhi-data-reports/resources?page=4.

16   United States Department of Labor, Bureau of Labor Statistics. (April 28, 2016). *Business Employment Dynamics*. Retrieved from https://www.bls.gov/bdm/entrepreneurship/entrepreneurship.htm.